André Lefebvre
and the cars he created for Voisin and Citroën

THE LIFE STORY OF A PASSIONATE AUTOMOTIVE PIONEER

Gijsbert-Paul Berk

Other great books from Veloce –

Speedpro Series

4-Cylinder Engine Short Block High-Performance Manual – New Updated & Revised Edition (Hammill)
Alfa Romeo DOHC High-performance Manual (Kartalamakis)
Alfa Romeo V6 Engine High-performance Manual (Kartalamakis)
BMC 998cc A-series Engine, How to Power Tune (Hammill)
1275cc A-series High-performance Manual (Hammill)
Camshafts – How to Choose & Time Them For Maximum Power (Hammill)
Competition Car Datalogging Manual, The (Templeman)
Cylinder Heads, How to Build, Modify & Power Tune – Updated & Revised Edition (Burgess & Gollan)
Distributor-type Ignition Systems, How to Build & Power Tune – New 3rd Edition (Hammill)
Fast Road Car, How to Plan and Build – Revised & Updated Colour New Edition (Stapleton)
Ford SOHC 'Pinto' & Sierra Cosworth DOHC Engines, How to Power Tune – Updated & Enlarged Edition (Hammill)
Ford V8, How to Power Tune Small Block Engines (Hammill)
Harley-Davidson Evolution Engines, How to Build & Power Tune (Hammill)
Holley Carburetors, How to Build & Power Tune – Revised & Updated Edition (Hammill)
Honda Civic Type R High-Performance Manual, The (Cowland & Clifford)
Jaguar XK Engines, How to Power Tune – Revised & Updated Colour Edition (Hammill)
Land Rover Discovery, Defender & Range Rover – How to Modify Coil Sprung Models for High Performance & Off-Road Action (Hosier)
MG Midget & Austin-Healey Sprite, How to Power Tune – New 3rd Edition (Stapleton)
MGB 4-cylinder Engine, How to Power Tune (Burgess)
MGB V8 Power, How to Give Your – Third Colour Edition (Williams)
MGB, MGC & MGB V8, How to Improve – New 2nd Edition (Williams)
Mini Engines, How to Power Tune On a Small Budget – Colour Edition (Hammill)
Motorcycle-engined Racing Car, How to Build (Pashley)
Motorsport, Getting Started in (Collins)
Nissan GT-R High-performance Manual, The (Gorodji)
Nitrous Oxide High-performance Manual, The (Langfield)
Race & Trackday Driving Techniques (Hornsey)
Retro or classic car for high performance, How to modify your (Stapleton)
Rover V8 Engines, How to Power Tune (Hammill)
Secrets of Speed – Today's techniques for 4-stroke engine blueprinting & tuning (Swager)
Sportscar & Kitcar Suspension & Brakes, How to Build & Modify – Revised 3rd Edition (Hammill)
SU Carburettor High-performance Manual (Hammill)
Successful Low-Cost Rally Car, How to Build a (Young)
Suzuki 4x4, How to Modify For Serious Off-road Action (Richardson)
Tiger Avon Sportscar, How to Build Your Own – Updated & Revised 2nd Edition (Dudley)
TR2, 3 & TR4, How to Improve (Williams)
TR5, 250 & TR6, How to Improve (Williams)
TR7 & TR8, How to Improve (Williams)
V8 Engine, How to Build a Short Block For High Performance (Hammill)
Volkswagen Beetle Suspension, Brakes & Chassis, How to Modify For High Performance (Hale)
Volkswagen Bus Suspension, Brakes & Chassis for High Performance, How to Modify – Updated & Enlarged New Edition (Hale)
Weber DCOE, & Dellorto DHLA Carburetors, How to Build & Power Tune – 3rd Edition (Hammill)

Those Were The Days ... Series

Alpine Trials & Rallies 1910-1973 (Pfundner)
American 'Independent' Automakers – AMC to Willys 1945 to 1960 (Mort)
American Station Wagons – The Golden Era 1950-1975 (Mort)
American Trucks of the 1950s (Mort)
American Trucks of the 1960s (Mort)
American Woodies 1928-1953 (Mort)
Anglo-American Cars from the 1930s to the 1970s (Mort)
Austerity Motoring (Bobbitt)
Austins, The last real (Peck)
Brighton National Speed Trials (Gardiner)
British and European Trucks of the 1970s (Peck)
British Drag Racing – The early years (Pettitt)
British Lorries of the 1950s (Bobbitt)
British Lorries of the 1960s (Bobbitt)
British Touring Car Racing (Collins)
British Police Cars (Walker)
British Woodies (Peck)
Café Racer Phenomenon, The (Walker)
Don Hayter's MGB Story – - The birth of the MGB in MG's Abingdon Design & Development Office (Hayter)
Drag Bike Racing in Britain – From the mid '60s to the mid '80s (Lee)
Dune Buggy Phenomenon, The (Hale)
Dune Buggy Phenomenon Volume 2, The (Hale)
Endurance Racing at Silverstone in the 1970s & 1980s (Parker)
Hot Rod & Stock Car Racing in Britain in the 1980s (Neil)
Last Real Austins 1946-1959, The (Peck)
MG's Abingdon Factory (Moylan)
Motor Racing at Brands Hatch in the Seventies (Parker)
Motor Racing at Brands Hatch in the Eighties (Parker)
Motor Racing at Crystal Palace (Collins)
Motor Racing at Goodwood in the Sixties (Gardiner)
Motor Racing at Nassau in the 1950s & 1960s (O'Neil)
Motor Racing at Oulton Park in the 1960s (McFadyen)
Motor Racing at Oulton Park in the 1970s (McFadyen)
Motor Racing at Thruxton in the 1970s (Grant-Braham)
Motor Racing at Thruxton in the 1980s (Grant-Braham)
Superprix – The Story of Birmingham Motor Race (Page & Collins)
Three Wheelers (Bobbitt)

Biographies

A Chequered Life – Graham Warner and the Chequered Flag (Hesletine)
Amédée Gordini ... a true racing legend (Smith)
André Lefebvre, and the cars he created at Voisin and Citroën (Beck)
Cliff Allison, The Official Biography of – From the Fells to Ferrari (Gauld)
Edward Turner – The Man Behind the Motorcycles (Clew)
Driven by Desire – The Desiré Wilson Story
First Principles – The Official Biography of Keith Duckworth (Burr)
Inspired to Design – F1 cars, Indycars & racing tyres: the autobiography of Nigel Bennett (Bennett)
Jack Sears, The Official Biography of – Gentleman Jack (Gauld)
Jim Redman – 6 Times World Motorcycle Champion: The Autobiography (Redman)
John Chatham – 'Mr Big Healey' – The Official Biography (Burr)
The Lee Noble Story (Wilkins)
Mason's Motoring Mayhem – Tony Mason's hectic life in motorsport and television (Mason)
Pat Moss Carlsson Story, The – Harnessing Horsepower (Turner)
Tony Robinson – The biography of a race mechanic (Wagstaff)
Virgil Exner – Visioneer: The Official Biography of Virgil M Exner Designer Extraordinaire (Grist)

General

11/2-litre GP Racing 1961-1965 (Whitelock)
AC Two-litre Saloons & Buckland Sportscars (Archibald)
Alfa Romeo 155/156/147 Competition Touring Cars (Collins)
Alfa Romeo Giulia Coupé GT & GTA (Tipler)
Alfa Romeo Montreal – The dream car that came true (Taylor)
Alfa Romeo Montreal – The Essential Companion (Taylor)
Alfa Tipo 33 (McDonough & Collins)
Alpine & Renault – The Development of the Revolutionary Turbo F1 Car 1968 to 1979 (Smith)
Alpine & Renault – The Sports Prototypes 1963 to 1969 (Smith)
Alpine & Renault – The Sports Prototypes 1973 to 1978 (Smith)
Anatomy of the Works Minis (Moylan)
Armstrong-Siddeley (Smith)
Art Deco and British Car Design (Down)
Autodrome (Collins & Ireland)
Autodrome 2 (Collins & Ireland)
Automotive A-Z, Lane's Dictionary of Automotive Terms (Lane)
Automotive Mascots (Kay & Springate)
Bahamas Speed Weeks, The (O'Neil)
Bentley Continental, Corniche and Azure (Bennett)
Bentley MkVI, Rolls-Royce Silver Wraith, Dawn & Cloud/Bentley R & S-Series (Nutland)
Bluebird CN7 (Stevens)
BMC Competitions Department Secrets (Turner, Chambers & Browning)
BMW 5-Series (Cranswick)
BMW Z-Cars (Taylor)
BMW Boxer Twins 1970-1995 Bible, The (Falloon)
BMW Cafe Racers (Cloesen)
BMW Custom Motorcycles – Choppers, Cruisers, Bobbers, Trikes & Quads (Cloesen)
BMW – The Power of M (Vivian)
Bonjour – Is this Italy? (Turner)
British 250cc Racing Motorcycles (Pereira)
British at Indianapolis, The (Wagstaff)
British Cars, The Complete Catalogue of, 1895-1975 (Culshaw & Horrobin)
BRM – A Mechanic's Tale (Salmon)
BRM V16 (Ludvigsen)
BSA Bantam Bible, The (Henshaw)
BSA Motorcycles - the final evolution (Jones)
Bugatti Type 40 (Price)
Bugatti 46/50 Updated Edition (Price & Arbey)
Bugatti T44 & T49 (Price & Arbey)
Bugatti 57 2nd Edition (Price)
Caravan, Improve & Modify Your (Porter)
Caravans, The Illustrated History 1919-1959 (Jenkinson)
Caravans, The Illustrated History From 1960 (Jenkinson)
Carrera Panamericana, La (Tipler)
Chrysler 300 – America's Most Powerful Car 2nd Edition (Ackerson)
Chrysler PT Cruiser (Ackerson)
Citroën DS (Bobbitt)
Classic British Car Electrical Systems (Astley)
Cobra – The Real Thing! (Legate)
Concept Cars, How to illustrate and design (Dewey)
Cortina – Ford's Bestseller (Robson)
Coventry Climax Racing Engines (Hammill)
Daily Mirror 1970 World Cup Rally 40, The (Robson)
Daimler SP250 New Edition (Long)
Datsun Fairlady Roadster to 280ZX – The Z-Car Story (Long)
Dino – The V6 Ferrari (Long)
Dodge Challenger & Plymouth Barracuda (Grist)
Dodge Charger – Enduring Thunder (Ackerson)
Dodge Dynamite! (Grist)
Draw & Paint Cars – How to (Gardiner)
Drive on the Wild Side, A – 20 Extreme Driving Adventures From Around the World (Weaver)
Ducati 750 Bible, The (Falloon)
Ducati 750 SS 'round-case' 1974, The Book of the (Falloon)
Ducati 860, 900 and Mille Bible, The (Falloon)
Ducati Monster Bible, The (Falloon)
Dune Buggy, Building A – The Essential Manual (Shakespeare)
Dune Buggy Files (Hale)
Dune Buggy Handbook (Hale)
East German Motor Vehicles in Pictures (Suhr/Weinreich)
Fast Ladies – Female Racing Drivers 1888 to 1970 (Bouzanquet)
Fate of the Sleeping Beauties, The (op de Weegh/Hottendorff/op de Weegh)
Ferrari 288 GTO, The Book of the (Sackey)
Fiat & Abarth 124 Spider & Coupé (Tipler)
Fiat & Abarth 500 & 600 – 2nd Edition (Bobbitt)
Fiats, Great Small (Ward)
Fine Art of the Motorcycle Engine, The (Peirce)
Ford Cleveland 335-Series V8 engine 1970 to 1982 – The Essential Source Book (Hammill)
Ford F100/F150 Pick-up 1948-1996 (Ackerson)
Ford F150 Pick-up 1997-2005 (Ackerson)
Ford GT – Then, and Now (Streather)
Ford GT40 (Legate)
Ford Model Y (Roberts)
Ford Thunderbird From 1954, The Book of the (Long)
Formula 5000 Motor Racing, Back then ... and back now (Lawson)
Forza Minardi! (Vigar)
France: the essential guide for car enthusiasts – 200 things for the car enthusiast to see and do (Parish)
From Crystal Palace to Red Square – - A Hapless Biker's Road to Russia (Turner)
Funky Mopeds (Skelton)
Grand Prix Ferrari – The Years of Enzo Ferrari's Power, 1948-1980 (Pritchard)
Grand Prix Ford – DFV-powered Formula 1 Cars (Pritchard)
GT – The World's Best GT Cars 1953-73 (Dawson)
Hillclimbing & Sprinting – The Essential Manual (Short & Wilkinson)
Honda NSX (Long)
Intermeccanica – The Story of the Prancing Bull (McCredie & Reisner)
Italian Cafe Racers (Cloesen)
Italian Custom Motorcycles (Cloesen)
Jaguar, The Rise of (Price)
Jaguar XJ 220 – The Inside Story (Moreton)
Jaguar XJ-S, The Book of the (Long)
Jeep CJ (Ackerson)
Jeep Wrangler (Ackerson)
Karmann-Ghia Coupé & Convertible (Bobbitt)
Kawasaki Triples Bible, The (Walker)
Kris Meeke – Intercontinental Rally Challenge Champion (McBride)
Lamborghini Miura Bible, The (Sackey)
Lamborghini Urraco, The Book of the (Landsem)
Lambretta Bible, The (Davies)
Lancia 037 (Collins)
Lancia Delta HF Integrale (Blaettel & Wagner)
Land Rover Series III Reborn (Porter)
Land Rover, The Half-ton Military (Cook)
Laverda Twins & Triples Bible 1968-1986 (Falloon)
Lea-Francis Story, The (Price)
Le Mans Panoramic (Ireland)
Lexus Story, The (Long)
Little book of microcars, the (Quellin)
Little book of smart, the – New Edition (Jackson)
Little book of trikes, the (Quellin)
Lola – The Illustrated History (1957-1977) (Starkey)
Lola – All the Sports Racing & Single-seater Racing Cars 1978-1997 (Starkey)
Lola T70 – The Racing History & Individual Chassis Record – 4th Edition (Starkey)
Lotus 49 (Oliver)
Marketingmobiles, The Wonderful Wacky World of (Hale)
Maserati 250F In Focus (Pritchard)
Mazda MX-5/Miata 1.6 Enthusiast's Workshop Manual (Grainger & Shoemark)
Mazda MX-5/Miata 1.8 Enthusiast's Workshop Manual (Grainger & Shoemark)
Mazda MX-5 Miata: The Book of the World's Favourite Sportscar (Long)
Mazda MX-5 Miata Roadster (Long)
Maximum Mini (Booij)
Meet the English (Bowie)
Mercedes-Benz SL – W113-series 1963-1971 (Long)
Mercedes-Benz SL & SLC – 107-series 1971-1989 (Long)
Mercedes-Benz SLK – R170 series 1996-2004 (Long)
MGA (Price Williams)
MGB & MGB GT– Expert Guide (Auto-doc Series) (Williams)
MGB Electrical Systems Updated & Revised Edition (Astley)
Micro Caravans (Jenkinson)
Micro Trucks (Mort)
Microcars at Large! (Quellin)
Mini Cooper – The Real Thing! (Tipler)
Mini Minor to Asia Minor (West)
Mitsubishi Lancer Evo, The Road Car & WRC Story (Long)
Montlhéry, The Story of the Paris Autodrome (Boddy)
Morgan Maverick (Lawrence)
Morris Minor, 60 Years on the Road (Newell)
Moto Guzzi Sport & Le Mans Bible, The (Falloon)
Motor Movies – The Posters! (Veysey)
Motor Racing – Reflections of a Lost Era (Carter)
Motor Racing – The Pursuit of Victory 1930-1962 (Carter)
Motor Racing – The Pursuit of Victory 1963-1972 (Wyatt/Sears)
Motor Racing Heroes – The Stories of 100 Greats (Newman)
Motorcycle Apprentice (Cakebread)
Motorcycle GP Racing in the 1960s (Pereira)
Motorcycle Road & Racing Chassis Designs (Noakes)
Motorhomes, The Illustrated History (Jenkinson)
Motorsport In colour, 1950s (Wainwright)
MV Agusta Fours, The book of the classic (Falloon)
Nissan 300ZX & 350Z – The Z-Car Story (Long)
Nissan GT-R Supercar: Born to race (Gorodji)
Northeast American Sports Car Races 1950-1959 (O'Neil)
Nothing Runs – Misadventures in the Classic, Collectable & Exotic Car Biz (Slutsky)
Off-Road Giants! (Volume 1) – Heroes of 1960s Motorcycle Sport (Westlake)
Off-Road Giants! (Volume 2) – Heroes of 1960s Motorcycle Sport (Westlake)
Pass the Theory and Practical Driving Tests (Gibson & Hoole)
Peking to Paris 2007 (Young)
Pontiac Firebird (Cranswick)
Porsche Boxster (Long)
Porsche 356 (2nd Edition) (Long)
Porsche 908 (Födisch, Neßhöver, Roßbach, Schwarz & Roßbach)
Porsche 911 Carrera – The Last of the Evolution (Corlett)
Porsche 911R, RS & RSR, 4th Edition (Starkey)
Porsche 911, The Book of the (Long)
Porsche 911SC 'Super Carrera' – The Essential Companion (Streather)
Porsche 914 & 914-6: The Definitive History of the Road & Competition Cars (Long)
Porsche 924 (Long)
The Porsche 924 Carreras - evolution to excellence (Smith)
Porsche 928 (Long)
Porsche 944 (Long)
Porsche 964, 993 & 996 Data Plate Code Breaker (Streather)
Porsche 993 'King Of Porsche' – The Essential Companion (Streather)
Porsche 996 'Supreme Porsche' – The Essential Companion (Streather)
Porsche Racing Cars – 1953 to 1975 (Long)
Porsche Racing Cars – 1976 to 2005 (Long)
Porsche – The Rally Story (Meredith)
Porsche: Three Generations of Genius (Meredith)
Preston Tucker & Others (Linde)
RAC Rally Action! (Gardiner)
RACING COLOURS – MOTOR RACING COMPOSITIONS 1908-2009 (Newman)
Rallye Sport Fords: The Inside Story (Moreton)
Roads with a View – England's greatest views and how to find them by road (Corfield)
Roads With a View – Wales' greatest views and how to find them by road (Corfield)
Rolls-Royce Silver Shadow/Bentley T Series Corniche & Camargue – Revised & Enlarged Edition (Bobbitt)
Rolls-Royce Silver Spirit, Silver Spur & Bentley Mulsanne 2nd Edition (Bobbitt)
Runways & Racers (O'Neil)
Russian Motor Vehicles – Soviet Limousines 1930-2003 (Kelly)
Russian Motor Vehicles – The Czarist Period 1784 to 1917 (Kelly)
RX-7 – Mazda's Rotary Engine Sportscar (Updated & Revised New Edition) (Long)
Scooters & Microcars, The A-Z of Popular (Dan)
Scooter Lifestyle (Grainger)
SCOOTER MANIA! – - Recollections of the Isle of Man International Scooter Rally (Jackson)
Singer Story: Cars, Commercial Vehicles, Bicycles & Motorcycle (Atkinson)
Sleeping Beauties USA – abandoned classic cars & trucks (Marek)
SM – Citroën's Maserati-engined Supercar (Long & Claverol)
Speedway – Auto racing's ghost tracks (Collins & Ireland)
Sprite Caravans, The Story of (Jenkinson)
Standard Motor Company, The Book of the
Subaru Impreza: The Road Car And WRC Story (Long)
Supercar, How to Build your own (Thompson)
Tales from the Toolbox (Oliver)
Taxi! The Story of the 'London' Taxicab (Bobbitt)
Toleman Story, The (Hilton)
Toyota Celica & Supra, The Book of Toyota's Sports Coupés (Long)
Toyota MR2 Coupés & Spyders (Long)
Triumph Bonneville Bible (59-83) (Henshaw)
Triumph Bonneville!, Save the – The inside story of the Meriden Workers' Co-op (Rosamond)
Triumph Motorcycles & the Meriden Factory (Hancox)
Triumph Speed Twin & Thunderbird Bible (Woolridge)
Triumph Tiger Cub Bible (Estall)
Triumph Trophy Bible (Woolridge)
Triumph TR6 (Kimberley)
TT Talking - The TT's most exciting era – As seen by Manx Radio TT's lead commentator 2004-2012 (Lambert)
TWR Story, The – Group A (Hughes & Scott)
Unraced (Collins)
Velocette Motorcycles – MSS to Thruxton – New Third Edition (Burris)
Volkswagen Bus Book, The (Bobbitt)
Volkswagen Bus or Van to Camper, How to Convert (Porter)
Volkswagens of the World (Glen)
VW Beetle Cabriolet – The full story of the convertible Beetle (Bobbitt)
VW Beetle – The Car of the 20th Century (Copping)
VW Bus – 40 Years of Splitties, Bays & Wedges (Copping)
VW Bus Book, The (Bobbitt)
VW Golf: Five Generations of Fun (Copping & Cservenka)
VW – The Air-cooled Era (Copping)
VW T5 Camper Conversion Manual (Porter)
VW Campers (Copping)
Which Oil? – Choosing the right oils & greases for your antique, vintage, veteran, classic or collector car (Michell)
Works Minis, The Last (Purves & Brenchley)
Works Rally Mechanic (Moylan)

www.veloce.co.uk
For post publication news, updates and amendments relating to this book please visit www.veloce.co.uk/books/V4244

Also available ... Apps – Download now from www.digital.veloce.co.uk
Hubble & Hattie
BATTLE CRY!
Also available ... eBook – Download now from www.digital.veloce.co.uk

First published in June 2009. Reprinted November 2014 by Veloce Publishing Limited, Veloce House, Parkway Farm Business Park, Middle Farm Way, Poundbury, Dorchester DT1 3AR, England. Fax 01305 268864 / e-mail info@veloce.co.uk / web www.veloce.co.uk or www.velocebooks.com. ISBN: 978-1-845842-44-4 UPC: 6-36847-04244-8 © Gijsbert-Paul Berk and Veloce Publishing 2009 and 2014. All rights reserved. With the exception of quoting brief passages for the purpose of review, no part of this publication may be recorded, reproduced or transmitted by any means, including photocopying, without the written permission of Veloce Publishing Ltd. Throughout this book logos, model names and designations, etc, have been used for the purposes of identification, illustration and decoration. Such names are the property of the trademark holder as this is not an official publication. Readers with ideas for automotive books, or books on other transport or related hobby subjects, are invited to write to the editorial director of Veloce Publishing at the above address. British Library Cataloguing in Publication Data – A catalogue record for this book is available from the British Library. Typesetting, design and page make-up all by Veloce Publishing Ltd on Apple Mac. Printed in India by Replika Press.

CONTENTS

Introduction 4

One	Prologue 6
Two	Under the wings of Gabriel Voisin. 11
Three	A short history of front-wheel drive 50
Four	An unfortunate episode at Renault 54
Five	Economic & social unrest.... 57
Six	Meeting André Citroën 58
Seven	Michelin steps in 73
Eight	World War II.. 89
Nine	Paris liberated 97
Ten	Enjoying life again 107
Eleven	Not for sale 129
Twelve	The Coccinelle project 130

Postscript 135
Lefebvre family tree 137
Heritage 137
Appendices 139
Thanks & Acknowledgements 143
Index 144

INTRODUCTION

LA MÉCANIQUE N'EST PAS UN MÉTIER, C'EST UNE PASSION.
MECHANICAL ENGINEERING IS NOT A PROFESSION, IT IS A PASSION.
– FRENCH WRITER PIERRE HAMP (HENRI LOUIS BOURILLON) 1876-1962

The majority of popular family cars today have front-wheel drive, an all-steel unit body, and independent suspension on all four wheels, technical features which play an important role in the safety of our modern automobiles, as they ensure predictable roadholding and good stability, and the cars' sturdy unit bodies give optimal crash protection.

However, in the early 1930s, the majority of car makers considered such concepts highly unrealistic, unnecessarily complicated, and too costly. Most cars those days had rear-wheel drive and a separate chassis and body. Only a few manufacturers offered independent front suspension, most opting for beam axles with cart springs front and rear. Only one per cent of all cars had front-wheel drive, and generally they were sports or racing cars.

The French automobile manufacturer André Citroën and his chief engineer, André Lefebvre, had a different idea. They wanted to build a new kind of family car: strong, low, and modern, and they were stubborn and courageous enough to do it their way. Although both men had the same goal, their motives were different. Citroën needed an advanced car to save his debt-ridden company and to outsell his arch rival, Louis Renault. Lefebvre wanted to prove that a popular, mass-produced, front-wheel drive passenger car was feasible; the more so as the same Louis Renault had previously rejected his proposal for such a car.

It's common knowledge that, together with his colleagues at Citroën, Lefebvre created the Traction Avant (1934), the TUB (1939), Citroën's first front-wheel drive utility van that was succeeded by the H and HY vans (1947), the Deux Chevaux (1948), and, last but not least, the DS (1955).

Many car connoisseurs are also aware that from 1923 to 1931, Lefebvre designed several highly original and outstanding competition cars and record-breaking automobiles for Voisin. He even drove some of these cars in races and during record attempts. It's obvious that during his 16 years with Gabriel Voisin he was very much influenced by the ideas of this illustrious aviation pioneer and car manufacturer.

The experience gained during that period gave Lefebvre the self-confidence to persuade his successive bosses at Citroën – André Citroën, later Pierre Michelin, then Pierre-Jules Boulanger, and finally Robert Puiseux and Pierre Bercot – that his unorthodox approach to automobile design was what the company needed.

Lefebvre's work for Citroën alone earns him a place of honour among the great automobile designers of the past century. The fact that most present-day cars still carry the DNA of his design philosophy makes him stand out amid other automotive pioneers and innovators. That is why it's incredible that so little is known about this fascinating and brilliant engineer.

There are two reasons for this. One is that in Lefebvre's time engineers and designers worked more or less incognito; in France, all designs and inventions automatically became the property of the employer. The second reason is that from 1958 onward Lefebvre suffered from an illness that gradually paralyzed the right side of his body, and made his speech incomprehensible, so he never had the opportunity to write or dictate his memoirs; besides, his real passion was designing automobiles, not self-promotion.

It is true, however, that many books about and by Gabriel Voisin, and about André Citroën, contain several mentions of Lefebvre. The first of the two-volume *Citroën, l'histoire et les secrets de son bureau d'études* by Roger Brioult, former editor of the French *Revue Technique Automobile*, is full of interesting anecdotes from Lefebvre's former colleagues and collaborators, which give a highly detailed insight to Lefebvre's innovative ideas and the way he worked.

Alas, Gabriel Voisin's fascinating autobiography *Mes mille et une voitures*, and Roger Brioult's book about Citroën's design department are out of print and were never translated into English. This book was written to pay tribute to André Lefebvre, the passionate pioneer who left such an important heritage for car enthusiasts around the world.

Over thirty years separate these two cars created by André Lefebvre. The reconstruction of the 1923 Voisin C6 Course or 'Laboratoire' by Philipp Moch, nose-to-nose with the ID owned by Citroën enthusiast Christian Le Baut. (Courtesy Hans Arend de Wit/Switchimage)

The three-quarter rear view of both cars shows the family resemblance, and demonstrates that Lefebvre remained faithful to the aeronautical engineering principles he shared with his mentor, Gabriel Voisin: lightness, a low centre of gravity, a long wheelbase, good weight distribution and effective aerodynamics. (Courtesy Hans Arend de Wit/Switchimage)

CHAPTER ONE

PROLOGUE

Paris, spring 1946

"What a handsome man," thought Monique Hebert. She was heading for the Gare de l'Est in the Métro, observing the couple opposite her. They were deeply engaged in a serious discussion and did not look at her at all.

When at the Gare de l'Est she boarded her train, she discovered that they shared the same compartment and were again sitting face-to-face. But this time he was alone and his grey eyes, shining like polished steel, were staring at her. Like every well-bred French girl she had learned from her mother always to avoid eye contact with strange men. But this time she could not avert her own gaze and soon he took the initiative and began the sort of conversation that strangers have on trains to pass the time.

However, before they knew it they were exchanging confidences as if they had known each other for years. Both had had their share of good and sad experiences. He told her that he worked at Citroën and was a widower; four years ago he had lost his second wife, who had died after a long illness. Now his cousin Annemarie, a stepsister of his mother, took care of his housekeeping. That was the lady she had seen in the Métro.

He made her laugh and she made him feel fully alive again. They were so absorbed in their animated conversation that they hardly noticed that their train had arrived at its destination. At the station – helping her out of the carriage onto the platform – he persuaded her to have dinner with him. It was what the French call a 'coup de foudre' – love at first sight. Four months later they were Monsieur et Madame André Lefebvre.

Being born on August 19, 1894, André Lefebvre belonged to a generation that grew up with the first motorcars and the first airplanes. His generation also witnessed the horrors of two world wars and great social changes.

During the last years of the 19th century motorcars were still a rare sight on the roads. But in France the 'automobile' caught the fancy of the wealthy and adventurous rather early. In July 1894, Pierre Giffard, the farsighted editor of the *Petit Journal*, although no auto fan himself, organised the Paris-Rouen run. It was the first official competition for mechanically-powered vehicles. The participants came with three- and four-wheelers, powered by steam, electric motors or petrol engines. Of the twenty-five starters, fifteen reached the finish. However, the publicity around this event set many wheels in motion.

André Lefebvre spent his earliest years in Louvres. Today, this village is one of the more affluent commuter suburbs north of Paris, situated in the pleasant rolling countryside of the Val d'Oise. In around 1900, however, Louvres was a small and somewhat isolated community, and France was still very much an agricultural nation, although the industrial age was well under way.

When Alfred Lefebvre, André's father, was promoted to the position of Chef de la Comptabilité et du Personnel (CFO today) at one of the leading Parisian manufacturers of ladies corsets, the family moved to the Rue Stephenson in the 18th arrondissement in Paris, not far from the Gare du Nord. André's mother was a trained midwife and also a knowledgeable herbalist.

The company Lefebvre senior worked for did very well. During the early years of the twentieth century, corsets were big business, and every self-respecting woman – especially those from the middle and upper classes – bought several each year – and they were not cheap.

André's mother, Clémence, supplemented the family income with her paramedical practice, and so the Lefebvres were in a position, financially, to give their children a good education. They stimulated their interests and allowed them to study the subjects they liked: André's sister, Jeanne, became a dental surgeon, whilst André had, even as a youngster, shown an outspoken talent for solving technical problems. He was very intelligent, but also a keen and practical tinkerer, and, like many French boys of his age, he was fascinated by those 'wonderful flying machines.'

THE 'ECOLE SUPÉRIEURE DE L'AÉRONAUTIQUE'

When André was accepted at the Ecole Supérieure de l'Aéronautique et de Construction Mécanique (Supaéro) in the rue de Clignancourt in Montmartre in 1911, the whole Lefebvre family was happy.

Colonel Jean-Baptiste Roche, a director of the Ecole du Génie at Versailles, who had spotted the need for qualified technicians in the young aviation industry, had founded the Supaéro college in 1909. As aviation was still in its infancy and most airplanes were constructed from steel wire, wooden slats and fabric, the curriculum covered a wide range of subjects, from theoretical lessons about the principles of flight, aerodynamics, thermodynamics, the mechanics of fluids, the properties of various materials – plus a lot of mathematics – to practical work on combustion engines, the construction of cells for wings, fuselages and balloons, and the use of small machine tools. In the course of two years its pupils were trained to become fully-fledged aeronautical engineers.

The rue de Clignancourt was within walking distance of André's parental home, but at that time Montmartre was a fascinating 'quartier' for a young student, one of the

Portrait of a youthful André by the French painter Vincent La Varenne.

The following portrait gallery spans a lifetime of challenges and opportunities, joys and deceptions, and some very daring and innovative automobile engineering. (Courtesy Collection family Lefebvre, Straza Photo Reportage, Citroën Communication & Ministère de la Culture – Médiathèque du Patrimoine, Dist. RMN)

cultural and artistic centres of 'la ville lumière.' Painters such as Marc Chagall, Fernand Léger, Pablo Picasso and Maurice Utrillo lived in this area with their girlfriends and models.

Montmartre also had a reputation as the scene of many bohemian parties and festivities. André had a healthy interest in attractive young females, and his self-assurance and penetrating look of his gleaming eyes melted the heart of many girls, and he in turn was easily seduced by their charms. But André was also an eager and serious student and in 1914 he qualified as Ingénieur d'Aéronautique.

A photo taken on the occasion of his graduation (Supaéro 1914).

Posing behind the steering wheel in one of the first Voisin cars (c1920).

Opposite: As team manager during a record attempt at Montlhéry (1929). (Courtesy Citroën Communication)

In immaculate white racing outfit. (Courtesy 'Strazza,' Milano.1923)

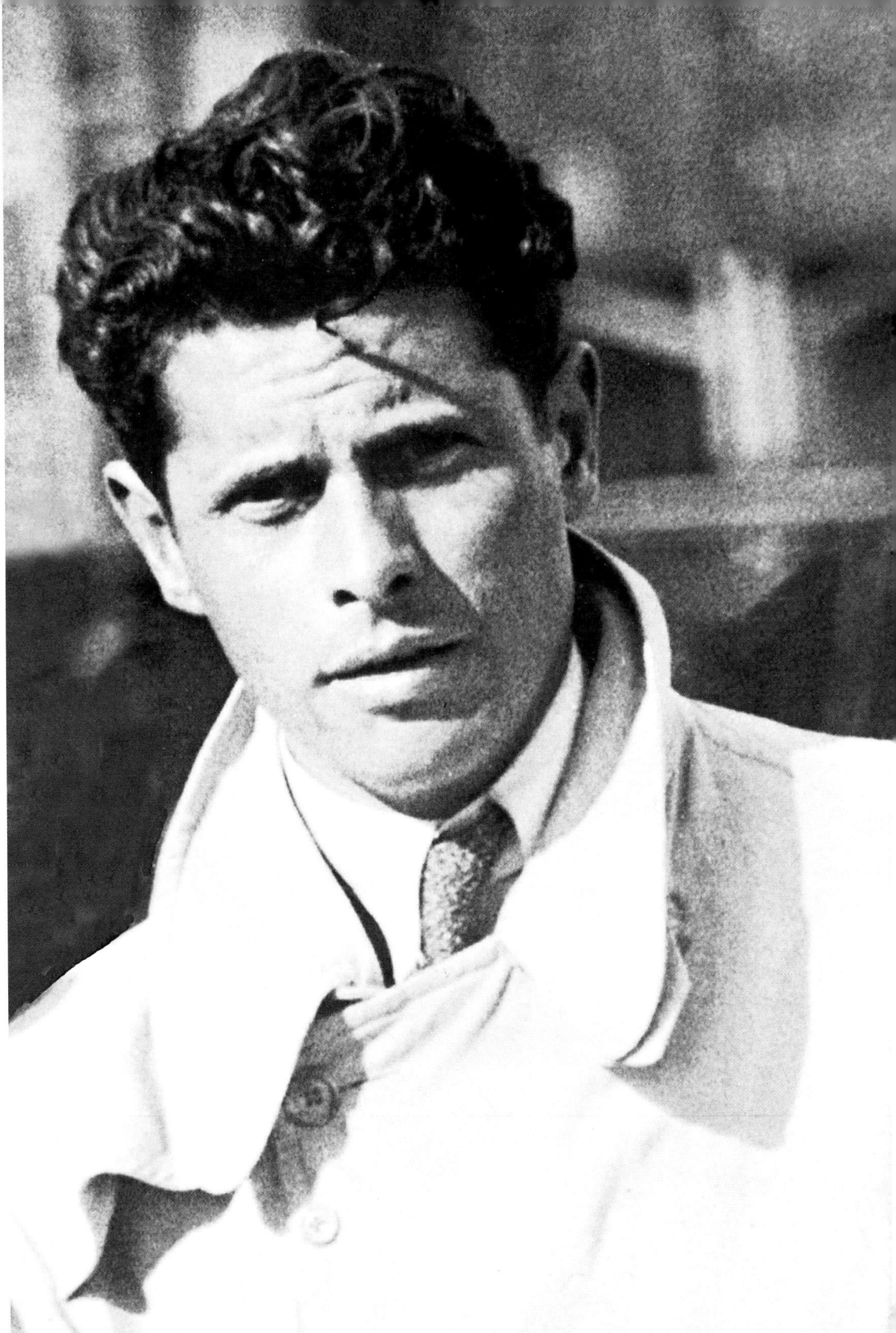

A passport photo (believed to be taken in 1934).

Relaxing whilst on holiday in the Loire region (1937).

Glamorous portrait by the famous Studio Harcourt (c1955).

Overlooking the Mediterranean coast.

CHAPTER

TWO

UNDER THE WINGS OF GABRIEL VOISIN

On August 3, 1914 Kaiser Wilhelm's Germany declared war on France. The next day the German Second Army crossed the border into Luxembourg and Belgium.

During the night of August 5, General Von Emmich attacked the city of Liége with a force of 30,000 men. Much to the surprise of the over-confident German staff, Von Emmich's troops sustained heavy losses and made little progress. Then the German army called in Zeppelins to drop bombs on the city and citadel to break the Belgian resistance. It was the first ever aerial bombardment in warfare history.

To the French War Ministry the message was clear: at that moment the 24 escadrilles of the French Armée de l'Air had only 158 planes and 5 airships at their disposal, so it was vital to establish an air force powerful enough to combat these German airships. To do this they needed all the pilots and airplanes they could get.

André Lefebvre was called up for military service. However, he was discharged for medical reasons, as he had become seriously ill with rheumatic fever. Fortunately, as one of the few graduated aeronautical engineers, he could be even more valuable to the French war effort working in the aviation industry than as a soldier or pilot. So, on the first of March 1916, Lefebvre started at the Voisin airplane factory.

His boss, Gabriel Voisin (1880-1973), was one of France's aviation pioneers. He had abandoned his architectural studies at the Beaux Arts in Lyon in order to get a job as a draftsman with the organisers of the 1900 World Exhibition in Paris. In one of the pavilions on the vast exhibition area beneath the Eiffel Tower he discovered the 'Eole,' a huge, bat-winged plane fitted with a four-blade propeller that was driven by a two-cylinder steam engine, and also met Clement Ader, its engineer/inventor, who, with his contraption, had 'flown' on October 6, 1890 over a distance of 50 meters on the estate of the Château d'Armainvilliers, near Gretz.

All of this had a profound impact on Voisin, who became fanatically fascinated by flying and flying machines. During Easter 1904 he was photographed while airborne in a glider plane doing a trial flight near Berck Plage. An enthusiastic young man named Jacques-Henri Lartigue – who would become one of the best-known photographers of his time – took the picture. Ernest Archdeacon, a wealthy lawyer and founding member of the Aero Club de France, who had sponsored Gabriel's flight, had the prints of these photos sent to all the members of his club and to the leading French newspapers. The ensuing publicity, and the proposal by Voisin to build a motorised airplane, led Archdeacon and some of his business friends to finance a Syndicat d'Aviation, and Gabriel Voisin was appointed as its engineer. In the years that followed he earned the reputation of being a highly imaginative and talented airplane designer.

When in 1911 Voisin launched the first plane with a metal frame, his competitors – who all used wood – considered this sheer madness. But Voisin's metal fuselage was one of the reasons why his planes became so popular with the flying schools that were training military pilots: contrary to wooden airframes, the metal ones did not warp when the planes stood overnight on a chill and damp airfield, and that saved a lot of time in the morning as trimming or adjustment was not necessary. Besides which, the pilots considered the Voisin planes to be very stable, predictable and reliable.

In October 1914 the French War Ministry decided that Voisin's design would be the standard machine for the Army Air Service to be used for reconnaissance and bombing. In a patriotic gesture Gabriel Voisin renounced any financial benefits from his licensing rights and so Voisin airplanes were produced by a number of other manufacturers also. Between 1914 and the armistice some 10,000 Voisin-designed machines took to the air, all manned by allied pilots, during which period, the Voisin factory situated at Issy-les-Moulineaux was the leading manufacturer of military aircraft in France.

Gabriel Voisin was a thin, bony and dynamic man with a strong personality. He could be very charming to women – especially if they were young and attractive – and to his clients, friends and equals. However, in those days many self-made industrialists sometimes abused their authority by treating their employees as might a drill sergeant in the army, screaming, cursing and shouting abuse. Voisin was no exception; he often called people 'imbécile' – including himself. He was very outspoken and never minced his words, but he was absolutely straight, both in business dealings and with his collaborators; he trusted other people to be as reliable and loyal as he was himself. In technical matters he was a genius, but he was also a rebel who preferred to be different. He lived with the conviction that his own – often unconventional – solutions were the best, and, as he concedes in his own autobiography, *Mes milles et une voitures*, he tended to be somewhat naïve as far as politics and commercial affairs were concerned.

In 1917 a businessman offered Voisin eight million francs for his factory (a real fortune in those days), and he spontaneously accepted this bid. Gabriel thought that with such capital he could realise an old dream and devote all his time and energy to experiments and inventions. For the execution of his ideas, and to help him with research and development work, he set up a small engineering workshop in Issy-les-Moulineaux, which he called his 'laboratoire.'

However, not long after the sale a delegation of former employees and suppliers visited him, urging him to turn back the clock as things were not going well at all; apparently, the new owner had no idea how to run a manufacturing company. Some time

Experimental World War I Voisin aeroplane type M or 'surbaissé.' It remained an experiment. (Courtesy Monde et Caméra No 13382)

A rare picture of the prototype of the Voisin type 12, a dual wing, four-engined bomber that Lefebvre worked on from 1917 till September 1918. It had four Hispano-Suiza engines, back-to-back, both sides of the fuselage. As it was not operational until September 1918, it never went into production. (Courtesy Collection family Lefebvre)

later the new owner approached Voisin and offered him the position of managing partner in his old factory, on condition that Voisin would refund six million francs. Gabriel Voisin felt emotionally responsible for the enterprise he had founded, and did not want to let down his former collaborators, so decided to return. His faithful bookkeeper verified that Voisin's payment of six million francs was duly incorporated in the capital of the company, but a few months later his new associate fraudulently transferred most of the money to another bank account and used it to finance other ventures. It took Voisin until November 12, 1918 to win his case in court and be reinstated as sole owner of his factory.

Voisin's other weakness (if one can call it that) was women; he was a passionate womaniser. Most females found him irresistible and easily fell for his charm. This regularly caused complications, especially if some women became jealous when he spent time with another conquest. He boasted in his autobiography that there was a period in his life when he regularly had three dinners in the same evening – two with mistresses and one with his wife. It cost him a lot of money, although he never gained much weight!

Head of the Voisin 'laboratoire'

When the young 'ingénieur' Lefebvre began working at the Voisin factory it was producing light bombers that also served for reconnaissance flights. In November 1916, French squadrons received their first Voisin night bombers. From 1915 onward Gabriel Voisin was busy experimenting with new types of landing gear. The type M looked like a typical Voisin dual wing 'pusher plane' with its radial water-cooled Salmson engine at the back of the cockpit. But, instead of the traditional four landing wheels, mounted on a frame that was fitted below the fuselage like the wheels of an old-fashioned pram, it had three landing wheels that were partly integrated in the fuselage. The aim was to reduce air resistance in order to achieve better performance without having to change over to more powerful engines. At about the same time Voisin constructed the type Q that had two M-type fuselages connected by a single lower wing. However, the Voisin M and the dual fuselage Voisin Q remained prototypes and never went into production.

One can assume that André Lefebvre assisted Voisin with the development of an undercarriage which was one of the first to have brakes, rubber suspension and shock absorbers. He must also have worked on the double-decker Voisin type 12, a large strategic bomber equipped with four Hispano-Suiza 220bhp engines, back-to-back at both sides of the fuselage, the front ones with pulling propellers and the rear ones with pushers. The machine was operational in September 1918, but by then nobody was interested anymore in such a military aircraft.

As Lefebvre gradually became more involved in the design and construction of the company's new planes, he proved not only a bright and inventive technician, but also a born leader, with the natural authority to convince his co-workers of what had to be done and why. Gabriel Voisin – in those days very much involved in what was going on in his workshops – soon became aware of this ability, which explains why when, in 1917 Voisin decided to establish his 'laboratoire,' he promoted this bright and promising engineer to head its team of eight qualified mechanics. What began as a straightforward working relation between the 'patron' Gabriel Voisin and his employee André Lefebvre would grow into a lifelong friendship between two men who shared the same passion for 'la belle mécanique.'

Years later Lefebvre told some of his colleagues at Citroën that, in the past, there had almost been an airplane constructed under the name Avions Lefebvre, and, as it was well known that Lefebvre had graduated as an aeronautical engineer, nobody was amazed or asked for details. So, two questions remain: who designed this aircraft and what happened to it? It is certainly true that after the sale of his factory, for a while legal problems prevented Gabriel Voisin from constructing or selling aircraft under his own name. But it is doubtful whether, during this time, Voisin and/or Lefebvre were actually engaged in designing or even thinking of building airplanes. A more likely explanation is that some confusion arose from the fact that the man who bought the factory from Voisin also happened to own the SARL (Société Anonyme à Responsibilité Limitée) Lefebvre. Theoretically, he could have applied for the type approval of a new plane under the name Avions Lefebvre, although there are no documents to show that he did so. And just to set the record straight, this new owner was not a relation and André Lefebvre never worked for him, as he stayed on with Gabriel Voisin's 'laboratoire.'

From Gabriel Voisin's *Mes 1001 Voitures* we know that during the First World War the bark of heavy guns could often be heard in the factory as Issy-les-Moulineaux was close to the firing line of German artillery. Fortunately, neither the production halls nor the laboratoire were ever hit.

After invading Belgium and northeastern France, the German First Army – under General Von Kluck – tried to encircle Paris from the east. By September 6, 1914, Kluck's troops had advanced to within 50km of Paris. The French capital was saved by the French Général Joffre and the military governor of Paris, Galliéni, deciding to ferry 6000 French reserve infantry soldiers to the front line in a convoy of Paris taxi cabs (most of them Renaults). This First Battle of the Marne culminated in a strategic triumph for the Allied forces, as the French army, together with the British Expeditionary Forces, succeeded in pushing back the Germans. But the toll was terrible with, it is believed, over 250,000 French military and civilian casualties. The Germans suffered heavy losses as well, although there are no official figures. It is also well known that during the last year of the war the Germans regularly bombarded Paris with their 'Big Bertha' gun, a 420mm 'siege howitzer' with a range of 100km that was responsible for the deaths of many civilians.

FROM AIRPLANES TO AUTOMOBILES

Long before the armistice of 1918, Voisin realised that the demand for military aircraft would take a sharp dive. After considering various alternatives, such as building large planes for civil aviation, producing motorised bicycles or small four-wheeled cycle cars (a predecessor of his later Biscooter), and constructing prefabricated houses, he decided to become an automobile manufacturer.

One evening Gabriel Voisin was having dinner in Maxim's, his favourite Paris restaurant, when a man by the name of Ernest Artault offered him all the drawings for the production of a luxurious automobile with a four-cylinder engine (Knight sleeve valve system), and four prototypes. The car was designed by his friend, Louis Dufresne, an engineer who had worked for Panhard.

The project had first been proposed to André Citroën, who was seriously interested and seemed willing to finance the prototypes. But after a visit to the USA, Citroën changed his mind and decided to convert his munitions plant to the production of automobiles that would sell in large quantities. He had aspirations to become the French Henry Ford and wanted to concentrate his efforts on popular models that could be mass-produced; clearly, André Citroën was no longer interested in the design of a luxury model.

Gabriel Voisin understood very well that he and his team knew everything about constructing airplanes, but next to nothing about manufacturing automobiles, and he also appreciated the silent power of the big Knight sleeve valve engine. He signed a contract to acquire all the rights and engaged Artault and Dufresne to help him get the car into production. This way Voisin saved himself a lot of time and money that would have been required to develop a car of his own design.

Early in 1918 the first machines and equipment for building the cars arrived at Issy-les-Moulineaux. At about the same time the construction of a fifth prototype was started: the first car to bear the name Avions Voisin. From then on the word Avions became linked with Voisin's former activities as an airplane manufacturer.

Fast forward in reverse

Voisin recalled in his autobiography: "At four o'clock on a cold and foggy morning the first chassis was ready for its maiden trip. It had no body; only a wooden bench. When I tried to drive off, the car surged backwards. I tried again, with the same result. The mechanics that had worked all night now stood around the car full of expectation.

"I then discovered that the rear axle had been fitted the wrong way round: this explained why the car reacted as if it had four reverse gears and one forward gear."

The incident had its positive side as well and Voisin insisted on continuing the trial run. Whilst driving backward at a relatively high speed on the icy and wet tarmac of his test track, he noticed that the car remained more stable during braking than when he drove forward at a much lower speed. As was usual practice in those days, his chassis was fitted with brakes on the rear wheels only, and Voisin decided that on future models he should fit brakes on the front wheels as well.

This first Voisin, the 4-litre M1, was still based on the Dufresne-Artaud design that had originally been developed for Citroën. The code letter M probably stood for Mors, the French luxury make that André Citroën had been closely involved with before WWI. The factory where once the Mors cars were made was now part of his company.

The M1 was a good car and mechanically conformed to the standards of its time, but Gabriel Voisin was a perfectionist and detected a number of weaknesses that Lefebvre and his crew had to rectify. Small changes to the engine gave the cars more power and greater reliability; in 1920, power went up from 80 to 100bhp. At the same time the type designation was changed to C1, and this C prefix would be used on all future Voisin models. Some claim that the letter C was chosen by Gabriel in memory of his deceased brother, Charles, with whom he had constructed a primitive automobile, nicknamed 'Char,' when they were both young boys. Others say that this is a nice romantic story, but that the C simply stands for chassis ...

Spiritual son

Voisin and Lefebvre did a lot of road testing together. From time to time they encountered serious technical problems that necessitated roadside repair, as Gabriel Voisin refused to go to local garages, fearing that these might discover the weak points in his cars. Some weekends they would drive as fast as their car would go from Paris to Cannes, where Voisin had a boat. At the Côte d'Azur they rounded up some attractive girlfriends and had a lot of fun. Then they would race back to Issy-les-Moulineaux. If we believe Gabriel's book, they often covered the almost 950km within 12 hours. Considering the road surfaces of that time, the cobblestones in many of the villages that they had to go through, the chances of a tyre blow-out and the fact that part of the route consisted of steep passes in the French Alps, achieving an average of nearly 80km/h must have entailed a lot of courage – and probably some reckless driving as well!

But that this was possible was proven on April 6, 1921 by Dominique Lamberjack, a friend of and dealer for Gabriel Voisin and Ettore Bugatti, when he was officially timed on a run from Paris via Fontainebleau, Auxerre, Chalon-sur-Saône, Grenoble. Sisteron and Digne. He arrived in Nice 11 hours 30min 40sec after he had left the French capital. With his 4-litre C1 Voisin, fitted with an aluminium factory body, Lamberjack not only bettered the previous record set by André Dubonnet with a 6.6-litre 32 CV Hispano-Suiza, but also established Voisin's reputation as a manufacturer of fast luxury cars, which boosted sales.

During their many test runs to get the cars behaving as they should, Voisin and Lefebvre discovered a number of fundamental laws of car design, and their years as aircraft builders helped them analyse the shortcomings and find remedies. As they discussed their findings, their differences in experience and education complemented each other and worked very well. Gabriel Voisin was a brilliant but intuitive and self-educated technical genius; Lefebvre had scientific training but was also highly intelligent and gifted with the creativity to translate Voisin's remarks into workable technical solutions. So it is quite logical that Gabriel Voisin – who only had one daughter – came to regard André Lefebvre as his spiritual son.

Gabriel Voisin had outspoken views about some design features that were equally important in aircraft as in cars. One of these was what he called 'centrage,' which means centring when translated, but for him it had a broader meaning: the precise concentration (distribution) of weight and (aerodynamic) forces. "A plane could never fly without centrage," he would say, "and a car without centrage is a danger to its driver."

According to Voisin, 'centrage' was a prime condition for good controllability, the importance of which was something that Voisin had learned during his career as an aircraft manufacturer. During pioneer days, a pilot needed his plane to let him feel when he reached the 'danger zone' and to react 'positively' to his input to regain control. Controllability meant safety, and, for this reason, pilots wanted planes that 'handled' well.

Voisin was convinced that the same principle applied to automobiles, and always reacted furiously when a journalist wrote that so-and-so had an accident because he or she had 'lost control' of their car.

One of the first Voisin automobiles, a C1 open tourer (1919-1920). (Courtesy Avions Voisin)

UNDER THE WINGS OF GABRIEL VOISIN

Four men who shared a passion for fast driving; from left to right: Gabriel Voisin, Dominique Lamberjack, César Marchand and André Lefebvre. (Courtesy 'Strazza,' Milano)

Discussing and evaluating the behaviour of a car with Gabriel Voisin after a test run. (Courtesy Collection family Lefebvre)

"Except when the driver has fallen asleep such accidents always have a technical reason," was his opinion: "lack of controllability."

AVIATION STANDARDS FOR SAFETY AND RELIABILITY

There is no doubt that André Lefebvre was greatly influenced by the theories and philosophies of his more experienced patron. This is understandable as their aviation backgrounds made both men highly sceptical of the established traditions of other automobile designers, many of whom had begun their careers as 'engine' men.

Voisin and Lefebvre were not primarily interested in engine performance, acceleration and speed. They were more preoccupied with safety and reliability than most of their colleagues. Therefore, chassis dynamics, ensuring controllability, and aerodynamic stability to reduce sensitivity to strong gusts of side winds, got high priority in all Voisin designs.

Their objectives of safety and stability led to a number of 'golden rules:'
• the mass (weight) of the engine and gearbox should be within the wheelbase
• the centre of gravity should be ahead of the middle of the wheelbase

- the centre of gravity must be as low as possible
- the aerodynamic centre of pressure should be behind the centre of gravity
- the brakes on the front wheels must be more powerful than those at the rear

Voisin's other design criteria were:
- the axis of the kingpins must coincide at road level with the centre of the front wheel tyres. In other words, he was a proponent of 'centre point' steering
- keeping down total vehicle weight
- an efficient aerodynamic profile combined with the smallest possible frontal area

These views were equally shared by Lefebvre.

It may surprise today's readers that the men did not develop theories about roll centres and wheel camber and their effect on cornering. But in the early 1920s, most cars still had rigid front and rear axles, so this was not yet an issue. However, when Lefebvre later started to develop cars with independent suspension, this matter became of great concern to him, especially while working on the Citroën 2CV and DS.

PREPARATION OF COMPETITION CARS

In those early days Lefebvre had little to do with the actual production of Voisin cars, still the responsibility of Dufresne. But the workload of the experimental department increased

Lefebvre developed the successful Strasbourg racers from the standard Voisin C3 chassis. This drawing of the 18HP chassis/type C3 Court (Short) was published in October 1922 by the French magazine Omnia.
1 View from the right side. 2 View from above. A 4-cylinder sleeve valve engine, bore & stroke: 95x140mm. B Horizontal carburettor. C 'Exhauster' fuel pump. D Four-speed gearbox. E Oil filler. F Batteries.

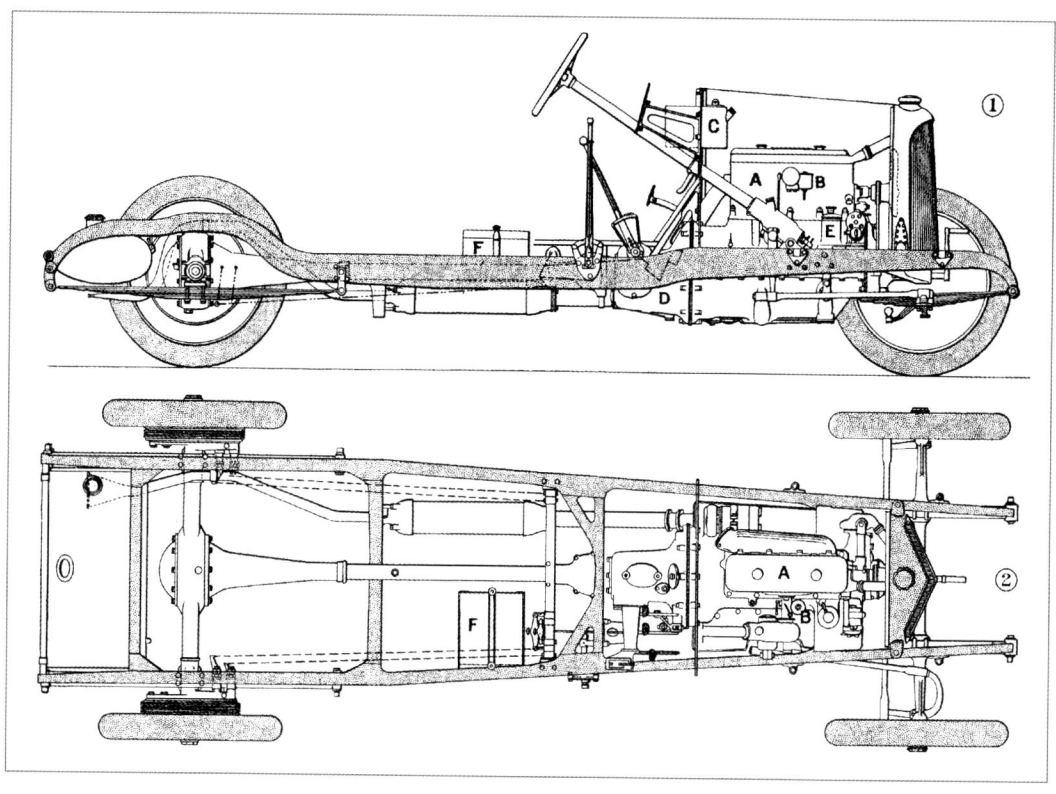

One of the 1922 Voisin C3 S (type GP de Strasbourg) competition cars during a test run with Henri Rougier at the wheel. (Courtesy Avions Voisin)

enormously, and Lefebvre also had to supervise the preparation of Voisin's competition cars. So at the end of 1920, Marius Bernard joined the team. Bernard had graduated as Ingénieur des Arts et Métiers in Lille, and was a gifted 'motoriste' (engine designer). Lefebvre, with his aviation background, had more experience with stress analysis, chassis design, aerodynamics and road behaviour. As both men were also skilled test drivers, they made a perfect team, though never became close friends. Bernard was probably somewhat jealous of Lefebvre, who remained Gabriel Voisin's favourite, his spiritual son. After Bernard became responsible for the manufacturing side, he would sometimes tease his colleague that the money needed for the cars Lefebvre designed was earned by the Voisin production models.

Between 1920 and the end of 1925, Voisin cars amassed more than 90 first prizes in racing events, with their biggest success the 1922 Grand Prix of the Automobile Club de France for touring cars at Strasbourg, when Gabriel Voisin was rewarded with an enormous silver trophy as his C3 S took the first three places.

André Lefebvre and his team at Voisin's development department were, of course, responsible for the preparation of these cars. With specially-designed magnesium pistons that increased compression ratio from 5 to 8, the 3969cc, four-cylinder sleeve valve engines developed around 120bhp at 3500rpm. The engine block and radiator were fitted some 20cm lower than in the standard C3 chassis, which not only brought down the centre of gravity (and improved roadholding), but also reduced overall height. Apart from being relatively light (the Voisins weighed just 1134kg), their bodies were designed to give minimal aerodynamic drag.

The ACF decreed that participating cars must have mudguards, and that coachwork had to be at least 130cm wide. Gabriel Voisin found this last rule ridiculous, and decided to fit his cars with aluminium four-seater torpedo coachwork that was only 90cm wide but had cigar-shaped bulges at both sides. This gave the least possible air resistance whilst still complying with the regulations; race organisers had to accept his entries but were not pleased ...

It has never been disclosed who came up with this ingenious and completely legal solution, which is reminiscent of the tulip-shaped body that Ferdinand Porsche designed in 1910 for his Prince Henry of Prussia Trial-winning Austro-Daimler, in order to circumvent a similar rule. However, it seems unlikely that Gabriel Voisin knew about this, as Porsche's

According to Philipp Moch, its present owner, this beautifully rebuilt Voisin C3 S is the car in which Henri Rougier won the 1922 Grand Prix de Tourisme at Strasbourg. Clearly visible is the cigar-shaped bulge at the side of the body which served to adapt the narrow aluminium coachwork to the width of 1m 30 that Automobile club de France race regulations required. (Courtesy Hans Arend de Wit/Switchimage)

Austro-Daimler dated from before the First World War, when Voisin was only interested in aviation and not yet in motor racing.

In any case, the Voisin C3 racers proved not only the fastest at the Strasbourg circuit, they were also very economical. In his memoirs Gabriel Voisin later wrote: "When our cars crossed the finish line there was sufficient fuel left from the allocated amount (based on a consumption of 16 litres per 100km) to wash the cars of our competitors."

THE AUTOMOBILE CLUB DE FRANCE BANS AERODYNAMIC EXPERIMENTS

The Sporting Committee of the Automobile Club de France did not appreciate Voisin's clever interpretation of its rules. When in December 1922 the regulations for the next year's Grand Prix were published, they required specific dimensions for the four-seater bodies, which put an end to aerodynamic experiments. As Voisin had already prepared his cars for the 1923 season by nibbling away another 100kg, and further reducing aerodynamic drag by changing the shape of the mudguards, Gabriel saw this as a personal snub. He wrote a sarcastic open letter to the ACF, denouncing its attitude to progress in automobile design. In the same letter he stated that he would not start in the race, but would instead engage four cars in the next Grand Prix de Vitesse.

This race was scheduled for July 2, 1923, and would take place on the Circuit de Touraine, a triangle of closed public roads just north of the city of Tours, passing through the villages of La Membrolle and Semblançay. The circuit had a length of 22.83km that had to be covered 35 times, to a total distance of 799.05km, with stretches where a speed of 200km/h could be achieved. Entry was open to machines with an engine capacity of up to 2 litres. A fierce battle was expected, as top drivers from several countries would compete for victory. At the time, this event had a media impact comparable with Formula 1 today.

What motivated Voisin to take on this challenge that was akin to hunting elephants with an air rifle? Was it the result of momentary pique or a desperate attempt to show that streamlining could compensate for the limited power of his sleeve valve engines? Either way, in his memoirs Gabriel admitted that, considering the time and money involved, his decision was indeed an 'unqualified stupidity.'

ANDRÉ'S BIG CHANCE!

For the ambitious and eager André Lefebvre, however, this 'unqualified stupidity' meant a chance to prove his worth, as he was to construct and test the cars for the Grand Prix de Tours – and had just six and a half months in which to do it. With youthful enthusiasm he conceived one of the most remarkable racing cars of its time.

The Voisin factory did not at that moment have an engine suitable for the Grand Prix de Vitesse, but Marius Bernard was already working on a replacement of the 1248cc engine in the Voisin C4 with a new, 1328cc, four-cylinder that had a bore of 62mm and a stroke of 110mm. For the C6 Course cars a new block was designed which had the same bore and stroke but two extra cylinders. The resulting six-cylinder had a cubic capacity of exactly 1984cc. Lefebvre and Voisin were well aware that their competitors' engines – which had poppet valves – could reach higher revs and thus would develop more power than their own sleeve valve machines were able to deliver, even if they could be slightly souped-up. The only way to compete with some success was to reduce to a minimum both the weight and aerodynamic drag of their cars.

Journalists wrote that the shape of the Voisin C6 Course resembled "an airplane without wings." Others called it the Voisin 'Laboratoire' because of its advanced concept. A few technical details: 1 Large drum brakes on the front wheels. 2 Propeller driving the water pump. 3 Radiator. 4 Six-cylinder sleeve valve engine and single plate clutch. 5 Wire mesh racing screen (can be folded down). 6 Fuel tank. 7 Aluminium and wood monocoque (unit construction), with the rear wheels within the body contours. 8 Spare wheel in tail. 9 Front track: 1.45m. 10 Flat and closed underside. 11 Wheelbase: 2.72m. 12 Underslung rear axle, no differential, rear track only 0.75m. Dimensions: length 4.53m, width 1.50m, height 1.05m, ground clearance 0.22m. Curb weight ± 660kg.

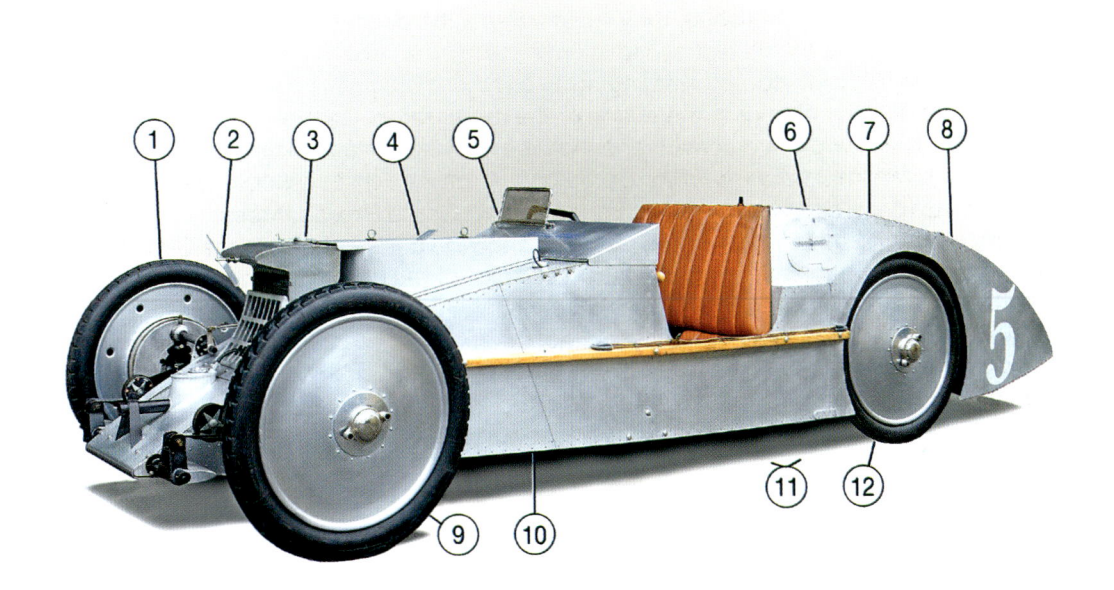

With its two Zenith carburettors the 1.992-litre six-cylinder sleeve valve engine developed 80bhp @ 4800rpm. But Gabriel Voisin instructed his drivers not to exceed 4000rpm. (Courtesy Hans Arend de Wit/Switchimage)

For this reason the Voisin C6 Course or 'Laboratoire,' as it later became known, was designed like the fuselage of an airplane. It had no conventional chassis, but was, in fact, the first racing car with a body-cum-chassis or monocoque construction; a sort of box consisting of a light ash frame, aluminium panels and a flat aluminium undershield. This structure, with its steel and wooden reinforcements, supported all of the mechanical parts such as the engine, transmission, and front and rear suspensions, its width dictated by the requirement that the cockpit should offer enough space for the driver and a riding mechanic. When the completed cars were officially weighed, the scales indicated 660kg, only 10kg over the minimum weight that the regulations of this Grand Prix decreed.

On the first prototype the front axle of the C4 was used, setting the front track at 1m 30. In order to reduce air resistance to a minimum, Gabriel Voisin and Lefebvre – experienced aircraft designers – used every trick they knew. The body got a long and tapering tail, and, at first, the track at the rear measured only 50cm. But, taking a fast corner on the road from Villacoublay to Issy during one of his trial runs, Lefebvre turned his Laboratoire on its side, luckily without too serious damage to himself or the car. After several more tests and by increasing the rear track bit by bit, Lefebvre found that 75cm of track provided sufficient stability. The rear wheels were then still just within the contours of the body. At the same time the front track was increased to 1m 45.

In 1992, the French Voisin expert Philipp Moch constructed an accurate replica of a C6 Course – using genuine Voisin parts and retracing its design from photos and personal notes from Gabriel Voisin himself – on no less than 100 square meters of new drawings. According to him, these cars had no differential. The rear axle housing, containing only the crown and pinion wheels, was made from aluminium, and had two vertically protruding parts that encased two thin strips of ash. The aim of this construction was to guide and limit the up-and-down movement of the rear axle unit with its simple quarter elliptic leaf springs. At the front these Voisin Grand Prix machines had half elliptic leaf springs and friction shock absorbers.

Lefebvre and his 'mécanos' worked practically day and night to get four cars ready for the race, systematically testing and improving every detail.

The six-cylinder was tuned to provide maximum power. It had magnesium pistons and provisions were made to prevent the sleeve valves from seizing and to keep down the temperature of the cylinder heads, even if this meant an increase of oil consumption. To minimise power losses the water pumps of the Laboratoires were driven by a small air propeller above the radiator. Bench testing showed that, with two big Zenith 36 HK

Some of the Laboratoires had a 'square' steering wheel with a flat top and bottom. Dashboard instruments included a clock. (Courtesy Hans Arend de Wit/Switchimage)

This picture shows the large, cable-operated, 'Perrot' drum brakes on the front wheels. (Courtesy Hans Arend de Wit/Switchimage)

The front suspension had leaf springs and the then usual friction-type shock absorbers. Note the wooden strengthening behind the rear of the spring mounting. (Courtesy Hans Arend de Wit/Switchimage)

With a rear wheel removed, it's possible to see details of the rear suspension and the underslung rear axle with its large brake drum. The photo also reveals the secrets of the monocoque body construction, the housing of the spare wheel, and location of the fuel tank just behind the seats. (Courtesy Hans Arend de Wit/Switchimage)

While the driver and mechanics look somewhat worried, Lefebvre seriously searches for the source of all the smoke. (Courtesy Sporting Magazine)

carburettors, at 4800rpm some 80bhp was available. Gabriel Voisin gave instructions that the drivers should not exceed 4000rpm, which reduced maximum power to 75bhp, resulting in a top speed of just under 175km/h. Not bad at all – but not enough!

The news that not one but two French marques were to participate with revolutionary streamlined race cars in the Grand Prix de Tours attracted a lot of attention in the press.

Gabriel Voisin had told his friend, Ettore Bugatti, about the advantages of aerodynamics, and 'Le Patron' of Molsheim entered four of his streamlined Type 32s that the journalists nicknamed the Bugatti 'tanks.' Their single overhead camshaft (SOHC) engines were developed from those of the eight-cylinder Type 30, and the cars had a conventional chassis frame under all-enveloping coachwork. With a wheelbase of just 2m, a total length of 3.80m, and a width of only 1.20m, they were very small cars with a minimal frontal surface, but with a total weight of around 750kg, they were heavier than the Voisins.

If we believe Bugatti experts Hugh Conway and Maurice Sauzay, Ettore did not have much experience of the basics of aerodynamics, and it seems that there was a fundamental error in the body design of these 'tanks.' Seen from the side their shape resembled the cross section of an airplane wing. This wing profile did indeed minimise drag, but also induced some lift, which made the car unstable and difficult to control at high speed: probably why the experienced Bugatti driver Pierre Viscaya left the road and crashed at Tours.

The C6 Courses were outclassed from the start by the limited power of their relatively slow turning engines. Bugatti's tanks had approximately 90bhp at their disposal and could easily reach 180km/h. The Sunbeam engine – with its double overhead camshafts

July 2, 1923. Le Jour de Gloire! André Lefebvre and his riding mechanic, Raphaël Fortin, waiting for their official 'weighing' at the town hall of Semblançay.
(Courtesy Sporting Magazine*)*

The four Voisins in front of their pit boxes at the circuit de Touraine. The C6 Course of Lefebvre (No 10) is behind number 12 driven by Duray. (Courtesy Agence M Rol)

André Lefebvre and Raphaël Fortin just before the start. In the background the Bugatti 'tanks.' (Courtesy Collection family Lefebvre)

Lefebvre driving at full speed past the grandstand. Note the blackened rear wheel. (Document courtesy Collection family Lefebvre, photo courtesy Sporting Magazine)

(DOHC) – developed 103bhp. And the Fiat, with its 130bhp supercharged eight-cylinder engine, could reach a top speed of over 195km/h.

Bringing the 'Laboratoire' over the finish line

Of the 18 starters only five reached the finish. The winner was Henry Seagrave whose Sunbeam averaged 121km/h. The Voisins of Rougier, Morel and Duray belonged to the unfortunate 13 cars that had to abandon the race.

The sole surviving Voisin – with starting number 10 – came in fifth place. It crossed the finish line after completing 798 kilometres at an average of 105km/h. At the steering wheel sat its designer, André Lefebvre, his courageous riding mechanic, Raphael Fortin, at his side. Both men were tired and dirty. When they took off their goggles they looked like owls because of the dust from the road that coated their faces.

It seems that Gabriel Voisin was rather pleased with the achievements of his 'spiritual

Congratulations! Of the four Voisins engaged at Tours, that which Lefebvre drove was the only one to finish. (Courtesy Maison Well)

son.' In his memoirs he wrote proudly: "Thirteen of our competitors, some of them the greatest names in the world of speed, had bitten the dust and we were amongst the survivors."

For Voisin the C6 Course, or 'Laboratoire' as this last name implies, was not only a racing car but also part of a research programme. The bitter lessons learned from the three C6 racers that had to give up with seized pistons and broken con-rods, helped Marius Bernard to redesign and improve these components, with the result that the later 2326cc, six-cylinders used in the C11, C14 and C15 Voisin chassis belonged to the most reliable engines of their time.

For the race on September 9, 1923 at Monza (Italy), the Voisin 'Laboratoires' had their wheel discs removed to improve brake cooling. Here we see Rougier in the Monza paddock. (Courtesy 'Strazza,' Milano)

Silvani in the Voisin No 3 made a good start leading Guyot (No 4), and Count Zobrowski (No 5). But the Voisin engines could not stand the pace at Monza. (Courtesy 'Strazza,' Milano)

The Italian Grand Prix, on September 9, 1923, saw three of the 'Tours racers' on the starting grid. This time Lefebvre did not drive in the race but accompanied the cars to the Monza track and acted as the team's chief mechanic. The drivers – Rougier, Duray and Silvani – made a good start and their cars seemed fast enough, but the engines did not stand the pace and none of the Voisins finished. However, in October of that year, Lefebvre made a good showing in the hill climb at Gaillon in northern France with a modified C6 'Laboratoire' powered by a 4-litre engine. With hindsight, it is obvious that this modification was a try-out for the next generation of sportscars that Gabriel Voisin had in mind.

Marriage to Claire

His successes as a designer and driver were not the only achievements that made Lefebvre a proud and happy man. In March 1923 he had also married Claire Grand, a pretty, charming and very intelligent young woman who worked as secretary to Gabriel Voisin.

Lefebvre had fallen in love with her and had wanted to marry her for a long time, but had been somewhat reluctant to ask because his first marriage had ended too soon and rather unhappily. He realised that when he married his first wife in 1916 they were both too young and inexperienced, simply wanting to continue to live the way they had in prewar Paris as sheltered and spoiled adolescents. In 1917, soon after the birth of their first son, Jean, his wife left both him and their infant child, returning, after a while, with a baby daughter, Alice, whom he acknowledged. But then she left again, leaving him in charge of the two young children. He often felt that he was partly to blame for this unfortunate situation, because his work with Voisin absorbed him so much and his first wife probably felt neglected. But André was six years older now, more mature and much wiser; Claire an understanding wife and pleasant company, and they enjoyed their life together. He also had a steady and interesting job, so the future looked bright.

Return to touring car races

At Issy-les-Moulineaux everybody agreed that the Knight engines were unsuitable as racing machines. Because of the double sleeve mechanism, these engines

On October 7, André Lefebvre participated successfully with a much modified C6 Course in a hill climb near Gaillon. The two-litre engine was replaced by a 4-litre unit. (Courtesy Sporting Magazine)

André – behind the open bonnet – and Claire, during a trip with their first car: an early Voisin that has only very rudimentary coachwork. (Courtesy Collection family Lefebvre)

Just before the start of de Grand Prix de Touraine. André is accompanied by two elegant ladies: the one on the left is his wife, Claire; the other is believed to be Madame Voisin. (Courtesy Collection family Lefebvre)

When André took Claire for a holiday to Quibéron in Brittany in 1924, their Voisin had a neat, but unpainted torpedo body. (Courtesy Collection family Lefebvre)

could never run at the same high revs their competitors achieved with double overhead (poppet) valves (see Appendix 1). To continue participating in races with a strict limit on cubic capacity would indeed have been an 'unqualified stupidity.'

However, Gabriel Voisin, who detested mechanical noise, did not intend to abandon his silent sleeve valve engines, and was wise enough to understand that his only option was to return to touring car races. The main event in 1924 for this category was the Grand Prix de l'ACF, on August 3 near Lyon, over 300km on a 24.5km long road circuit. Voisin entered five cars in three different categories, and Lefebvre's experimental department was ordered to construct these completely new machines.

By now André Lefebvre had shown that he was able to design potential winners, and that he and his team could work extremely fast; they had built the 1923 racers in record time. He was also a capable and fast driver

With Claire and dog around 1928. (Courtesy Collection family Lefebvre)

who could successfully compete with experienced professionals. Gabriel Voisin not only endorsed but even encouraged Lefebvre's unorthodox approach to car design, and the dedicated craftsmen and mechanics in his workshop respected him and followed his instructions to the letter.

Designing the new cars Lefebvre applied the lessons he had learned while building and driving the first 'Laboratoires,' so in a number of technical details they resembled the C6 Course, although their basic layout was totally different. To comply with the

Artist's impression of a small Voisin sports car. It is believed that Gabriel Voisin intended to market Lefebvre's small voiturette as the C10, but the project was abandoned.

Gabriel Voisin asked Lefebvre to prepare five cars for the Grand Prix de Tourisme at Lyon in 1924. One 10CV Voiturette, one for the category Voitures Légères, and three for the category Voitures. For all these machines Lefebvre used an aluminium monocoque body construction quite similar to that of the C6 Course. From left to right: the cars of Rougier, Lefebvre, Gaudermen, Morel and Piccioni. (Courtesy Agence Rol, Paris)

In the paddock at Lyon, Lefebvre looks on while his mechanics check his small Voisin Voiturette No 1. (Courtesy Cycles, Motos & Voitures)

regulations they had to be fully-fledged four-seaters with near similar dimensions at front and rear tracks, and with mudguards. Lefebvre developed a new monocoque structure, inspired by aircraft technology and consisting of a lightweight skeleton made up from ash strips that were glued together with steel reinforcements, as on the cars that had run in the Tours Grand Prix. Stress-bearing aluminium panels were then screwed and riveted onto this frame.

THE 'SCANDAL' OF THE GRAND PRIX DE L'ACF

Because of this construction the cars had no conventional chassis, and this caused quite an uproar. One of the French motoring journals had the headline 'The scandal of the Grand Prix de l'ACF,' its editorial suggesting that these chassis-less vehicles should be disqualified. The author had probably remembered some French army regulations, dating from 1902, which specified that an automobile must consist of 1) an engine, transmission, steering mechanism, springs, axles and wheels; 2) a chassis to support these components, and 3) the coachwork.

The Sporting Committee of the Automobile Club de France had the wisdom and courage to ignore the article; it's easy to appreciate that its members were reluctant to again cross swords with Gabriel Voisin about his advanced concepts in automobile engineering ...

Apart from their dimensions, all of the Lyon GP Voisins looked quite similar; relatively low with short bonnets. As on the Tours cars a small air propeller was fitted in front of the radiator to drive the water pump. Plunging body panels below the radiators completely covered the front axles.

Other characteristic features were the narrow, teardrop-shaped mudguards, those at the rear ending at nearly the same level as the pointed tails. Because lightness and aerodynamic functionality rather than fashion dictated their shape, these Lyon cars cannot be described as elegant; even then they were considered strange and ugly. But the sturdiness and low drag of these crab-like tourers was never questioned, nor was there any doubt about the reliability of their power units.

The race was run in two heats and the cars divided into three categories: voiturettes (400-1000kg); voitures légères (100-1400kg), and voitures. Voisin entered one car in the first category to be driven by Lefebvre. According to the book, *Automobiles Voisin*, by Pascal Courteault, this C10 or 'Petit Laboratoire' had a four-cylinder engine of just 1475 litres. Then came the C8L for the category up to 1400kg with a 1996 litre, four-cylinder unit delivering 6 bhp at 2500rpm. The three C9s or 'Grands Laboratoirs' were equipped with a long stroke 3885cc, four-cylinder engine that developed 130bhp at 3500rpm.

The Voisin C8 sport scars, with their short bonnets and large radiators, were more functional than elegant.

Lyon 1924 and Morel in the 18HP Voisin C8 for the category 'Voitures Légères' 1000-1400kg. (Courtesy Agence Rol, Paris)

The engine bay of a 4-litre C8 L. Note the propeller-driven water pump and the use of strips of wood to strengthen the aluminium monocoque body. (Courtesy Agence Rol, Paris)

Apparently, Voisin intended to sell a limited number of lookalike replicas of these ultra lightweight touring cars to clients who wanted better performance. It is known that the factory had publicity material made for the small C10, but there are no records to show that any cars were ever sold.

Their participation in the Grand Prix de l'ACF was not quite the success the Voisin team had hoped for. Rougier flooded his engine at the start; his own fault, as he had ordered his mechanic to fit a different carburettor, but it cost him over half an hour. During the night he tried to make up for lost time, and drove his car into a ditch. Gauderman made the fastest lap at 97.8km/h, but with a lead of ten minutes one of his tyres burst, and it took him twenty minutes to change his damaged wheel. Then Morel lost precious time – and almost certain victory – when a pit marshal forced him to fix a loose mudguard. André Lefebvre drove the small C10 with great determination, but, plagued by a jamming starter, did not cover the required distance during the first heat. Nevertheless, Gauderman and Piccioni finished with their Voisin in second and third places in the category 'voitures,' and Morel came in fourth in the category of up to 1400kg.

Stolen victory

Gabriel Voisin wrote in his book that his initial satisfaction over the race results was completely spoiled when he discovered that the winning Peugeot, driven by Dauvergne, was based on a Voisin design. According to Voisin, one of his former collaborators had taken the drawings with him when he left Issy-les-Moulineaux to work in Sochaux.

Amazing, because he must have been well aware that when Dufresne moved to work for Peugeot, an immense amount of engineering know-how went with him.

However, Voisin's anger was understandable. In those days it was customary for employee inventions or designs to remain the property of the employer. Besides, it was not the first time that another car manufacturer had infringed Voisin's intellectual property. During a factory stocktake, it was found that a very special car had disappeared; a lightweight 10CV prepared by Lefebvre, and overall winner of the 1924 Circuit des routes pavées in the north of France. Albert Decarme, Voisin's administrator, heard on the grapevine that it had been bought by Renault for a hundred thousand francs. Gabriel Voisin could not believe this; it seemed such an exorbitant sum, representing around twice the price of a new six-cylinder 14CV chassis! Furthermore, he knew that Renault never paid a penny for other people's inventions.

Therefore, he personally questioned Louis Renault, whom he knew quite well, because during WWI he had bought many aviation engines from him. The 'emperor' of Billancourt swore that he had absolutely nothing to do with such a transaction, and even seemed rather upset and promised to investigate. A few days later Renault phoned and told Voisin that the thieves had offered the car to four major French manufacturers. It was like an auction: the highest bidder would get it. Shamefully, he admitted that his research department had indeed made the best offer, and in order to discover its secrets, the car had immediately been taken to pieces.

THE CHALLENGE OF THE SPEED RECORDS

After the GP de Lyon, Gabriel Voisin withdrew his company from participation in races, instead, concentrating on challenging world records. In his memoirs he explains that one of the reasons for this was his discovery of industrial espionage by one of his esteemed competitors. His other argument sounds more rational: "Considering the effort and cost of participating in these races, the risk that after 600 kilometres the certitude that a victory may evaporate by a difference of a few seconds, exasperated me."

Had he been completely honest he would have added that, at the time, establishing speed and endurance records was the latest fashion, especially since earlier that year when Alexandre Lamblin opened his Autodrome de Linas-Montlhéry. This new banked oval track near Paris had, like its older counterpart at Brooklands in Britain, everything needed for such ventures. The architect, Raymond Jamin, had calculated the slope of the banked curves in such a way that cars weighing 1000kg could attain a speed of 220km/h, without risk of tipping over the top of the banking.

Being a new phenomenon, successful record attempts got a lot of coverage in the French press. Suppliers of oil, tyres, sparkplugs, components and accessories would see their names in the articles describing the achievements, encouraging them to pay their share in collective advertisements. French manufacturers such as Roland-Pilain, Renault and Panhard were the first to make use of the publicity Montlhéry offered.

LIKE RIDING OVER A ROUGH SEA

For André Lefebvre, who got the job of designing and building the record-beating car, his boss' decision meant a totally new challenge – and not a simple one.

Thanks to Gabriel Voisin's autobiography, we know a little about the problems encountered in developing the car. In the introduction of his chapter about the record attempts Voisin wrote: "Only those who, during twenty-four hours have driven full throttle at over two hundred kilometres an hour on the Montlhéry track, can judge what this kind of performance means."

They did a few trial runs. In Gabriel Voisin's own words: "that should have been

In the spring of 1925 the first Voisin record car was ready; André Lefebvre poses proudly behind the wheel of his latest design. This machine had a sturdy ladder-frame chassis, and the 4-litre four-cylinder engine plus gearbox was mounted practically amidships, so the driver sat just in front of the rear axle. (Courtesy L'album du fanatique de l'automobile*)*

enough to discourage us. The oval track of Montlhéry is well made; its smooth concrete surface looks perfect. But at two hundred kilometres an hour this surface changes into one comparable to a rough sea. After some forty minutes the roller bearings in the transmission start to spit out their contents into the carter! And within an hour bits and pieces of the engines tend to drop onto the road. The strong vibrations also affect axles, suspensions, steering, tyres and wheels."

It is certain that for Lefebvre and his team, building the first Voisin record car was quite a disconcerting experience. The car had a conventional ladder-type chassis, reinforced in the midsection, half-elliptic springs, a beam axle at the front and a rigid rear axle housing. According to Serge Pozzoli, who made an extensive study of Voisin's record cars for the French magazine *L'Album du fanatique de l'Automobile*, Lefebvre used a number of elements from the chassis of the car Morel had driven in the 1924 Grand Prix de l'ACF. Its wheelbase measured 3m, its front track 1.30m, and its rear track 1.25m.

Many mechanical parts, such as the engine and gearbox, were derived from the C5

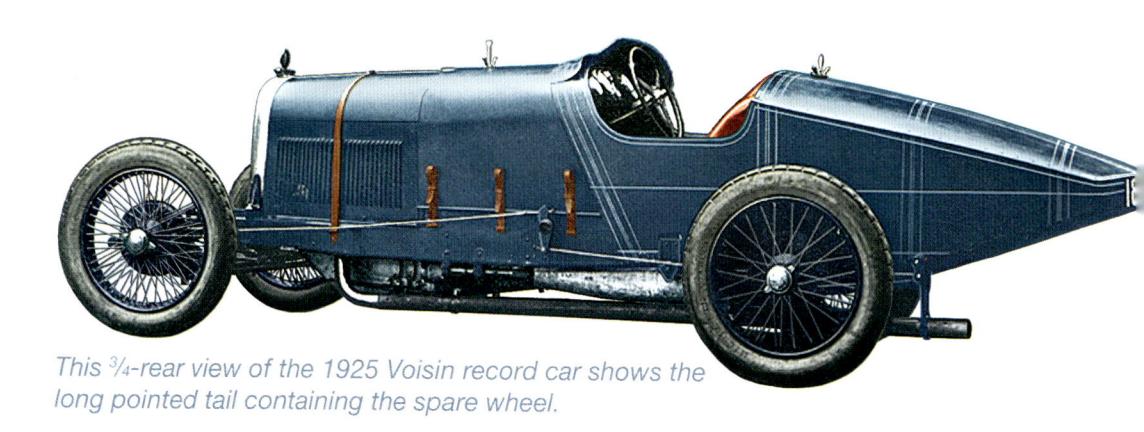

This ¾-rear view of the 1925 Voisin record car shows the long pointed tail containing the spare wheel.

Voisin production cars. The four-cylinder had a bore of 95mm and a stroke of 140mm, giving a cubic capacity of 3969 litres. With a compression ratio of 6.5:1, it developed between 110 and 120bhp. The engine was placed almost amidships the chassis, with the aim to get the masses well centred within the wheelbase; for the same reason the radiator was mounted behind the front axle. The driver sat just in front of the rear axle.

To save weight the engine had no starter motor, the idea being that the car could be push-started after each pit stop. The lightweight construction of the aluminium body clearly reflected some of André Lefebvre's design principles.

But it did not look very aerodynamic. True, it had a tapered tail that housed a spare wheel. but the radiator stood up as straight as on the Voisin touring models. The body was also decorated with the same sort of 'Scottish' pinstripes. With the large oil tank filled, plus 100 litres of petrol on board, the car weighed some 1200kg.

A TERRIFYING MAIDEN TRIP

The car's maiden trip on the Montlhéry track revealed some alarming faults.

At two hundred kilometres an hour, one drives rather high on the steep banking of the oval, which means that the centrifugal forces are transformed into a down force that has the same effect as extra weight. Voisin wrote: "The leaf springs sagged, the axles touched the chassis and the thrashing that followed caused as much damage as if the car had been attacked with a power hammer. The axles bent, the steering became dangerously vague, the car tore itself to pieces and the spokes of the wheels penetrated through the rims." In other words, the trial run was a disaster and Voisin seriously considered abandoning the project.

With due respect for the technical talents of the engineers at Voisin's laboratoire, it is evident that they had badly miscalculated the flexibility of the springs in conjunction with extra load caused by the down force on the banking, and axle oscillation at high speed. They probably thought that 'soft' leaf springs would better absorb the undulations of Montlhéry's bumpy surface.

With hindsight, the mistakes made with the first Voisin record machine are quite understandable. In those days the way cars behaved under difficult conditions was very much 'terra incognita,' and the only way to find a solution for a technical problem was by trial and error, learning from experience.

ABOLISHING THE GEARBOX TO SAVE WEIGHT

In Issy-les-Moulineaux they learned fast. A war council consisting of Gabriel Voisin, André Lefebvre and Marius Bernard analysed the problems, and concluded that, to pursue their ambition, the car had to be lightened, engine power increased, and the suspension system adapted in order to be able to absorb the important down force on the banking.

Within three weeks the engine was modified to develop 130bhp at 3500rpm. It was calculated that, during the record runs, it would be necessary to change wheels at least every three hours, as, at speeds of over two hundred kilometres an hour, tyres would not last much longer.

During these tyre changes they would also be able to refuel the car. As the acceleration after such a pit stop had only limited influence on the average speed, Voisin suggested abolishing the gearbox, saving 54kg. To make up for the lack of indirect gears while gathering speed in direct drive, the single plate clutch was replaced by an air-cooled multiple disc unit that could better withstand the heat of some clutch slip.

Because of the banking, cornering at Montlhéry causes less centrifugal force than on a flat road, and so front and rear track was reduced to 1.10m, giving shorter, stronger axles, a smaller frontal area, and less weight. The suspension system was improved

Marchand, Julienne and Lefebvre (in white racing overalls) before their first attempt at Montlhéry on August 8 1925. (Courtesy Sporting Magazine)

by fitting auxiliary leaf springs that came into action when the (centrifugal) down force increased the load; a system comparable to that used on heavy lorries.

FULL THROTTLE AT MONTLHÉRY

On August 8, 1925 Lefebvre, Marchand and Julienne began their record attempts at Montlhéry with the Voisin 18 CV SS; their intention was to beat the record set by Woolf Barnato in his 3-litre Bentley when he had averaged 152.930km/h over 24 hours. At its first attempt the Voisin team established two world and ten international records.

Unfortunately, after 16 hours and 5 minutes (2435.95km, with an average speed of 153.237km/h), Julienne had to stop the car because of an oil leak from a ruptured oil cooler, caused by vibration. The supplier, Chausson, replaced it with a stronger unit and, together with Lefebvre's team, devised a 'floating' mounting with rubber silent-blocks. On September 25 the car was back on the track and the official timekeepers of the Association Internationale des Automobile-Clubs Reconnus, Carpe, De Thuau and Delpeyroux started their stopwatches again.

Within six hours the Voisin drivers had established another five international records, the most impressive of which was the 6 hours world record covering 1032.280km (average speed 172.046km/h). The previous record, by Garfield on a Renault, stood at 985.010km (164.168 km/h). Lefebvre drove the last three hours himself.

Although in Voisin's own words these successes did not generate many commercial benefits, he was determined to continue his pursuit of a 24 hour record. One of the reasons for this was that he wanted to demonstrate the power and endurance of the latest six-cylinder engine they had developed for the new C12 passenger cars.

So on October 11, 1926, another Lefebvre-designed machine took off at Montlhéry. As it had a new 'underslung' chassis it was much lower than its predecessor. The leaf

The second record attempt took place on September 25, 1925. Marchand waits for the signal to start. Lefebvre (in light raincoat) stands next to the car. (Courtesy Sporting Magazine)

springs of the front suspension passed through the front axle; a setup, it seemed, inspired by Bugatti. At the rear the leaf springs were attached to the chassis by a bracket in which the upper leaves could slide. To reduce weight the car had no brakes on the front wheels. The body was more streamlined than the previous one and showed that Lefebvre had

Unique photos of a change of driver on a cold morning at Montlhéry in October 1925. Marchand comes in for a pitstop and Lefebvre (in white overalls) waits eagerly to take over ... (Courtesy Sporting Magazine)

... he jumps into the cockpit, while the mechanics check and refuel the car.
(Courtesy Agence Rol, Paris)

Seated behind the steering wheel, ready to resume the record run.
(Courtesy Sporting Magazine)

acquired a lot of knowledge about the aerodynamic requirements of a record machine. The vertical radiator was placed behind a large cowling at the front of the bonnet; a longer sloping tail covered the spare wheel.

Lefebvre's own experience as a racing driver showed in the design of the cockpit. The dashboard, with all its instruments, occupied the left side of the cockpit, and was slightly inclined towards the driver, just as in some BMWs during the nineteen eighties. Marchal took three records – among them the international record for 100km with an average of 185.48km/h – but, despite its many modifications and two carburettors, the 4880cc, six-cylinder engine delivered insufficient power to try for world records: it needed more time and work to achieve the necessary performance.

Above: Lefebvre and his team with the sleek Voisin record contender that was completed early in 1926. From left to right: Julienne, Marchand, Rogé, Vialet, Lefebvre, Bernard, Fortin and Roux. On October 11, Marchand established four new distance records, but Gabriel Voisin realized that this engine did not deliver enough power and lacked the potential for international records. (Courtesy Agence Rol, Paris)

The six-cylinder of the 1926 record machine was based on the 4.5-litre Voisin production block, enlarged to a capacity of nearly five litres and equipped with two Zenith carburettors.

The chassis of the 1926 Voisin record car was 'underslung' to reduce its height, and its shape was more aerodynamic than that of its predecessor. The aluminium body still had a large air intake for cooling. Interesting detail: the front springs passed through the front axle, just as on a Bugatti.

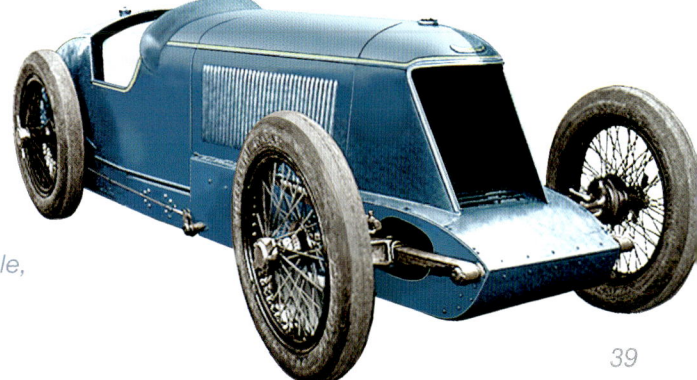

MERGING TWO FOUR-CYLINDER BLOCKS INTO AN EIGHT-CYLINDER

Slightly disappointed, Gabriel Voisin decided to try again with an engine specially designed to fulfil his ambitions. He asked Lefebvre to mount two four-cylinder blocks one behind the other on the same sump. Including its dynastart at the front of the crankshaft, this new, eight-in-line engine measured over one-and-half meters. A bore of 95mm and a stroke of 140mm gave a cubic capacity of 7938. Equipped with two large Zenith carburettors, it produced some 200bhp on the test bench.

The new chassis resembled the previous one, but was, in fact, a totally new construction, adapted to the size and power of the larger engine. Lefebvre and his team also modified the body to suit the longer chassis. Its bonnet was stretched, the nose made somewhat longer and more rounded, and the size of the air intake was reduced. Just as on the first Laboratoires, a small air propeller drove the water pump. This propeller was mounted very low down on the panel covering the front axle, and was later replaced by a conventional engine-driven water pump. The tail was shortened and got a more pronounced downturn.

ORGANISING THE 24 HOUR ATTEMPT

The car was taken to Montlhéry for a tryout on April 11, 1927. Two days later César Marchand officially established two new world records: 100km at 205.268km/h and 100 miles (160.93km) at 206.885km/h. Over the following months several more records were

Gabriel Voisin told Lefebvre to construct an eight-in-line engine by using two four-cylinder blocks of the cars that had raced in the Grand Prix at Lyon, and mounting them, one behind the other, on the same sump. This resulted in a capacity of nearly eight litres. The new car made its first record runs on April 11, 1927. The photo shows Marchand ready to go, getting some last minute advice, while Lefebvre (in light raincoat behind the car) seems to be praying for good results. (Courtesy Sporting Magazine)

Gabriel Voisin in the pit box at Montlhéry amidst his drivers Marchand, Morel and Kiriloff; Lefebvre on the left. During 1927 the Voisin team collected an impressive number of speed records, among them the international 24 hours record at 182.660km/h (113.50mph).

A proud trio: André Lefebvre sitting on the rear wheel; César Marchand at the steering wheel, and Lefebvre's colleague and good friend, the engineer Anthony (Tony) Philipon, behind the car.

broken and, by the end of spring, Voisin had 8 world records to his name.

In view of the forthcoming Paris Motor Show in October, he also wanted the additional publicity of a 24 hour record, and so on September 26 and 27, under unfavourable weather conditions, Marchand, Morel and Kiriloff finally set off again. Nine new world records were added and they bagged the coveted 24 hour world record for Voisin, covering a distance of 4,383.851km with an average speed of 182.651km/h (112.50mph)!

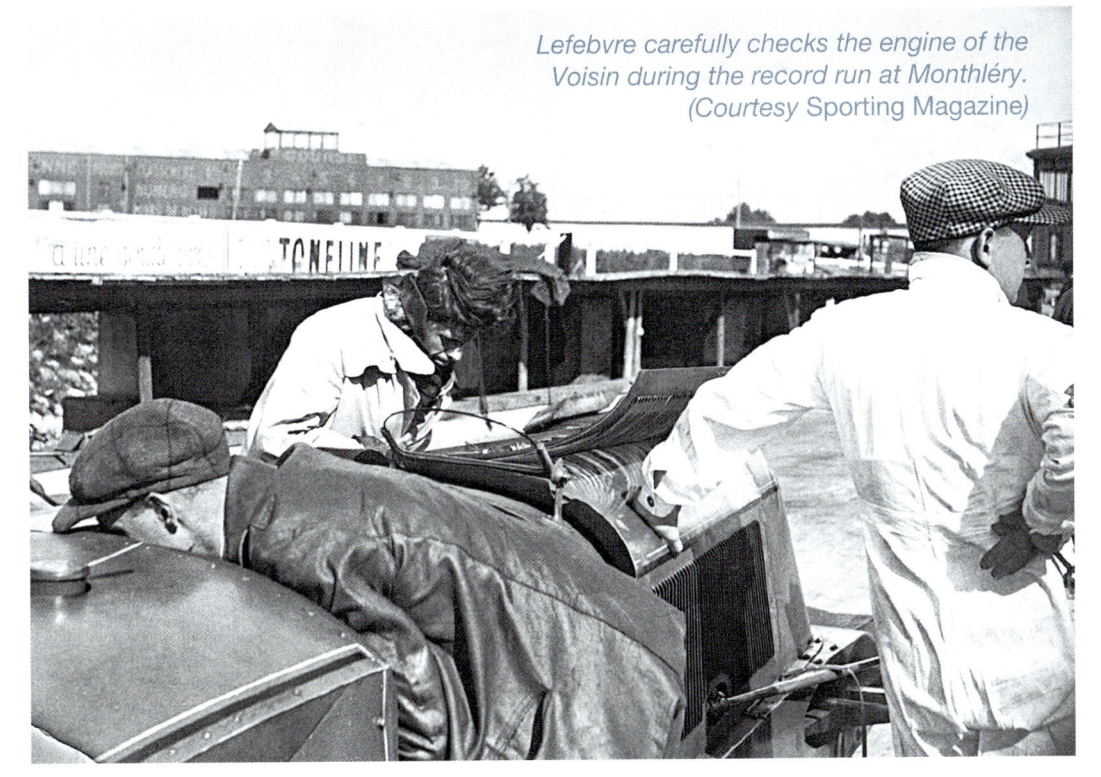

Lefebvre carefully checks the engine of the Voisin during the record run at Montlhéry. (Courtesy Sporting Magazine)

This time André Lefebvre did not drive, although, as team manager, he supervised the entire operation, assisted by two colleagues, engineers Fernand Vialet and Anthony (Tony) Philipon. During the record runs the pit area at Montlhéry resembled a small army camp, complete with barracks, tents, lorries, and lots of people. In addition to officials and timekeepers from the Automobile Club, and the team of Voisin mechanics, there were specialists from all the supporting companies, such as Yacco, the oil supplier, Dunlop, which took care of the tyres, Ponsot, a small manufacturer that produced the sparkplugs, and Zenith for the carburettors and fuel system. Lefebvre was responsible for the wellbeing of the car and its drivers, liaison with the representatives of the suppliers, and the logistics and organisation of the pit stops. Every 90 minutes the car came in for a change of driver and tyres; every 3 hours to refuel and refill the engine with new oil, heated beforehand to the right temperature. And this during 24 hours ...

Improving production models

Lefebvre and his colleagues were not only building and tuning record cars; Gabriel Voisin constantly demanded improvement to his existing passenger car range, as well as development of new engines and chassis.

During the 'golden days,' from 1920 to 1928, the Voisin automobiles belonged to the European top league, with a client list that read like the *Almanac de Gotha* and included a number of royal families. Président Millerand of France drove a Voisin – as did ministers of various countries – and also ambassadors, important industrialists, business tycoons and well-known artists, such as Rudolph Valentino – who had several – Joséphine Baker and Mistinguett.

All Voisins were expensive, and some more than others. Commercially, the most successful Voisin models were the mid-range 2.3-litre, six-cylinder C11, and its successor, the C14. During their five year production run from 1926 to 1932 some 3975 were sold (35 per cent of Voisin's total production over 20 years).

To prove their performance and reliability, Gabriel Voisin asked the Automobile Club de France to choose one of the cars at random from his depot. After being run in it was driven for one hour at full throttle on the Montlhéry track. From a standing start it covered 124.48km.

Gabriel's friend, the architect Noël Noël, designed most of the factory coachwork for these relatively small cars. To keep weight down Voisin used mainly aluminium for most body panels; only the mudguards were made of steel. Some of these standard factory bodies weighed no more than 140kg. Often erroneously called 'Lumineuses' – which was, in fact, the name of only one of the body styles – they were quite 'en vogue' with the liberal professions. The famous architect Le Corbusier had one and, in 1928, photographed his Voisin in front of the ultramodern Villa Stein that he had designed. This picture was later published in a magazine article about contemporary architecture.

1928 seemed to begin rather well. César Marchand, who, at a speed event near Lugano (Switzerland), had shown that the eight-cylinder record car was capable of 234km/h, clocked up a new record at Montlhéry with an average of 121.491km/h. Then, while trying again on July 25th, he had a tremendous crash when a tyre burst at high speed. Looking at photographs of the wreck it is hard to believe that he escaped alive; even so, he had to spend several weeks in hospital to mend his broken ribs, collarbone and pierced lung. The car was a total write-off.

Yacco comes to the rescue

It was not only Marchand's accident that dampened Gabriel Voisin's enthusiasm for further record attempts: he also had serious personal and financial problems.

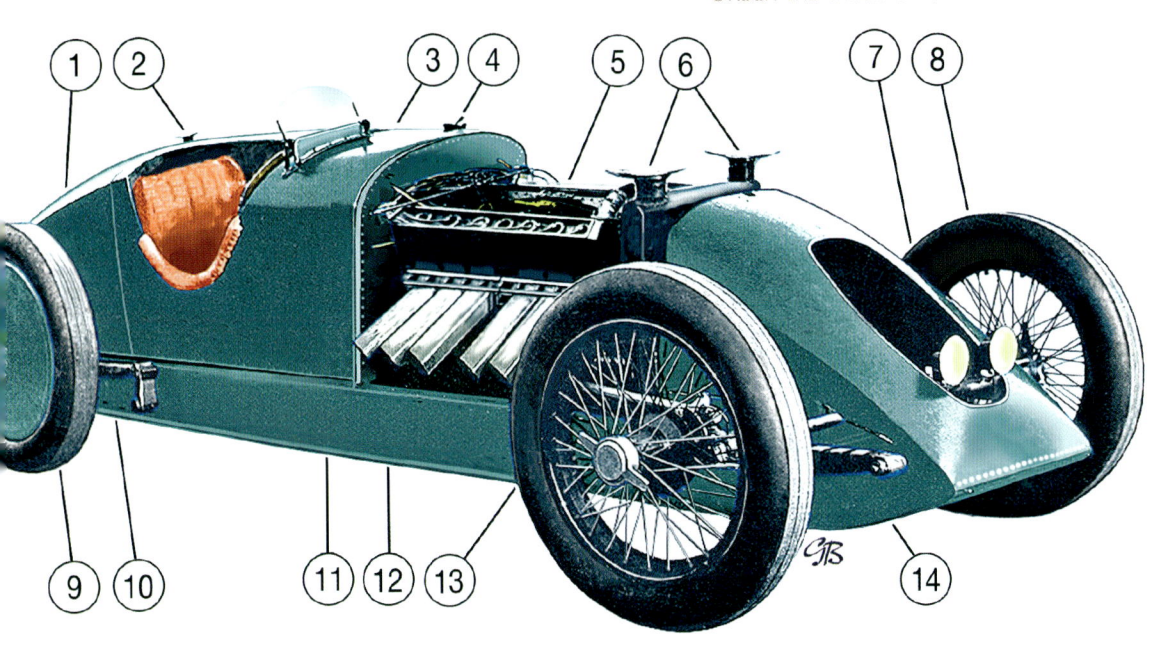

Details of the V12 record Voisin for 1929.
1 Spare wheel in tail. 2 Fuel tank behind driver. 3 Dashboard. 4 Filler cap for oil reservoir. 5 Twelve-litre V12 sleeve valve engine (100km/h at 1000rpm). 6 Radiator caps (dual water pumps). 7 Auxiliary headlights. 8 Wire wheels (no brakes on the front wheels). 9 Rear axle on top of the leaf springs. 10 Wire wheels covered by aluminium discs. 11 'Ladder-frame' chassis. 12 No gearbox (multiple disc clutch). 13 'Dyna-starter' at the front of the crankshaft. 14 Front axle on top of the leaf springs. Total weight: about 1950kg. Top speed: over 220km/h. World record at Montlhéry: September 16-26, 1929 – distance 31,965km (average speed 133.187km/h).

One of the company's loyal sponsors was the oil supplier Yacco, which always got a great deal of publicity from Voisin's exploits at Montlhéry. When its managing director learned why Voisin intended to abandon his pursuit of new world records, he offered to share in the cost of developing a new car.

However, there was one obstacle. The public utility company Gaz de Paris was promoting a substitute for petrol – called benzol and made from coal tar – and its management had let Yacco know that it was willing to participate in the sponsorship, on condition that the Voisin would run on a mixture consisting of two thirds petrol and one third benzol. Grateful to have found sources that were prepared to pay the wages of the employees of his Laboratoire, Gabriel Voisin accepted.

He outlined his new goal to Lefebvre and Bernard and instructed them to build a new record machine, the target being 40,000 kilometres or once around the earth! In the raw reality of record runs it meant over 15 days and 15 nights on the tortuous concrete bowl at Montlhéry, at speeds of up to 160km/h. For this particular machine Gabriel Voisin suggested that they should develop a V12 engine by using two six-cylinder blocks on a common light metal carter. This concept was not, in fact, entirely new for Voisin, as, at the Paris Motor Show of 1921, his company had already exhibited a C2 chassis with a 3.85-litre V12.

The new 12-cylinder had a capacity of 11.660 litres. This metal brute was fed by

For the 1929 car Lefebvre experimented with various tails. This one improved aerodynamic stability but increased drag. (Courtesy Avions Voisin)

This was the reason why Lefebvre decided to revert to the long sloping rear end already used on previous record Voisins. (Courtesy Avions Voisin)

The dashboard instruments were tilted towards the driver, reflecting Lefebvre's own racing experience. (Courtesy Avions Voisin)

two big Cozette downdraught carburettors – one for each cylinder block. Gabriel Voisin confessed in his memoirs that they had no test bench at Issy-les-Moulineaux on which to measure the precise power output, but he estimated that it delivered around 250bhp at very low rpm. The gearing of the rear axle allowed the record car to do 100km/h at 1000rpm.

A large dynastart at the front of the crankshaft made push starts superfluous. There was no gearbox, the engine transmitted its power through a heavy-duty clutch made up from steel discs with bronze linings. The underslung ladder-frame chassis bore an obvious similarity to the 1927 machine, but was even lower and reinforced with extra transverse beams at the front. To create room for the steering column and the legs of the driver, the engine was mounted slightly off centre. Again, the front wheels had no brakes.

Lefebvre did a lot of testing to find the best aerodynamic shape for the body. He experimented with a high tail to get more stability, but ended up by reverting to a rear end resembling that of the previous machine. Although the Montlhéry track would be illuminated during the record run, the car was fitted with two small headlamps.

DELIGHT AND DISAPPOINTMENT

At two o'clock on September 16, 1929, the record car moved off. Three of the drivers were veterans at Montlhéry: César Marchand, who had completely recovered, André Morel and Serge Kiriloff. The fourth was Leroy de Présalé, the son of one of Voisin's business relations, and an enthusiastic and promising young racing driver.

The mighty V12 had two Cozette carburettors – one for each cylinder block – and developed over 250bhp on a mixture of petrol and benzol.

Preparation for this attempt was even more professional and power generators provided electric light around the banking and in the paddock area; there was even a first aid post and a medical team, because Marchand's accident was still a recent memory. André Lefebvre was again in charge of pit organisation. To limit tyre wear and fuel consumption the drivers had instructions not to exceed 1800rpm. The target

André Lefebvre at Montlhéry between drivers César Marchand (left) and Leroy de Présalé.

of 40,000km and the benzol mixture made provision for regular maintenance and small adjustments essential, and two teams of mechanics were especially trained for these jobs, equipped with thick, heat-resistant gloves to work on the red hot V12. Nevertheless, some pit stops took around an hour. But everything went according to plan and existing records were scattered like leaves in the autumn wind when the Voisin set no fewer than 17 new world records.

Then, on September 25, just before the distance of 35,000km was reached, the rim of a front wheel collapsed. The car overturned but Serge Kiriloff, who was driving at that moment, was thrown free and escaped with minor injuries. The only victim was the 40,000km record, because the car was too badly damaged to continue.

The Voisin had officially clocked up 31,965km in 10 days at an average speed of 133.187km/h, an endurance record that no-one else could claim. The big V12 had performed remarkably well on its petrol/benzol mixture, needing an oil change only twice and consuming about 25 litres of fuel every 100km.

Unfortunately, a rumour was spread in the press that the engine had exploded. Gabriel Voisin was furious, and asked officials of the Automobile Club de France to take apart the machine to verify that all of the engine components were in perfect working order, after which the record car was rebuilt and proudly displayed on the Voisin stand at the Paris Motor Show in October 1929.

Shortly after this Motor Show closed its doors, the New York stock market crashed: October 24, the first day of real panic, is remembered as 'Black Thursday.' Major banks and investment companies bought a record 12,894,650 shares in an attempt to shore up prices and stop the slide. But on 'Black Monday' the panic continued, and on 'Black Tuesday,' October 29, share prices collapsed completely and many people faced ruin. In one brutal stroke the Wall Street Crash marked the end of the Roaring Twenties. At first its impact was mainly felt in the USA, but soon the tidal wave of depression swept the rest of the world. As a direct result – and not surprisingly – sales of expensive luxury automobiles suffered badly.

Around the world in 15 days

The financial situation of the Voisin company – already in bad shape before the market collapse – did not permit the building of another completely new record machine. Gabriel Voisin was determined to be the first manufacturer to set a world record over 50,000km. Not only did he need the publicity, it had also become a personal obsession. Fortunately his friend, Monsieur Dintilhac, the president of Yacco, shared his enthusiasm for these record attempts and the attention they received in the motoring press, and

The 1930 Voisin record car at full speed on the Montlhéry banking: it looks about as aerodynamic as a brick! But money was scarce and Gabriel Voisin was convinced that for the 50,000km record reliability was more important than excessive speed. For their next attempt he decided that Lefebvre had to prepare a C18 'Diane' Chassis with a V12 engine and a standard two-door factory body. (Courtesy Album Yacco)

UNDER THE WINGS OF GABRIEL VOISIN

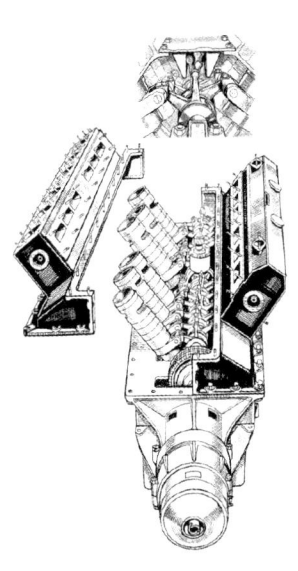

This exploded view of the V12 Voisin engine – with one of its blocks partly removed – reveals the mechanism of the Knight system. The small drawing shows details of the eccentric shaft and the rods that move the sleeves up and down, with the safety device that would prevent damage to the eccentric shaft mechanism in case of sleeve seizure. The drawing is from a reprint of an article in The Autocar, *published by Automobiles Voisin UK.*

The oil company Yacco not only sponsored the record attempt, it even bought the car. However, Lefebvre was responsible for its preparation and technical support during the event. Here we see him with the management of Yacco in their pit at Montlhéry. (Courtesy Album Yacco)

Both Yacco and Voisin claimed that during the 50,000 kilometres record run no oil changes took place, although the car was thoroughly checked during each of the approximately 200 pit stops and driver changes. (Courtesy Album Yacco)

47

so proposed that his company would buy a chassis from Voisin and pay all the expenses. Lefebvre got the task of overseeing the mechanical modifications and preparation and testing of the car, and was to assist the team during the event. For practical and commercial reasons it was decided that the record car should as much as possible resemble one of Voisin's production models.

The 1929 experience had shown that, for an endurance record, a good cruising speed was more important than a high top speed, and work started on a production C18 chassis, codenamed 'Diane,' with a wheelbase of 3.58m. As reliability was the main objective, its standard 4.885-litre V12 was only slightly modified, alterations that had mainly to do with the fact it had to run on a petrol/benzol mixture as Gaz de Paris had again joined Yacco as a sponsor. The chassis was fitted with a two-seater body from the 'Châtelaine' series, but without its mudguards and running boards. Its luggage trunk was sacrificed to make room for two enormous, barrel-shaped fuel tanks located just above the rear axle.

Reassuring pit signal: "Tout marche Bien" (All goes well). On 27 September, 1930, Voisin achieved his ultimate world record: 50,000 kilometres in 17 days. (Courtesy Album Yacco)

Between September 7 and 25, 1930, César Marchand and his brother Eduard Marchand, Leroy de Présalé, and Co van Doorninck, Voisin's agent for the Netherlands, took the big car around the Montlhéry track with the regularity of a French Comtoise clock. In 15 days they covered 43,737km, the coveted equivalent of one trip around the world! When on the 17th day, after 50,000km the Voisin passed the timekeeper's box, it had averaged 119.948km/h. Mission accomplished! Even if it was to be the last of Voisin's world records, the wave of publicity it created attracted worldwide attention. One of the 89 V12 C18s produced was purchased by the royal family of Thailand.

It is clear that during the first half of 1930 Lefebvre was heavily involved in this superb achievement. However, reading Gabriel Voisin's *Mes 1001 voitures*, it would seem that, at about the same time, he and Lefebvre were already toying with ideas for an experimental front-wheel drive car.

UNDER THE WINGS OF GABRIEL VOISIN

1930 publicity poster by Yacco highlights the successful record run.

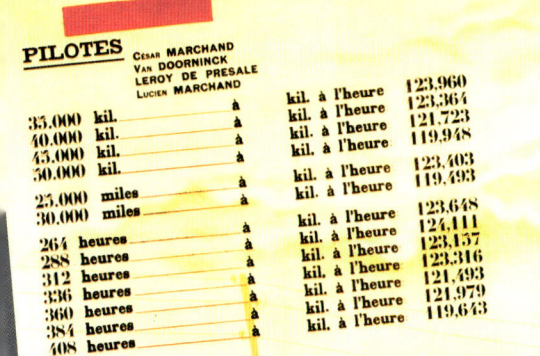

1930 Voisin advertisement.

Chapter THREE

A SHORT HISTORY OF FRONT-WHEEL DRIVE

After the automobile had outgrown its origins as a horseless carriage, the majority of cars manufactured in Europe and the USA had the engine at the front and rear-wheel drive. However, around the mid-twenties, a number of progressive automotive engineers began to experiment with different drive train solutions. They were divided into two camps, but had the same objectives: to provide more interior space, better aerodynamics, and lower the centre of gravity of their cars by getting rid of the traditional driveshaft between the engine and the wheels that propelled the car.

ALL AT THE REAR ...

At the 1921 Berlin Automobil Ausstellung the German engineer Edmund Rumpler introduced a revolutionary rear-engined car. His 'Tropfenwagen' was shaped like the gondola of an airship. During WWI, Rumpler had manufactured the 'Taube' airplane, designed by Igo Etrich, but, like so many aircraft manufacturers, had to switch to peacetime production. Unfortunately, Rumpler's aerodynamic automobile, although technically very advanced, did not suit the public taste. He sold a few to a taxi company in his home town of Berlin, but his factory ran into financial difficulties and Rumpler was forced to sell his patents to the Benz company, which then developed a rear-engined racing car. However, Rumpler's ideas inspired others: Austrian-born Hans Ledwinka, working for Tatra in Czechoslovakia, the British airship designer Sir Denniston Burney, Emile Claveau in France, Dutch-born John Tjaarda, employed by the American coachwork company Briggs, William B Stout, who designed the Scarab, and, last but not least, the eminent Dr Ferdinand Porsche, to name but a few, firmly believed in the 'all in the tail' formula of the engine at the back driving the rear wheels.

... OR EVERYTHING IN FRONT?

Other visionary engineers became ardent supporters of 'everything in front.' As a matter of fact, front-wheel drive was not a totally new idea: as early as 1896, in France Charles Jeantaud built a two-seater with a transversal electric motor driving its front

Early French front-wheel drive Latil was built in 1899 in Marseille. (Courtesy Fondation Berliet)

wheels. Three years later Georges Latil, another Frenchman, produced a small front-wheel drive runabout, powered by a petrol engine.

In 1904 the brilliant but almost forgotten American engineer John Walter Christy constructed a racing car with front-wheel drive and a transversally mounted engine. Christy raced it himself in the 1907 Grand Prix of Dieppe (France), and again in 1909 on the 'brick yard' track of Indianapolis (USA), where he established the record for the quarter mile with a speed of 156km/h.

During the late twenties front-wheel drive became big news again, probably due to the American racing car builder Harry Miller, who incorporated in his designs some of the ideas and experiences of his compatriot and old friend John W Christy.

The 1927 Miller front-wheel-driven 'Detroit Special' caused a great sensation and attracted enormous publicity at the Indianapolis 500, and proved fast and reliable.

The US automobile and aviation tycoon Errett Lobban Cord – then owner of Auburn, Duesenberg and Lycoming – was so impressed that he signed an agreement with Miller to use his front-wheel drive transmission system for the new Auburn L29. Cord introduced this long, low and impressive eight-cylinder luxury car in 1929, just two months before the Wall Street Crash; a most unfortunate start for this timeless American beauty.

Another front-wheel drive car that became the victim of the ensuing crisis was the Ruxton, which started life as a concept car, sponsored by the Budd company in Philadelphia to promote its patented system for unit body construction. It was designed by William J (Bill) Muller and Joseph Ledwinka. Ledwinka was Edward Gowan Budd's right-hand man and technical director. A number of financiers established a consortium that convinced the automaker Moon to manufacture the luxurious Ruxton. But after a few hundred cars were produced the bottom dropped out of the stock market and all further activities were cancelled. It did not take long for the tidal wave of doom caused by the American economic crisis to reach European shores, but, in contrast to the USA, front-wheel drive made its first impact in a small and cheap popular car. Danish-born Jørgen Skafte Rasmussen was the founder of German DKW motorcycles. Company publicity eulogised its machines as 'Das Kleine Wunder' (the small wonder), but the name also became a pun: Das Kreng Weigert (the rotter refuses). In 1928, Rasmussen began to manufacture small open cars in his Spandau factory with a 0.584-litre, two-cylinder two-stroke engine driving the front wheels. They were an instant success.

At the Berlin Automobil Ausstellung of that same year one of Germany's most innovative engineers, the ex-WWI pilot Hans Gustav Rohr presented a prototype of a front-wheel drive saloon with a 2.25-litre eight-cylinder engine.

After Rohr's own venture ran into financial difficulties he became technical director of Adler in Frankfurt, where he designed the front-wheel drive Adler Trumpf. In 1933, these Adler cars were also produced under licence in France by Rosengart, which marketed them as the 'Supertraction,' and in Belgium by Imperia which called them the 'Albatros.'

SUCCESSES AT LE MANS

Jean-Albert Grégoire was a young French engineer, and owner of the Garage des Chantiers in Versailles. He delighted public and press by successfully participating with his extremely low front-wheel drive Tracta Gephi in the 24 Heures du Mans of 1927, 1928 and 1929, as well as other races. What the cars lacked in speed on the straights they made up for in the corners, thanks to their outstanding roadholding. Grégoire had designed them himself, using small four-cylinder engines manufactured by SCAP (Société de Construction Automobile Parisienne). One of his reasons for entering these cars in competitions was to promote the homokinetic Tracta driveshaft joints that he had developed together with his business partner, the inventor Pierre Fenaille.

Another front-wheel drive sports car ran in the 1928 Le Mans endurance race: the British Alvis TA FWD driven by Major Maurice Harvey and Harold Purdy. Then there were the French Bucciali brothers who, from 1926, regularly exhibited one of their impressive front-wheel drive prototypes at the Salon de l'Automobile in Paris, with the objective of selling the complete design to a manufacturer.

In 1929, Paul-Albert Bucciali contacted the Voisin factory because he wanted to install a 4.9-litre Voisin V12 in the front-wheel drive show car for the 1931 exhibition. Gabriel Voisin then sold him the engine type 18 H no 40048. One of the technical features of Bucciali's advanced design was a drivetrain with a very clever but compact transversally mounted four-speed gearbox. The Voisin engine – originally designed for a rear-wheel drive chassis – had to be adapted to this gearbox, which meant that the flywheel and the clutch housing had to be moved to the front of the chassis. It is hardly conceivable that Bucciali staff did not discuss the technical implications with Voisin and Lefebvre. Bucciali's chief engineer, who had some experience with other engines designed for rear-wheel drive, decided to turn the V12 Voisin back to front; that doing so reversed the crankshaft rotation as well did not bother him at all, because the transmission unit was designed to compensate for this.

THE MYSTERIOUS FRONT-WHEEL DRIVE VOISIN

From his biography we learn that Gabriel Voisin was quite taken by the possibilities of front-wheel drive. He wrote: "The system has the following merits: 1) It makes it easier to lower the centre of gravity and bring it forward. 2) It will free us from that unbelievable stupidity: a transmission shaft and tunnel between the engine in front of the driver and the driven wheels. 3) Front-wheel drive will increase the interior space of the body, reduce the car's weight and diminish the cost price."

According to this book Voisin himself also experimented with front-wheel drive*. For a power plant he chose a new V8 engine, using two four-cylinder blocks (from the existing 10CV), mounted under 90 degrees on the same aluminium carter. Thicker inner sleeves reduced cubic capacity to 3.2-litres. At 4000rpm this machine developed about 100bhp. Voisin gives other details about his front-wheel drive design as well; for instance that the low, underslung chassis had a ground clearance of only 13 centimetres, and that it had an electromagnetic Cotal gearbox, the semiautomatic transmission that was also available

Tragic timing: two months after the front-wheel drive Auburn Cord L-29 was introduced, the New York stock market crashed. (Courtesy Free Library of Philadelphia)

*Note: Gabriel Voisin's Mes mille et une voitures was published in the early nineteen sixties, by which time he was nearly eighty years old. Besides, along with his factory he had also lost his archives, and had no records to fall back on, so may have confused some of his early experiments with more recent experiences.
Because there have been front-wheel drive Voisin cars, albeit much later, during postwar years the concept of his minimalist C31 or 'Biscooter' was just as original as his ideas for a number of large and luxurious machines in prewar days. Voisin constructed several prototypes successively to transport two, three or four people, plus a narrow single-seater intended for use by postal services. It is possible that the latter did not need a differential. Voisin's Biscooter was exhibited at the 1950 Salon du Cycle et de la Moto in Paris, where it attracted great interest. Its dry weight was just 175kg and it was powered by an air-cooled,

on other Voisin chassis. What happened to this unusual automobile remains a complete mystery; it certainly never went into production.

Philippe Ladure, president of the association Les Amis de Gabriel Voisin, and an expert on the achievements of this extraordinary French airplane and automobile manufacturer, says that he has indeed seen drawings of the V8 engine that Gabriel Voisin tells about in his book. These were shown to him by Eugène Lamy, one of the engineers then responsible for its design, who told him that this engine was intended for a new Voisin model. However, Ladure thinks it unlikely that Voisin or Lefebvre ever completed such a evolutionary front-wheel drive prototype; firstly, because around that time (1930) Voisin simply did not have sufficient financial means for this sort of experiment, and secondly, because Gabriel's authority in the factory was dramatically curtailed as he had handed over day-to-day management of his company to a Belgian consortium (see page 54).

Lefebvre's son, Michel, confirms Ladure's doubts: "I was only about seven or eight years old at the time, but I remember quite well that we lived at 175 Rue de la Convention in Paris. Most evenings after dinner my father would sit at the large drawing board he had installed in his study next to our bedroom. There he worked on his front-wheel drive 'pet' project till our mother told him it was time to come to bed. Most evenings and during the weekends he would be sketching, making technical drawings and calculations. As far as I know all this took place when he no longer worked with Voisin. But one cannot exclude that Gabriel Voisin and my father did discuss the possibilities of a front-wheel drive car, and even made some preliminary studies.

"However, I have never heard my father talk about testing or driving such a revolutionary Voisin car, so I do not believe that it ever got much further than a number of blueprints. But it is true; Gabriel Voisin and my father were constantly exchanging ideas on technical matters, and I am convinced that my father even showed him his drawings for the front-wheel drive car that eventually would become the Traction Avant. They remained very close, even long after my father had left Voisin."

Michel also recalled that his father always used the same type and make of lead pencil for his drawings or to make notes; dark brown wooden pencils No 110, made by L & C Hardtmut in Czechoslovakia. He bought them in large quantities. "At school some of my classmates were very envious of the pencils I brought from home, and once I even had a fight with another boy who tried to steal my pencil." Michel Lefebvre still has one in memory of his father.

The Bucciali TAV8-32 had a V12 Voisin engine driving the front wheels. The low body was a creation of the French coachbuilder, Jacques Saoutchik. (Courtesy Saoutchik)

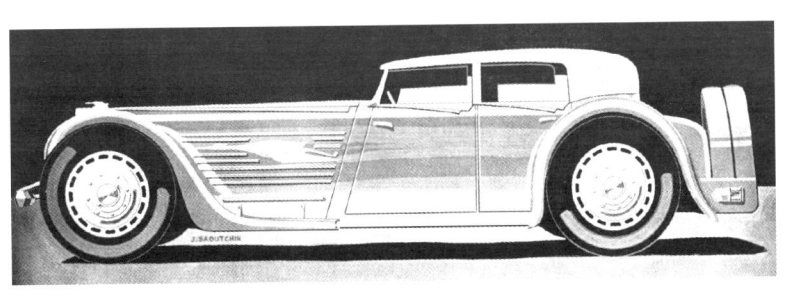

two-stroke motorcycle engine of just 125cc, manufactured by Gnome & Rhône. This company, which had taken over the Voisin factory, also produced a small number of these cars. But Gnome & Rhône had been nationalised and was by then integrated in the Snecma (Société nationale d'étude et de construction de moteurs d'aviation), presently part of SAFRAN.

It seems that there was disagreement about the project and, in June 1953, Gabriel Voisin sold the manufacturing rights to Autonacional SA in Barcelona. In collaboration with the Spanish engineer Damien Casanova, the structure was modified and the Gnome & Rhône engine replaced by a 197cc air-cooled, single cylinder made in a former Hispano-Suiza plant, under licence from the British motorcycle manufacturer Villiers. Up until 1958 Autonacional produced many thousands of these sympathetic runabouts under the name Biscuter Voisin.

CHAPTER FOUR

AN UNFORTUNATE EPISODE AT RENAULT

Construction and preparation of the successful racing machines, record cars and other Voisin prototypes had, of course, enormously enhanced the reputation of their talented designers. As even in those days headhunting was an established practice (though not known by that name), André Lefebvre and his colleague, Marius Bernard, had regularly been approached by other car manufacturers. But loving their work at Voisin and being utterly loyal to their 'patron,' they had systematically refused these offers.

However, circumstances changed, and not in a positive way when financial difficulties forced Gabriel Voisin to accept a merger proposition made by a Belgian consortium, which already had a majority shareholding in Minerva and Imperia. The company was renamed Société Commerciale des Automobiles Voisin, and was also to produce Imperia cars for the French market.

But almost as soon as the ink on the contract had dried the problems began. The men from the consortium practically took over the factory and more or less evicted Gabriel Voisin. Unfortunately, the money they had promised to inject into the new company never materialised.

With great regret Gabriel Voisin advised André Lefebvre and Marius Bernard to look for another employer. Bernard left for Lancia, which was building an assembly plant in Bonneuil-sur-Marne near Paris: producing the small Lancia Augustas as Belnas in France would make them commercially more competitive, as at that time the French automobile market was 'protected' by high import tariffs.

The board of Lorraine-Dietrich in Argenteuil invited Lefebvre for talks, during which he discovered that this famous French manufacturer with several racing successes at the 24 Heures du Mans to its name also suffered from financial malaise. The future of La Lorraine as a car-maker did not look very promising, and three years later the company abandoned production of automobiles altogether to concentrate on aeronautic construction and military equipment.

On May 4, 1931 André Lefebvre began work for Louis Renault (1877-1944). François Lehideux,

Working on the big eight-cylinder rear-wheel drive Renault gave Lefebvre little satisfaction. (Courtesy Renault Communications)

54

Renault's right-hand man (he was also married to a daughter of Louis' deceased brother, Fernand), offered him the job of second-in-command to Charles Serre, head of Renault's development department.

Lehideux and Lefebvre – practically the same age and of similar background – knew each other and got on well. Lehideux was convinced that to go forward the Renault company needed a younger, more dynamic and professional technical staff to replace the 'old guard' of his uncle's cronies.

Indeed, Louis Renault was an absolute autodidact, a genial inventor and a great industrialist, but he lacked formal technical training and most of his closest collaborators had no better education in engineering than he had himself.

Charles Serre had been 'discovered' by Louis Renault at the firm of Durand, which had cut the gears for the first Renault car, where he worked as a draftsman. He was a pleasant man and a dedicated worker, but no visionary engineer. He had been engaged by Renault when he was only sixteen, and by faithfully following the wishes and ideas of his patron over the next thirty years, was promoted to the position of chief engineer.

A HEAD-ON COLLISION WITH HIS BOSS

Lefebvre was given the task of developing and improving the Reinastella, successor to the large 40CV model. The Renahuit was a huge and heavy conventional rear-wheel drive design, and Lefebvre, who was obsessed with the idea of a light front-wheel drive car, was bored to death by the job.

Serre tried to dissuade Lefebvre from talking to their boss about his 'revolutionary' ideas, as he feared Renault's reaction. But André Lefebvre, remembering his frank technical discussions with Gabriel Voisin, went against Serre's fatherly advice.

It is said that Louis Renault told Lefebvre: "I won't waste five minutes on such nonsense." Lefebvre, who could be hot-tempered when he felt he had been treated unfairly, replied by telling Renault what he thought of his antiquated engineering ideas. The meeting between the two men ended in a shouting match, and shortly afterwards Louis Renault ordered François Lehideux to "get rid of that man."

According to André Lefebvre's son, Michel, Lehideux deeply regretted the incident, and told Lefebvre "Go home, you can work there. Avoid meeting my uncle and take your time to find a new employer."

Renault's refusal to listen to Lefebvre's proposition was, of course, rather foolish, and his reaction – if things really happened that way – was graceless indeed. But placed in an historic context, Renault's reluctance to invest in the development of a car with this new and unproved technology is also quite understandable, especially in view of the economic situation at that time.

In the early thirties, 99 per cent of all cars had a front-mounted engine driving the rear wheels. Front-wheel drive was only successful in small sports cars such as the Tracta and Alvis, or in competition machines like the American Miller Indianapolis racer. Other FWD experiments – such as the French Bucciali or the American Auburn and Ruxton – had not survived the economic crisis.

It is also true that Louis Renault was averse to any new idea that he had not thought of himself, or had already been proved by others. Furthermore, he had developed dictatorial tendencies, indeed behaving as the 'Emperor' of Billancourt: in his organisation nobody dared contradict him.

Perhaps Lefebvre would have done better to listen to Serre. In his book about Louis Renault, Anthony Rhodes tells how the collaborators from the technical department had learned to handle him: "If one of them had a solution to a given problem by which he set great store, he knew it would be fatal to suggest it. Renault would immediately point out its disadvantages and turn it down. One had to approach him with two, three or even four alternative suggestions and announce them in reverse order of importance, keeping the true solution till last. Renault would immediately dilate the defects of the first suggestion; nor was the second, he would say, much better; nor the third. But the fourth – ah! did the man not see that this was obviously the answer? Anyhow, on February 2, 1933, Lefebvre's employment at Renault was terminated.

There is a rather cynical postscript to this unfortunate episode, however. In August 1961, Renault – by then the Régie Nationale des Usines Renault, RNUR – introduced the front-wheel drive R4, as successor to the popular rear-engined Renault 4CV and a direct competitor of the successful 2CV that Lefebvre had designed for Citroën.

Technical journalists immediately observed that some of the construction details of Renault's first front-wheel drive car bore a marked resemblance to those of André Lefebvre's original Citroën Traction Avant. The choice of a drivetrain layout with the gearbox in front of the small four-cylinder was, of course, quite logical. The economic advantages were obvious, because this combined engine/transmission unit was similar to that used in the rear-engined Renault Dauphine, and could thus be manufactured on the same production lines. But the independent front suspension with longitudinal torsion springs, in combination with transverse torsion springs at the rear, seemed a belated tribute to Lefebvre's clever idea to concentrate the suspension forces over a small section of the floor panel. Renault had every right to use this solution, of course, as it had never been patented by Citroën ... and Lefebvre had probably designed it whilst still employed by Renault.

CHAPTER

FIVE

ECONOMIC & SOCIAL UNREST

During the early years of the 1930s the world's economical climate deteriorated fast, and the recession in the USA also had serious repercussions in Europe.

The Germans were still licking their wounds after their defeat in 1918, and, after the Wall Street Crash, a number of American banks – which up until then had financially supported Hindenburg's government – could no longer provide credit, meaning that Germany was faced with tremendous debt, and was also unable to finance its repair payments. The situation became critical when the large Donat bank in Berlin had to close its doors, precipitating a run on other banks, increasing pressure on the mark and forcing the government to take severe measures to curtail the exodus of German capital. According to many historians, growing economic and monetary uncertainty was instrumental in the landslide victory of the Nazi party in the Reichstag elections of July 31, 1932: five months later Hitler became Reichskansler.

The economies of other European countries were also seriously affected by the crisis. Early in 1931, Britain introduced import tariffs to combat unemployment and protect its native manufacturers and agriculture. On September 21, Chancellor of the Exchequer Phillip Snowden announced that the country was abandoning the gold standard, whereupon the pound sterling devaluated by 20 per cent, all of which made export to Great Britain a lot less lucrative.

The ever-changing French government did not take any special measures to protect the country's industry or promote employment – it hardly had the time! – but lack of stable leadership, plus the fear of unemployment and poverty, caused increasing social unrest. Cabinet changes and presidential inaugurations followed each other so rapidly that it seemed like a dreadful charade of musical chairs: the cabinet of Raymond Poincaré was replaced in December 1930 by one formed by Pierre Laval; on February 21, 1932 the senate sent Laval away and chose André Tardieu as his successor; in May 1932 the French president, Paul Doumer, was murdered by a madman of Russian origin.

After the elections that month, Edouard Herriot took over as prime minister. Herriot's cabinet fell six and half months later, to be replaced by one formed by Joseph Paul-Boncour. Edouard Daladier drastically changed this cabinet on February 7, after a mob of 40,000 right-wing activists stormed the Palais Bourbon, seat of the French chamber of representatives. The police opened fire on the demonstrators, and 15 people were killed and 2000 wounded. In reaction the French labour unions called for a general strike in protest against the growing fascism in their country; as the social climate worsened, the economy suffered, too. It was a vicious circle …

Chapter

SIX

MEETING ANDRÉ CITROËN

When Gabriel Voisin heard about Lefebvre's predicament he was reminded of a recent conversation with André Citroën, who told him in confidence that, at the Paris Motor Show of 1934, he intended to introduce a revolutionary new car with the engine driving the front wheels. However, he complained that his engineering team had not tackled this project with the necessary enthusiasm and vigour, and now they were hopelessly behind schedule. Remembering this, Voisin immediately phoned Citroën: "I know just the man you need, he worked with me. I also know that he is at present looking for a job!" A meeting between the two Andrés was arranged.

André Citroën (1887-1935) had, within a time span of just ten years, become one of France's most prominent automobile manufacturers. After the armistice in 1918, he had converted his factory at the Quai de Javel in Paris – where, during the war, he had produced 23 million shells – to manufacture automobiles. He hired Jules Salomon, the well-known engineer who had designed the small Le Zèbre car, and adopted the mass production techniques he had seen in the US and which he had already used in his ammunition factory.

The first Citroën, the seductively-priced 10CV, was an immediate bestseller. From its introduction in June 1919 to the end of 1921, some 24,000 were made. Only the acclaimed 5CV Cloverleaf topped this with a production run of no fewer than 80,841 units.

André Citroën had a genius not only for optimising production processes, but also for organising sales. A born marketeer, with an infallible intuition for what the public wanted, he combined an inexhaustible imagination with a flair for public relations, his sometimes daring publicity stunts making his a household name, not only in France, his native country, but throughout the world.

After he had acquired the licensing rights from American coachwork supplier E G Budd Mfg Co in Philadelphia in 1923, Citroën was the only manufacturer in Europe to offer closed all-steel, four-door saloons. By 1925, Citroën – selling 61,487 units a year – was France's leading maker of popular family cars. Four years later, a growing model range gave an output of 102,891 units per annum, nearly double Renault's production of 54,117 passenger cars.

The tide turned

During the early thirties the tide turned, and car sales slipped in an alarming way from over 100,000 in 1929 to just 48,027 in 1932. In 1925, Citroën's company had made a record profit of around one hundred million francs, but lately registered only losses. With the investments he made to modernise his factory, his debt increased every day, and slowly accumulated to over 125 million francs.

André Citroën had the reputation of being a gambler. An optimist by nature, he was convinced that the economic crisis – which had hit the car industry so hard – would be followed by better times. In preparation of them, Citroën had completely rebuilt his Quai de Javel plant; the one thing he was desperate for now was a totally new car, and one with such outstanding qualities that it would immediately outsell all its competitors, and which was so advanced that it could continue in production for a number of years. To pay Budd for the manufacturing rights, and to amortize his huge investment in large presses and machinery, Citroën needed to produce at least 300,000 more or less identical bodies.

FASCINATED BY FRONT-WHEEL DRIVE

During one of his last visits to Budd in the USA, technical director Joseph Ledwinka had shown André Citroën the advanced prototype of the new 'Ruxton.' This car had a very low, four-door body integrated with the chassis, and its engine drove the front wheels.

Moreover, 'le colonel' Pierre Prévost, one of Citroën's trusted technicians, had personally tried out Grégoire's front driven 'Tracta Géphi' sports car. When Prévost, not an easy man to satisfy, stated that he was quite impressed by its road behaviour, this also fired André Citroën's imagination.

His new popular car should have front-wheel drive, he decided. What further whetted his appetite was that, in 1932, Lucien Rosengart offered him a partnership in the manufacture of a front-wheel drive car, designed by new chief engineer Hans Gustav Rohr under a license contract that Rosengart had obtained from the German company Adler Werke. Ambi-Budd, the German subsidiary of Budd in Philadelphia, had been involved in the development of its chassis and four-door body. Citroën was tempted, but said no: he did not want to be associated with Rosengart and, besides, refused to become dependent on a German company.

Alas, Citroën's own technical and commercial staff did not share his conviction that front-wheel drive – a revolutionary but unproved solution – would boost sales and save the company. Then André Lefebvre stepped into his office ...

André Citroën was favourably impressed by Lefebvre. This smart, self-confident engineer spoke with great conviction about his ideas for a modern front-wheel drive automobile; he had all the details in his head, and even had some drawings to show. His enthusiasm was contagious. When André Citroën told Lefebvre about his contract with the American Budd company which made it possible to manufacture monocoque bodies, Lefebvre told him that he had already designed chassis-less racing cars for Voisin in 1923 and 1924.

It did not take long for André Citroën to realise that he needed this engineer as much as the man needed a top job. He promised Lefebvre absolute freedom to form his own team of engineers, draftsmen and mechanics to help him develop and build prototypes: he could select the best men from the technical staff. Lefebvre had only to report to one person: André Citroën himself. But time was pressing! On March 12, 1933, André Lefebvre officially began the third job in his career: 'ingénieur' at Citroën.

One can imagine that his sudden arrival at the top echelon of the experimental department did not please everybody in the company. Many of Citroën's loyal staff belonged to the 'old school,' and did not share André Citroën's conviction that an unorthodox car could turn the tide of slipping sales.

Although Lefebvre had no official title – today, he would be called the 'project manager' of a 'task force' – some resented his appointment on personal grounds. Maurice Broglie, Director of the Bureau d'Etudes, was openly hostile because he had no authority over this 'intruder.' Broglie had also come from Renault to Citroën, and, as an engineer, was nearly as conservative as Serre, though dedicated to André Citroën and a good technician. Broglie never drove a car, and some said this was because he did not have a driving licence.

He challenged Lefebvre about why front-wheel drive should be preferable to rear-wheel drive. Without saying a word, André took a matchbox from his pocket, shook out a matchstick, stuck that vertically in the box and placed the box on a glass table. He invited Broglie to move the box by pushing it from behind with the matchstick; the box immediately drifted off course. Lefebvre demonstrated to Broglie that if the matchbox was pulled instead of pushed, it would proceed in a straight line, after which, nobody had any doubt about who was the real leader of the Bureau d'Etudes.

BIRTH OF THE TRACTION

For the first time in his life Lefebvre was confronted with the petty jealousies that exist in most large organisations. He was too busy to bother with this, though, and was able to win people over to his point of view.

Also for the first time in his life he was to design a car that had to be mass-produced, which certainly posed some extra challenges. Fortunately, at Citroën there were sufficient specialists with experience in this field, and, as we know, Citroën had a contract with American coachwork specialist Budd concerning the manufacturing process of his all-steel bodies.

A RACE AGAINST THE CALENDAR

During the first meeting of Lefebvre's 'task force,' André Citroën personally briefed its members. According to his 'Cahier des Charges,' the new car, codenamed PV (Petite Voiture), was to be a 7CV ('Chevaux Vapeur' = the French fiscal horsepower) four-door family saloon with room for four to five people, a dry weight of 800kg, top speed of 100km/h, and petrol consumption of 7lt/100km when driving long distances from Paris to Bordeaux for example. It would have superior roadholding, thanks to front-wheel drive and a low centre of gravity. Independent suspension would ensure the comfort of its passengers, hydraulic brakes and a steel unit body their safety. The style of the coachwork was to be modern, but Citroën did not want any fancy streamlining, because this could deter customers.

Citroën also insisted that the price should not exceed 15,000 francs, but this was an overambitious target and Citroën's cheapest model sold for 19,500 francs.

However, one thing was certain: the car had to be ready for the Paris Motor Show in October 1934, which gave the factory just 18 months. It would be a race against time ...

AN UNPLEASANT SURPRISE

André Citroën had another surprise in store: the PV would have an automatic gearbox to make it the easiest car to drive with only an accelerator and a brake pedal. For this reason he engaged the services of Dimitry Sensaud de Lavaud, an inventor who, for years, had been experimenting with automatic transmissions and who had recently developed a kind of fluid-drive system. Sensaud de Lavaud could afford his experiments because his family had amassed a great fortune planting coffee in Brazil.

Lefebvre was sceptical. He had met Sensaud de Lavaud several times, as, in the mid-twenties, Gabriel Voisin had allowed the inventor to try out his automatic gearbox on a Voisin chassis. This had proved to be an ingenious, but very complicated mechanism that needed continual adjustment, even with the large and powerful Voisin engines. Voisin had therefore opted for a combination of a mechanical gearbox coupled to an electromagnetic-operated planetary unit manufactured by Cotal. Now, Sensaud de Lavaud proposed an automatic gearbox based on what sounded like an hydraulic torque converter. Hopefully, this new transmission would function better.

LITTLE DEVIL

If Lefebvre appreciated that his task would be extremely difficult, he never complained, as he rather liked challenges. Broglie, official Director of the Bureau d'Etudes, allotted him a corner in an old building in the Rue du Théâtre, once the factory where Mors automobiles were built. Within a few weeks this experimental workshop was as busy as a beehive.

At first, Lefebvre only had the assistance of Fortin, his faithful mechanic at Voisin, and Monteil, a draftsman who had followed him from Renault. Soon, some Citroën engineers joined the team: Maurice Julien, a mathematical genius; Alphonse Forceau, a mechanical engineer of outstanding quality; draftsmen/designers Oudart and Léonzi; Swiss engine specialist Théo Nordlinger, and Georges Sallot. Sallot was a self-educated technician who had joined Citroën in 1923, knew his way around and was just as keen to try out something new as Lefebvre, soon becoming his right-hand-man. It was not long before the team's enthusiasm attracted specialists from other departments as well.

Lefebvre hardly ever bothered about formal procedures but, thanks to his charm and wit, mostly got what he wanted – and fast! He personally oversaw everything that had to do with the PV, apparently everywhere at once. Behind his back André Citroën called him the 'little devil.'

One of his collaborators compared André Lefebvre with the conductor of a symphony orchestra, directing a composition he had written himself. He knew every note by heart and expected that all his musicians should play the score precisely the way he had in mind.

Lefebvre demanded professional capability, enthusiasm and dedication, and had little patience with those who were slow to follow his explanations. He had an outspoken aversion to engineers who were merely theoreticians, or those who claimed "We have always done it that way." He inspired his collaborators to be inquisitive and innovative; to understand how something had to function and be able to make it work.

His management style was very modern, certainly for those days. Every morning he held a short meeting with a number of his colleagues, engineers and draftsmen in order to evaluate progress and problems. When he wanted something done he gave a detailed outline and then asked: "Who will tackle this job?" He hardly ever gave a direct order.

NO RUNNING BOARDS REQUIRED

In August 1933, Lefebvre's team had two prototypes ready, and André Citroën took his wife, Giorgina, along to have a look at them. He set great store by her opinion because he knew from experience that women played a decisive role in the purchasing process of cars. When Madame Citroën noticed the absence of running boards she asked her husband about it. He replied proudly that these were not needed: their new 7CV would be the first family car in the world you did not have to climb into, as it was possible to just slide into the seat as easily as into an armchair at home!

If the static presentation was successful, the first trial runs were a catastrophe. Nearly everything that could break, broke. Louis Robin, one of the engineers involved in this project, remembered how at that time some five to six prototypes were simultaneously tested at Montlhéry, each carrying four sacks of sand to represent three passengers. The test programme comprised 20,000km at top speed on the oval track or the adjoining road circuit. Test drivers were relieved every five hours or after around 500km.

Lefebvre, who knew Monthéry very well from his Voisin days, regularly came to see how the cars were doing. Often the test teams confronted him with hair-raising tales of broken driveshafts and front suspensions, brakes that overheated, wheels that had broken free and, in some cases, cracks in the body structure.

Fortunately, there were no serious accidents. The test drivers were professionals who knew how to react when their cars shed some parts. And Lefebvre always remained unruffled; his reaction was: if, on a prototype, things break, you can redesign and strengthen them, but if they don't break they are probably too strong and too heavy. How to find out? Weight and strength were two of his main preoccupations, but they were not the only ones.

French fries

Lefebvre asked Forceau to evaluate Sensaud de Lavaud's hydraulic gearbox. Forceau reported that its principle was based on an invention dating from 1902 of a German marine engineer by the name of Föttinger, and Dimitri de Sensaud had added a turbine that ran as a freewheel within the casing of the 'fluid flywheel.' In theory, this would increase engine torque, though Forceau feared that, given its size and the limited torque of the relatively small engine in the PV, it would not perform well enough. The power losses of the hydraulic turbine also made it practically impossible to meet the fuel consumption targets set by André Citroën; moreover, it would be expensive to mass-produce.

Charles Brull, head of the department that bench-tested all components, confirmed these conclusions, and the test drivers discovered that the hydraulic transmission was utterly unpredictable as, after some distance, sometimes it would completely refuse to move the car any further! The reason for this was that, when the oil in the turbine casing heated up, system efficiency diminished dramatically. And the oil got hot, very hot, in particular when driving in a mountainous region. Someone in the Bureau d'Etudes joked: "If you like French fries, put a few potatoes in the turbine and take the car up the hill at Meudon. When you reach the top they will be crisp."

Abandoning the automatic

Even if everyone on his technical staff was convinced that it would be a mistake to continue with the Sensaud de Lavaud gearbox, nobody could persuade André Citroën to accept that this was so. When Lefebvre told him about the shortcomings of the system he replied: "You solve them, you are the engineer!" And when Brull presented his condemning report, Citroën was furious and told him that he must have been drunk during the tests!

André Citroën was too eager to equip his new car with this automatic gearbox. Together with its inventor he had tried it himself and found it worked very well! Around the end of February 1934, he invited several bankers for a private demonstration, intending to convince them of the qualities of the new car, so that they would lend him money till it was in production and sales profits would allow him to pay them back. The plan backfired badly: the automatic transmission failed and left the moneymen stranded. It was a bitter disappointment for André Citroën; he summoned Broglie, Brull and Lefebvre to his office and ordered them to prepare a conventional gearbox.

The men at the Bureau d'Etudes had foreseen their boss' change of heart, and, as they feared that it would cause insurmountable delays in the test programme, had already persuaded Citroën's gearbox specialist, Camusat, who was recovering at home from an accident, to return to his office – even if he had to come in a wheelchair. As both his arms were in bandages, Camusat could hardly lift a pencil, but under his guidance, and with practical suggestions from Forceau, within record time his draughtsmen designed an alternative transmission; a mechanical three-speed box with a conventional single dry plate clutch that perfectly fitted within the front-wheel drive concept. The position of the gear lever in the middle of the dashboard, and the complicated system of rods (called the 'Eiffel tower') that manipulated the gears were thought up by André Lefebvre. Two weeks after André Citroën decided to abandon Sensaud's transmission, the first PV prototypes ran with a manual box.

Problems with driveshaft joints

This took one problem from Lefebvre's shoulders. However, another would haunt him til after the Traction Avant went into production: the durability of the driveshaft joints.

Front-wheel drive means that engine power is transmitted to the wheel hubs, which also steer the car. Therefore, these wheels must be able to swivel horizontally through an arc of at least 40 degrees around their kingpins. Conventional cardan – or universal joints as used in the transmission of rear-wheel drive cars – are not suitable, because in a bend (when the driveshafts have to work at an angle) such simple joints induce an irregular rotation of the driven wheels. As the angle increases (sharper bends), the more pronounced this phenomenon becomes. The only solution is to either fit double cardan joints at the wheel side, which somewhat reduces this unpleasant characteristic, or, even better, homokinetic – ie constant – velocity joints that are completely free of this vice.

It is known that André Citroën had already decided to produce a front-wheel drive car some time before Lefebvre joined the company. When he became aware that the German car manufacturers DKW and Adler used the 'Tracta' transmission joints patented by Gregoire and Fenaille in their front-wheel drive cars, he immediately contacted the engineer Jean-Albert Grégoire to begin negotiation over royalties. As a result, the first PV prototypes were equipped with homokinetic 'Tracta' joints.

Then Grégoire made a terrible mistake, as he admitted in his book *50 Ans d'Automobile*. Together with Charles Rivolier, who worked for him at Bendix France, the company that was to manufacture the 'Tracta' joints, Grégoire 'improved' construction of the joint, with the objective of simplifying installation during assembly of the front axle unit.

It was a great disappointment when Citroën test drivers reported that these new so-called 'revolving' joints had to be replaced at between 5000 and 10,000 kilometres. Brull's bench tests showed why. Turning at full lock, the joints became so hot that they spewed out their grease; lack of lubrication then destroyed their revolving parts.

In the above-mentioned book, Grégoire bitterly complains that Lefebvre did not grant him sufficient time to find a remedy for what, in his view, was simply a production fault, but he should have realised that André Lefebvre was committed to the irrevocable deadline that André Citroën had set. Grégoire also suggests that his 'Tracta' joints became the victim of a conflict of interest within the Bendix Company: according to him, the bosses of Bendix France, Baptistin Boetto and Henry Perrot, were afraid of upsetting relations with Citroën's technical staff, as this might mean losing an important customer for their brakes. So they asked Grégoire to cease in his attempts to sell Citroën the Tracta joints.

In his book, *Best Wheel Forward*, Grégoire also tells of a meeting in 1934 with Mr Kliesrath, one of the directors of Bendix Aviation, the American mother company of Bendix France, who told him in no uncertain terms that he preferred the constant velocity ball-joints made by Weiss.

Further experiments

In the meantime, Kasimir, a buyer for Citroën of machine equipment in the USA, informed Citroën's production manager, Houdin, that he could secure a contract for the manufacturing rights of the American 'Rzeppa' constant velocity joint, which, because of its construction, seemed less prone to overheating. However, there was a drawback: in sharp bends the bearing balls that embedded the node rattled, and Citroën's test drivers complained that the noise was similar to that which marbles might make if dropped into an empty chamber pot! Besides, it was difficult to get the machines which manufacture these joints delivered in time.

As a last resort it was decided to ask Gleanzer, the company that always had supplied Citroën with universal joints for its rear-wheel driven models, to come up with a solution. The Gleanzer-Spicer joints that were finally adopted followed the double cardan principle, and were – strictly speaking – not homokinetic. But at least they posed no serious problems ...

THE TRACTION'S INCREDIBLY SHORT GESTATION TIME

Many have wondered how André Lefebvre and his team could have developed a car as revolutionary and epoch-making as the 'Traction Avant' in just over 13 months, because only some 404 days had passed since March 12, 1933 – when Lefebvre began to work at Citroën, and April 18, 1934 – the date of the official presentation of the Citroën 7CV – after which, production began and the first cars were driven to the dealers.

Today, even with the high-tech help of computers and Cad Cam systems, the process of developing a new car intended for mass production still takes at least 36 months!

In his well-documented book, *Citroën: l'Histoire et les Secrets de son Bureau d'Etudes* (Tome 1), Roger Brioult comes up with eight explanations:

- André Lefebvre was a genius
- He had carte blanche from André Citroën, and no 'administrative' responsibilities
- He knew how to explain clearly to his collaborators what had to be done
- In those days people worked fast, and sometimes for very long days; when a job had to be finished, working days of ten to eleven hours were not unusual
- Everybody in the team believed in Lefebvre and his Traction Avant
- Lefebvre had thoroughly thought out most of the details of the car, so was able to quickly resolve any problems that arose
- He had already made many of the drawings for the front-wheel drive car before he came to work for Citroën
- André Citroën and André Lefebvre were equally impatient to get the car into production

Gabriel Voisin, in his memoirs, even provides a ninth explanation:
- Lefebvre and his closest collaborators continued to work during the summer months of 1933, while at the Citroën factory most of those opposed to his front-wheel drive project went off to enjoy their holidays. Even given these considerations, it was still quite an accomplishment.

It's only fair to add that some of the elements which Lefebve and his engineering team used for his new car had been on the drawing boards at Citroën before he came to work there. This was certainly the case for the engine and also probably the independent front suspension with its torsion bars. From January 1934, the rear-wheel driven Citroën 10 NH Légères and 15 NH had a front suspension arrangement similar to that of the Traction Avant.

Then there were the very many people, both at Citroën and at Budd in Philadelphia, without whom Lefebvre could never have achieved his target in time. Some of them have already been mentioned, but there are others who also made important contributions to the PV project. If Lefebvre could have written his own biography he would surely have paid tribute to these men.

A TRIBUTE TO HIS COLLEAGUES

Maurice Sainturat was a top-notch engineer who had worked for Delage and Hotchkiss. He was quite a character, and liked to do all his drawings and calculations in the evenings at home, surrounded by his purring cats. Was that why his new Citroën engine ran so smoothly?

His four-cylinder began life with a capacity of 1298cc, subsequently increased to 1303 litres, then 1529 litres and finally 1911cc. In 1933, it was very much a 'state of the art' machine: it had overhead valves, a separate cylinder head, and wet cylinder liners to facilitate overhaul, which was to remain in production for over 30 years.

Sainturat's four-cylinder unit also served as the point of departure for the 3822 litre OHV V8 engine that was fitted in the '22.' This super-ambitious version of the 'Traction Avant' (with a top speed of 140km/h) was exhibited at the 1934 Paris Motor Show. However, this model silently disappeared from Citroën's sales brochures after Michelin took over management of the company.

Flaminio Bertoni, the talented Italian-born sculptor and stylist/designer, worked for a number of well-known coachbuilders before coming to Citroën. He had been employed by Carrozzeria Macchi in Varese (Italy), and in Paris by Manessius, Rothschild et Fils, and Sical. In 1931, Sical produced a small series of special bodies for Citroën C6 chassis that Bertoni had designed, which was how the French car manufacturer discovered him. His colleagues at Citroën nicknamed him 'il signor' because of his singsong Italian accent.

As a stylist Flaminio Bertoni certainly matched the creativity that André Lefebvre showed as an engineer. He translated many of Lefebvre's rough sketches into fine artist's impressions, superb scale models, full plan drawings and plaster mock-ups. Although Bertoni had only a limited knowledge of car technology, he often added his own ideas to those of Lefebvre, and, aesthetically, most of them were an improvement. He was a tireless worker who made hundreds of studies and was responsible for the final shape of the Traction Avant body.

The story goes that, after André Citroën had rejected three proposals for the coachwork of the new PV, Bertoni, in the course of one Saturday night, modelled with his hands a new, scale mock-up from plasiline, a sculptor's wax. The next Monday he and Raoul Cuinet, his superior in the coachwork department, presented it to their patron. When André Citroën saw it he became so enthusiastic that he invited them both to his apartment in the rue Octave-Feuillet, to show it to his wife. She did not hide her admiration either and that night André Citroën told their son, Maxime, that the body of his next car would look like 'the shell of a tortoise.'

André Citroën also gave Bertoni a salary increase of 1000 francs.

Raoul Cuinet, his assistant Pierre Franchiset, and the engineers at Budd also earned Lefebvre's gratitude. After the draftsmen from Cuinet's coachwork department had painstakingly transformed Bertoni's sketches into detailed technical 1/1 drawings, on November 18, 1933 he and Franchiset embarked with all the plans to the USA. Because of their great expertise in manufacturing steel bodies, Budd had again been engaged by Citroën to supply the production tools and dies for the new car. In Philadelphia Cuinet and Franchiset discovered that all of the metric measurements on their blueprints had to be converted to feet and inches. As Citroën was an old and valued customer, the management of Budd did everything to help.

A great number of modifications were needed to make the Citroën body suitable for mass-production. The first prototypes had been hand-built in France by specialised craftsmen and mechanics, which explains why their bodies comprised many small parts. But, for both economical and technical reasons, the production coachwork had to be made from the largest pressings practicable, as larger panels require less labour-intensive welding operations and also improve torsional strength. The engineers at Budd were masters in the art of the optimal use of sheet metal: the door cutouts in the huge panels that formed the complete sides of the body were used to make smaller parts, and the same was done with the metal from the window cutouts in the doors.

Cablegrams

To inform all concerned about the changes that either Lefebvre and his team or the experts at Budd considered necessary, some form of day-to-day contact with the home front in Paris was vital, but, in 1933, this was no simple matter. Cuinet and Franchiset found that the telegraph was the most reliable and fastest form of communication; using cablegrams – as such messages were called in those days – they also discovered a way to get round the six hour time difference between France and the USA. By sending off their reports in the evening, they would get replies early the next morning. Sometimes, however, electric storms over the Atlantic made the directives they received impossible to decipher and then they had to try again. The manager of the Atlantic Club Hotel in Philadelphia, where they stayed, told them that never before had any of his guests received such a constant stream of cablegrams.

The setup worked well and just three weeks after their arrival, the so-called 'Kellering' models – the three-dimensional mock-ups that served as the master for the steel dies – were ready for inspection. Cuinet then returned to France and Franchiset remained in Philadelphia to oversee the manufacture of the dies and the special production machines.

Pierre Lemaire, a professor in Lyon, and engineer Paul d'Aubarède were the French inventors of the flexible engine mountings used for the original floating engine. They first sold their patent to Chrysler in the USA, which meant that Citroën had to pay a lot of money to the American automaker in order to obtain the manufacturing rights for France, so he could introduce his (rear-driven) 1932 models with the novelty of a 'moteur flottant.'

However, on the Traction Avant prototypes it became apparent that the 'moteur flottant' system was not suitable for a combined engine and transmission unit driving the front wheels as, at certain speeds, the entire front end of the car began to dance up and down. Citroën engaged the services of Pierre Lemaire and Paul d'Aubarède, who then – together with Maurice Julien – developed a completely new type of flexible engine mounting for the PV. They called it the 'Système Pausodyne,' Greek for 'I soothe the pain.'

Roger Prud'homme, a veteran of Citroën's Croisière Jaune, was a first-rate mechanic and an outstanding organiser. In 1933, he joined the Bureau d'Etudes and became responsible for the workshop that prepared and repaired the prototypes. As such, he worked closely with Pierre Prévost, head of the test drivers. Of course, he also regularly reported to André Lefebvre, and from time-to-time gave him invaluable practical advice. Prud'homme, a resourceful troubleshooter, often came up with solutions nobody else had thought of, which Lefebvre appreciated very much. It is evident that the men had great mutual respect, and André's son, Michel Lefebvre, who, in the fifties, worked in Prud'homme's department, confirms this.

RAVE REVIEWS

On Wednesday April 18, 1934 – only four days after type approval had been granted by the Service des Mines (the French road transport authority) – André Citroën officially unveiled the new 7CV Traction Avant in his showroom on the Place de l'Europe in Paris. That same day 300 cars left the factory, driven away by Citroën's dealers.

The next day photos and descriptions of the Traction Avant figured on the front pages of most French newspapers. In the press the 'Sept Chevaux' was praised for its daring design, and the many original technical solutions never before seen in a family car. The

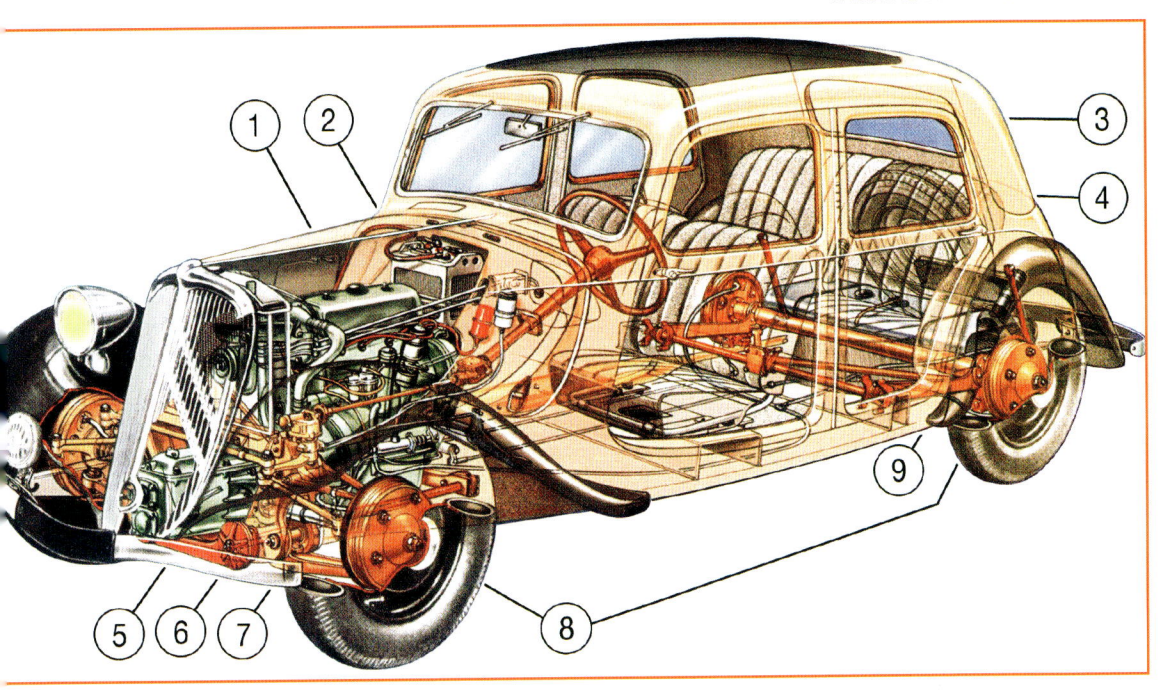

In 1934, Citroën's front-wheel drive 7CV Traction Avant set a new standard for family cars. Some of its technical details: 1 Water-cooled four-cylinder engine with push-rod-operated overhead valves, cast-iron block with wet 'changeable' linings. 2 Accessible six-volt battery in the engine compartment. 3 Steel monocoque (unit construction) four-door body. 4 Spare wheel on tail panel (from 1935 onward on luggage lid). 5 Three-speed gearbox at the front of the engine (synchronized on second and third), gear change on dashboard. 6 Independent front suspension with longitudinal torsion bar springs, friction dampers (from April 1935 onward hydraulic shock absorbers). 7 Front-wheel drive. 8 Hydraulically-operated drum brakes on all wheels. 9 Rear suspension with trailing arms and transverse torsion bar springs. (Drawing courtesy Citroën Communication)

influential journal *L'Auto* even called it 'sensational.' Lefebvre's brainchild got enthusiastic reviews but nobody mentioned his name as its creator. That was not customary in those days: it was André Citroën's new car and he got all the credit.

Only a few weeks before, on March 24, André Citroën had already assembled his most important dealers – some of whom were also shareholders – in his office at the Quai de Javel. He promised them a preview of the car he was going to launch, followed by lunch, with the intention of boosting morale and diverting attention from rumours about his financial difficulties. And, of course, he and his commercial director, André Pommier, were also eager to hear their reaction to the new car.

The presentation was orchestrated with all the attention to drama and detail that used to characterise such Citroën events. The guests were chauffeur-driven to the nearby Rue Cauchy, where they were shepherded into an inconspicuous building. In the middle of a small hall stood a spotlighted 'Sept Chevaux.' The moment they saw the Traction Avant all of the dealers fell silent. Then somebody asked: "How do you get into such a low car?" This was the signal for André Citroën to invite the Polish Count Chopsky, a six feet tall giant who worked in Citroën's export department, to take his place behind the steering wheel. When the Count sat down and stretched his long legs without any problem, the dealers applauded as if they had witnessed a circus act.

67

A well-known publicity photo from 1934 shows that the new Citroën Traction Avant had the 'horse' (engine and transmission) in front of the 'carriage' (body). As horse-drawn vehicles were then still a common sight in rural France, this was a very clever way to explain that – for automobiles, too – it is more logical to 'pull' than to 'push.'
(Courtesy Citroën Communication)

The Conservatoire Citroën at Aulnay-sous-Bois still keeps a display similar to the one which was used for the 1934 photo of the 'horse.' This allows study of the subframe with the engine/transmission unit, the front suspension arms, and front-wheel drive components. (Courtesy Hans Arend de Wit/Switchimage)

Right: Even in 1938 FWD was still considered a 'Unique Selling Proposition.' A Citroën advertisement from those days says: "Front-wheel drive glues the car to the road."

It was a big day for André Lefebvre. Proudly strutting around the car, he highlighted all its technical features and advantages. Front-wheel drive allowed the coachwork – and the centre of gravity – to be lowered whilst retaining the interior headroom found in conventional cars: and this without sacrificing ground clearance. The low roofline combined with the flat underside also reduced aerodynamic drag, resulting in economic fuel consumption. Independent suspension at the front, and a suspension at the rear with trailing arms, not only improved comfort but also handling. The torsion springs were anchored in such a way that suspension forces were absorbed in the strong midsection of the body, to

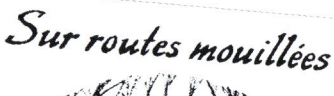

Independent front suspension

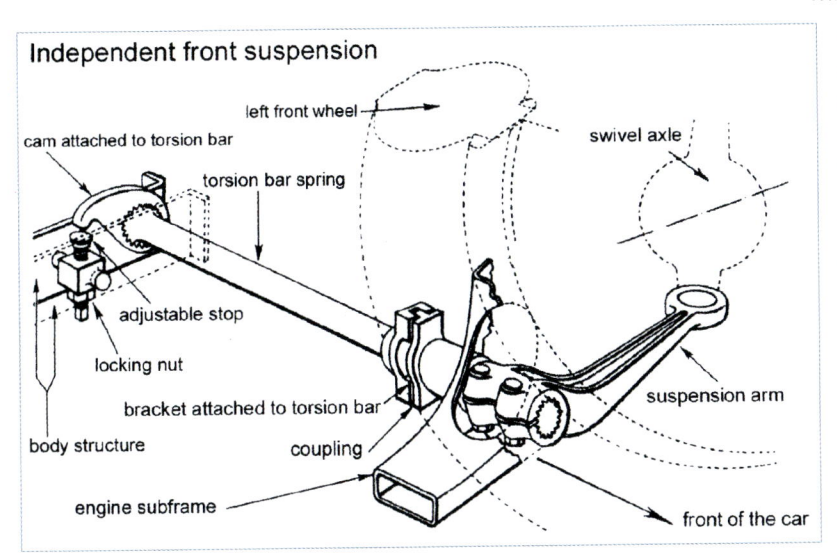

(Labels: cam attached to torsion bar; left front wheel; swivel axle; torsion bar spring; adjustable stop; locking nut; bracket attached to torsion bar; suspension arm; body structure; coupling; engine subframe; front of the car)

Diagram showing attachment of the torsion (bar) springs of the front suspension. (Drawing from Citroën service manual)

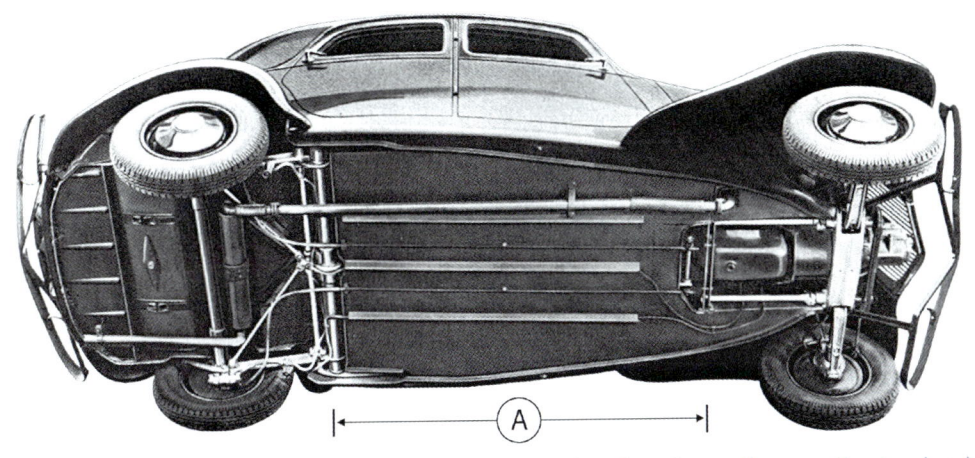

One of the hidden design secrets of Citroën's Traction Avant was the way the torsion bar springs were mounted. The two longitudinal torsion bars for the front suspension were anchored in the body near the footwell, whereas the supporting arms and transverse torsion bars for the rear suspension were mounted below the rear seat. Concentrating most of the suspension forces in the relatively small area of the floor of the passenger compartment reduced the stress-bearing area and provided optimal torsional stiffness.

In the wind tunnel at Chalais-Meudon (France), the Citroën TA proved to have less air resistance than most of its contemporary competitors. The explanation: A Front-wheel drive and the monocoque body enabled Lefebvre to achieve a practically flat underside. B Front-wheel drive also permitted a lower roofline, so the TA had a smaller frontal area. (Courtesy Soufflerie Aérodynamique de Chalais-Meudon)

During the early thirties André Citroën imported huge and – in those days – ultra modern presses and electric welding rigs from the US to manufacture the monocoque body of his new Traction Avant. The presses could produce a complete car side in one stroke. (Courtesy Citroën Communication)

The monocoque or unit construction gave a strong but light body structure, whilst providing extra safety for passengers. (Courtesy Citroën Communication)

To demonstrate the sturdiness of its monocoque coachwork, Citroën had a new 7CV Traction Avant driven over a cliff. After a fall of eight meters and several somersaults, the passenger compartment was not damaged and the doors could still be opened. (Courtesy Citroën Communication)

prevent flexing of the monocoque construction. The position of the gearbox in front of the differential and engine brought the centre of gravity as far forward as possible, thus obtaining the best traction and optimising straight line stability, even in strong side winds.

What he did not tell them – because they could see it for themselves – was that the low body made the car look much sportier than the conventional 'berlines' (four-door family saloons) of its competitors.

Most dealers were enthusiastic, though not all of them. Those from rural areas wondered how to sell such a revolutionary automobile to their affluent but conservative gentleman farmers and country notables. When Citroën announced that the car would retail at 17,600 francs, still other dealers feared for their profit margins, but, as Jacques Borgé and Nicolas Viasnoff have remarked in their book *La Traction*, "they had nothing to worry about; most of them would make a fortune with this new car."

Sadly, the financial benefits would come too late for André Citroën, however ...

A DISASTROUS DECISION

Not long after the successful dealer presentation, André Citroën visited the workshop of the Bureau d'Etudes to see how things were progressing. Prud'homme told him that over the last months his men had worked more than ten hours a day, including Saturdays and Sundays; could he give them two days off? Citroën replied: "My dear Prud'homme, it is not a question of days, it is a matter of hours."

Indeed, given his desperate financial situation – he urgently needed the cash to pay his suppliers – Citroën's impatience to rush his new car into production is understandable. Nevertheless, and with hindsight, this was a disastrous decision. In mid-April 1934, the Quai de Javel factory began to turn out 100 units a day; a month later, output had reached 300 a day. But the effort needed to manufacture this new and unorthodox car in a completely fresh factory, and in quickly increasing numbers had dramatic consequences, as these early models suffered from all kinds of teething troubles. The hydraulic brake system proved unreliable, front wheels came off on their own, torsion springs and transmission shafts snapped like matchsticks, windshields leaked and doors flew open. Some of these faults were the result of inadequate testing; others were caused by insufficient time given over to properly train the workforce, and by a lack of quality control. The problems not only considerably harmed the reputation of the newborn Traction Avant in this critical stage, but also meant that Lefebvre's team and the production engineers had again to do overtime to get things right.

TURNING FORTY

August 19, 1934 was André Lefebvre's 40th birthday. For most men, this is an occasion to reflect on their achievements, and Lefebvre had many reasons to be pleased with himself, both personally and professionally. He was happily married to Claire, they had two healthy sons and lived in a pleasant house. Against all the odds he had been able to realise his dream: his design of an advanced front-wheel drive car was actually being mass-produced in the Citroën factory. Amongst his colleagues he was considered to be one of the most innovative automobile engineers in Europe.

But the stress of the last few years was beginning to show. When something or somebody made him nervous he would rapidly blink his eyes and jut his jaw forward, just like his old mentor Gabriel Voisin used to do. And at the Bureau d'Etudes, new projects meant that the workload was still increasing.

ALL SET FOR THE PARIS MOTOR SHOW

For the Salon de l'Automobile in the Grand Palais in October 1934 André Citroën and

From 1931, Yacco became the official sponsor of Citroën's record runs, and all of the record cars were successively named Rosalie. From 17 to 21 July 1934, Rosalie VII – based on a 7CV TA 'faux cabriolet' – covered the distance of 16,010km at an average speed of 111.185km/h. Although this was a new international record, the main objective was to prove the reliability of the recently introduced front-wheel drive Citroën. César Marchand, André Lefebvre's comrade from his racing days, organized the event, and drove the '7' as well. (Courtesy Citroën Communication)

Lefebvre and his colleague, Leon Renault, during a test drive of a pre-production TA 11 'Normale' in the mountains. Even then automobile manufacturers tried to disguise future models during test runs on public roads. The bonnet 'embellishments' of this Citroën prototype closely resemble those of a competitor, the Fiat-Simca Ardita. (Courtesy Collection family Lefebvre)

his commercial director, André Pommier, were determined to exhibit not only their 7CV but a whole range of new front-driven Citroëns.

For Lefebvre, Cuinet and their teams this meant developing two longer and wider versions of the '7.' The 11CV (later named the 11B), with a wheelbase of 3.09m for the berline and 3.27m for the nine-seater 'familiale,' would be powered by the same 1911cc four-cylinder engine as the 7 Sport (later the 11BL). The wider bodies would also serve for the '22,' which was to be equipped with a 3822cc V8, also designed by Sainturat. André Citroën was not satisfied with only four-door 'berline' bodies, but also wanted a smart two-door cabriolet and a so-called faux-cabriolet or coupé for all these versions. In no time Flaminio Bertoni, assisted by Jean Daninos, came up with a very elegant design for these two-door bodies. The floor section, mudguards and bonnet, plus a lot of other body parts, were identical to those of the 'berlines.'

André Lefebvre must have been aware that Citroën's plan to refinance his company was rejected by both the banks and the French government. His relationship with André Citroën had never been as convivial as that with Gabriel Voisin, but they met regularly, as Citroën liked to visit the Bureau d'Etudes to inspect the prototypes his engineers were working on. Lefebvre highly appreciated the man, just as did most of the staff at Citroën, and not only admired him for his tenacity and optimism, but also for his outgoing manner and pleasant behaviour to his employees. And, like most people, he observed that their patron was obviously tired, losing weight, and sometimes looking pale and old. This filled him with great compassion.

CHAPTER SEVEN
MICHELIN STEPS IN

After the banks and the government refused to help, André Citroën turned to the Michelin family. He contacted Edouard Michelin's son-in-law, Pierre Bourdon, whom he knew quite well, as they had travelled together on a mission to the USA. Michelin was not only the largest tyre manufacturer in France, but also one of Citroën's major creditors.

Edouard Michelin, the seventy-four year old co-founder of this family business, sent his son, Pierre Michelin, and his right-hand man, Pierre Jules Boulanger, to Paris with instructions to find out what could be done to save Citroën and Michelin's financial stake in that company. Within weeks – even before the Paris motor show opened – a small army of inspectors and engineers from Michelin invaded the factory at the Quai de Javel. These men were instantly recognisable, as they wore clear blue dustcoats to protect their suits and poked their noses in everything. A stream of reorganisations in most departments, intended to improve efficiency and reduce the payroll, followed this episode, which naturally created a lot of unrest amongst the workers at Citroën. Even Lefebvre must have been worried about his future: was production of the Traction Avant to continue? And what would happen to the jobs of those who worked at the Bureau d'Etudes?

From December 21, 1934, the Société Anonyme André Citroën was officially in juridical liquidation (receivership). A new (temporary) board of directors represented Citroën's three most important creditors: Pierre Michelin for Michelin, Paul Franzen for the Banque Lazard Frères, and M Du Castel for the Comptoir Sidérurgique, a syndicate of French steel manufacturers.

ANTOINE HERMET SAVES THE TRACTION

If the Michelins and their advisers did not doubt the industrial potential of the Citroën factory, they were – understandably – not as convinced of the prospects for the new front-wheel drive car. Was it worthwhile investing in its further development? They instructed Antoine Hermet to asses its possibilities.

Hermet had begun his career in the Michelin competition department, and had later introduced a quality control system at Clermont-Ferrand; he was also an experienced test driver. In his biography about André Citroën Jacques Wolgensinger states: "Hermet was a colourful figure who never took off his wide-brimmed cowboy hat. When he presented himself at Citroën, Maurice Norroy, the technical director, Maurice Jouffroy, responsible for quality, and Pierre Prévost, the chief of the road-testing team were far from co-operative." Nevertheless, Hermet made a favourable judgement of the car: "It is a remarkably good automobile, provided they get the bugs out and make it reliable." Thus, Hermet saved André Lefebvre's creation. Later, Hermet was appointed head of Citroën's quality inspection department.

That both men had been absolutely right in their conviction that the front-wheel drive design would be successful was confirmed by the figures in Citroën's annual report of 1936, when sales of the Citroën Traction Avant alone resulted in a net profit of eighteen million French francs.

For the record, the last Traction Avant left the factory at the Quai de Javel on July 25, 1957. In the twenty-three years and four-and-half months since its introduction, no fewer than 759,123 units of this legendary model were produced, not only in France, but also Belgium, Britain and various countries outside Europe. Apart from Ford's illustrious model T, it was at that time the first car that had sold for so long and in such numbers.

New masters

On March 6, 1935, Pierre Michelin wrote to his father, Edouard, that he had asked André Citroën not to come to the factory anymore, because as long as Citroën was regularly seen in the workshops, many employees still considered him the 'Patron.' Although Citroën had no longer any function on the management committee, some of his former staff members refused to accept orders from anyone else, especially if they considered that these were not in their own (short-term) interest: change always breeds resistance. The end result was that André Citroën's presence made it difficult for Pierre Michelin and Pierre Boulanger to push through a number of urgent reorganisations. Besides, André Citroën was obviously in poor health and badly needed to take some rest.

Apparently, André Citroën reacted very badly to Pierre Michelin's request that he stay away, accusing him of a breach of confidence and betrayal, regarding Michelin's suggestion as a sort of 'coup d'état.' This was, of course, unjustified as Pierre Michelin and Pierre Boulanger, at that time acting as interim managers on behalf of the creditors, simply wished to keep the factory running and improve its profitability, so that Automobiles Citroën might survive the financial crisis.

In December 1935 – around one year after André Citroën had applied for bankruptcy and six months after his unexpected death (July 3, 1935) – the Michelin family became the majority shareholder and 'de facto' owner of the Société Automobiles André Citroën. Pierre Michelin was officially appointed Président Directeur Général and Pierre Boulanger became Directeur Général (managing director).

Drastic measures

The financial overhaul of the company had dramatic consequences for a great many employees, who were made redundant or forced to accept lower wages. Between September 1934 and January 1935, the workforce was reduced from 25,000 to 18,000, and by June 1936 just 11,500 workers remained. After abolishing overtime, the monthly payroll figure was reduced to roughly half of that in 1934.

At the same time Michelin and Boulanger scrapped all expenses that they considered unnecessary. They terminated the contract for the illuminated letters 'Citroën' on the Eiffel Tower; the prestigious showroom on the Place de l'Europe was closed, and all activities that were not to do with the core business of an automobile manufacturer – such as the taxi and bus companies – were sold. The British Caledonian group bought Citroën's insurance business.

Another measure designed to improve the cash situation was to diminish raw material stocks, components and unsold cars. André Citroën's wildly optimistic forecasts for the Traction Avant had created a stock of 7304 unsold units – worth over 108 million francs

– in 1934. After Michelin took over, production volume more closely followed the reality of the order books.

It was also essential to reduce the production cost of the Traction. In the beginning it took 955 hours to manufacture one complete body. Considering that this was the first time that Citroën had produced 'monocoques,' this was not so bad, and once sufficient experience had been acquired this time was reduced to around 580 hours, or approximately 10 per cent less than it took to produce the old 'Rosalie.' Eventually, when all of the modern American machinery and equipment was finally installed and functioning, the coachwork department succeeded in producing one unit in 445 hours, which explains why, in 1936, Citroën was able to reduce the price of the Traction, which of course had a positive effect on sales volume and profit margin.

IMPROVEMENTS AND EXPERIMENTS

Apart from the necessity to speed up production and implement a more rigid system of quality control during the various phases of the manufacturing process, the Traction also required a number of technical changes, and André Lefebvre and his collaborators had to redesign a number of parts to improve reliability and drivability.

The monocoque structure was strengthened, and Pierre Franchiset replaced the moleskin-covered mid-section of the roof with a steel panel and, together with Bertoni, redesigned the rear end. The luggage compartment – in the first series only accessible by folding forward the back of the rear bench – got a lid that opened from the outside. It was hinged at the underside and could be lowered to a near horizontal position to accommodate larger goods. The spare wheel was mounted onto this new luggage lid.

One of the major mechanical improvements consisted of replacing the worm and cam steering box – inherited from former rear-drive Citroën models – with a completely new rack and pinion system that improved steering precision. The idea was thought up by André Lefebvre and Georges Sallot, with the latter responsible for its execution. Sallot also redesigned the rear axle. The axle's new cross profile was both lighter and stronger. Lefebvre enthusiastically sought a way to reduce intrusion of the engine block into the passenger compartment, in an effort to increase footroom in the wide-bodied 11B, thus allowing three people to be seated in the front. He toyed with the idea of a transverse engine layout, and also thought about fitting the differential partly under the crankshaft of the engine. But top management refused to go along with these proposals, as such fundamental modification of both power plant and body required large investment that it was not prepared to make.

THE TUB: CITROËN'S FIRST FRONT-WHEEL DRIVE VAN

While Lefebvre and his team were constantly improving the existing Traction models, Pierre Michelin and Pierre Boulanger proceeded with internal reorganisation of the company, resulting in a clear description of the tasks and responsibilities of each department, ensuring that everybody knew who was accountable for what. They also began to establish a product strategy for the near and long-term future.

At a staff meeting in early December 1935, replacement of Citroën's utility vans was on the agenda. These vehicles, with payloads of 500kg and 850kg, were built on the conventional rear-wheel drive chassis, which was also used for the larger Citroën 7UA and 11UA 'Rosalie' passenger cars. But now that the Traction Avant was selling well, production of these older models would be terminated.

MARKET RESEARCH

Before taking any decision about these new vans, Pierre Michelin wanted to know more about the wishes and requirements of their intended users, and insisted on a survey amongst potential buyers. In the USA most manufacturers of fast-moving goods already carried out this kind of market research, but, as far as is known, it was the first time that a European automobile manufacturer tried to find out what his customers really wanted.

Fortunately, Citroën already had the means to do this as, in order to generate a constant stream of information about customer satisfaction – especially useful during the Traction Avant's early days – Pierre Boulanger had implemented a 'Service des Enquêtes sur Routes' similar to the one at Michelin. This consisted of a small team of travelling investigators, headed by Jacques Duclos, which visited Citroën dealers and owners all over France, then directly transmitted their findings to the general management. Now, the team was asked to do a survey amongst owners of light utility vehicles in order to ascertain their needs.

In the spring of 1937, Citroën's management had accumulated a complete file that contained all the basic requirements that customers sought, from which it appeared that replacement of the 500UB was unnecessary, as the long wheelbase 'Familiale' version of the 11B Traction could be transformed into a 'Commerciale' with a similar volume and payload. However, Lefebvre at the Bureau d'Etudes had to design a successor for the 850UB, which would be mainly intended for urban deliveries.

The specification of the brief was:
- a smaller turning circle than that of existing utility models
- a lower and larger loading area, easily accessible from the driver's seat
- a full height sliding door at the curbside
- total access to the loading area from the rear
- the back doors, when opened, should not jut out into the street by more than 80cm

For reasons of production cost a maximum number of components from the Traction Avant passenger cars were to be used.

TRENDSETTING SHOEBOX

André Lefebvre and his team had the first prototype of the TUB (Traction Utilitaire Basse: front-wheel drive utility vehicle for the lower market segment) ready in the autumn of 1937. The Bertoni-designed body, with its forward control cab, looked just like a 'shoe box on wheels,' but, as a delivery van, this new Citroën was a trendsetting masterstroke, the archetype of all modern light vans: it was also one of the first commercial vehicles to be equipped with a lateral sliding door.

Unlike the front-wheel drive Citroën passenger cars, which had the engine behind the transmission, the 7CV 1628cc four-cylinder was mounted in front of the three-speed gearbox-cum-differential. These engines were known as the MI (Montage Inversé) and were essentially similar to those used in the last of the rear-wheel driven Citroëns, the 7UAs. The driver of the TUB sat more or less on top of the left front wheel. Thanks to a wheelbase of 2.35m the turning circle measured only 1.80m, substantially less than that of its rear drive predecessors. With a total length of 4.04m, the TUB was also shorter, but offered more loading space. Its interior was 1.75m high and 1.77m wide (1.32m between the rear wheel wells), and the flat floor was long enough to transport a horse.

Front-wheel drive, independent front suspension with torsion springs, and hydraulic brakes were logical design features, and all of these components were shared with the Traction Avant. But at the rear the TUB had a beam axle with conventional half elliptic leaf springs. The Bureau d'Etudes also chose to use a conventional ladder-frame chassis and not a monocoque construction. Apart from the fact that tooling costs for a unit body were considered too high, a chassis allowed clients to order a custom-made body from one of

Lefebvre was not only responsible for the development of original family saloons, but also for Citroën's first front-wheel drive, cab-forward van, introduced in 1939 after years of intensive market surveys. (Courtesy Citroën Communication)

The compact TUB (Traction Utilitaire Basse) used many components of the Traction Avant. The driver sat just over the front wheels. (Courtesy Citroën Communication)

As it was equipped with the powertrain of the 7CV Traction Avant, French police forces found the TUB's performance disappointing when used as a personnel carrier. (Courtesy Citroën Communication)

The TUB had an excellent loading volume and, thanks to its sliding side door and large tailgate, easy access to the loading area. It could be used for urban deliveries and also by farmers who wanted to transport cattle. (Courtesy Citroën Communication)

the many 'carrossiers' that still existed in France in those prewar years; for its standard TUB Citroën 'outsourced' all of the bodywork to the coachbuilder Fernand Genève.

Before giving the green light for production of the TUB, Pierre Boulanger instructed the 'Service des Enquêtes sur Routes' to show one of the prototypes – or photos of it – to a selection of prospective customers to check that it was really the sort of van they wanted. Today, a 'consumer clinic' is an established procedure in the automobile industry, but in 1938 it was a novelty.

Those who saw the TUB for the first time usually said: "What an ugly thing." However, once the advantages of the van were demonstrated, opinion generally became more favourable. On May 12, 1939, the TUB got its type approval from the French Services des Mines, and production started on June 5. Its sale price was set at 36,000 francs – quite a lot of money in those days!

Lacklustre performance

The TUB was not an immediate bestseller. Price and shape were drawbacks, as was the lacklustre performance of the 7CV engine. In an interview about the TUB in the French magazine *Citro-Passion*, Georges Toublan, one of the collaborators of Boulanger's 'Service des Enquêtes sur Routes,' is quoted as saying: "During my last surveys I had discovered that the police in Marseille were very interested in such a compact van. They intended to use it as a personnel carrier. So as soon as the TUB went into production I contacted the local dealer and made an appointment for a test drive with the Chief Commissioner. The police officers praised its space and manoeuvrability, but were disappointed with its performance when driving with ten policemen on board." Toublan explained the situation to his superiors at the factory and suggested that, for the police forces, a number of these TUBs might be equipped with the more powerful 11CV engine. Alas, he was told that this was not feasible, as the Bureau d'Etudes was opposed to such modifications.

However, on February 13, 1940, the Services des Mines homologated the 11-T série U, fitted with the larger engine. Needless to say, Georges Toublan, by then serving in the French army, felt deeply let down when he heard about this.

The lifecycle of the TUB was cut short by the outbreak of WWII. According to the factory, 1748 TUB's were built between 1939 and 1941, 50 of them with the 11CV engine, allowing an increased payload of 1200kg. These figures may not be 100 per cent accurate, as during the German occupation nobody cared much about the reliability of production quantities, and the Germans were obviously not interested in the TUB. However, certain documents show that, during those years, Citroën delivered a number of ambulances on the TUB chassis with the type designation TAMH. It is also known that, in 1941-1942, Fenwick transformed about 100 TUBs to electric traction.

PJB is appointed PDG

On December 29, 1937, Pierre Michelin was killed in a road accident when his car crashed between Briare and Montargis, after, it is believed, he hit a patch of black ice on this part of the Route Nationale 7. For his father, Edouard Michelin, by then already 78-years old, the death of his last surviving and very promising son was a terrible loss.

André Lefebvre was also saddened by this tragedy. At first, he had been rather upset by the ruthless reorganisation ordained by Pierre Michelin and Pierre Jules Boulanger, but had come to understand that these changes were absolutely essential for the company's survival. In time, he and Pierre Michelin developed a mutual liking, the more so as they shared a passion for cars. Pierre Michelin was very interested in automobile design, and often visited the Bureau d'Etudes to look at the projects they were working on and to chat with Lefebvre. Both men enjoyed discussing new technologies and the future of the automobile. Pierre Michelin, who was nine years younger than his top engineer, greatly admired Lefebvre's past achievements, original ideas, and the way he inspired his team.

He prompted Lefebvre to visit not only the yearly French motor show, but other European exhibitions as well, to see for himself what their competitors were doing. He particularly insisted that Lefebvre should go to the Berlin Automobil Ausstellung, because, at that time, it was the showcase of the German car industry and was where things were happening. The German government had just begun construction of a network of autobahns, and the automobile engineers in that country were developing new cars that could cruise at high speed while remaining economical on fuel. Scientists and specialists in aerodynamics, such as Paul Jarray, Reinhard König-Fachsenfeld and Professor Wunibold Kamm of the Stuttgart University, were advising Adler, BMW, Maybach and Mercedes, and even assisting their technical staff with wind tunnel experiments. In 1936, 1937 and 1938, a number of German car-makers and coachbuilders displayed some very advanced streamline bodies at their national motor show. There, Lefebvre saw confirmation of some of the ideas he and Gabriel Voisin had nursed for many years with regard to aerodynamically-shaped automobiles.

According to his sons, during one of these visits to Berlin, André Lefebvre made the acquaintance of Ferdinand Porsche, creator of, amongst others, the Volkswagen, and Auto Union's racing and record cars. Lefebvre did not speak any German but Porsche, who was born and educated in Austria (in his youth, still part of the Hungarian-Austrian Empire), spoke some French. Although Lefebvre was convinced that cars should have front-wheel drive and Porsche designed his cars with rear engines, it seems they got on quite well, as both employed unconventional engineering solutions and agreed on the importance of a low centre of gravity and good aerodynamics.

Pierre Michelin also arranged regular meetings between Lefebvre and the research engineers at his father's tyre company in Clermont-Ferrand. These experts were developing and testing the – then, still secret – Michelin Pilote tyres and wheels. Lefebvre was fascinated by all these experiments and learned a lot about tyres and the influence of their characteristics on the behaviour of a car on dry and wet roads. His colleagues in Paris sometimes joked that he was becoming more of a Michelin engineer than a Citroën engineer!

From February 1938 onward, all Traction models were fitted with larger mudguards to accommodate the new Pilote tyres and their characteristic wide rim wheels, which had a noticeably positive effect, not only on comfort and ride but on braking and cornering also.

Pierre Jules Boulanger – who was always referred to by his initials, PJB – succeeded Pierre Michelin as Président Directeur Général (PDG) of Automobiles Citroën. For André Lefebvre and his team at the Bureau d'Etudes, this made little difference: Boulanger had been Pierre Michelin's right-hand man and Citroën's General Manager, and so was quite familiar with all of the projects they were working on.

THE SIX-CYLINDER '15'

Although in 1935 Pierre Michelin and Pierre Boulanger had jointly taken the decision to discontinue development of the Citroën 22 with its V8 engine, Boulanger had reacted favourably when, shortly before his death, Pierre Michelin proposed the production of an upmarket version of Lefebvre's Traction Avant with a six-cylinder engine. Except for some minor modifications, such as a longer bonnet, a larger radiator and slightly modified front mudguards, the body of the six-cylinder was identical to that of the long wheelbase, four-cylinder Traction 11B.

As it was not a totally new concept, but an evolution of the existing four-cylinder

This cutaway drawing of the six-cylinder Citroën '15' (in this case, a 1950 model with a larger boot and stronger bumpers) reveals the strengthened front suspension and drivetrain. In the separate enlargement is the rubber-cushioned transmission joint developed for Citroën by André Lefebvre's colleagues at Michelin. (Illustrations courtesy L'Automobile (France) & The Motor (UK)

The Citroën '15' was a large and roomy car, integrating the new six-in-line engine of 2.657-litres developed by Maurice Sainturat in the wide body of the TA 11 Normale. With a total length of 4m 76, it was 11cm longer than the 11 Normale (21cm longer than the 11 Légère), and weighed 1335kg. This French Citroën 15 is not to be confused with the Light 15, made in the Citroën factory at Slough (Great Britain), which was, in fact, a four-cylinder 11CV with right-hand steering, and an interior adapted to British taste. In accordance with the British (taxable) horsepower rating, it was called the Light 15.

The Citroën '15' – Quinze in France – quickly earned a reputation as 'la Reine de la Route' (The Queen of the Road). Thanks to its superb road-holding (due to a low centre of gravity and front-wheel drive), it could achieve higher averages than many more expensive luxury saloons with bigger and more powerful engines. Soon, it also became the favourite car of French bank robbers ... (Courtesy Citroën Communication)

models, André Lefebvre's official role in its development was rather limited, and he acted more as a consultant than design chief. The bulk of the work was carried out by the Service des Méthodes, the department responsible for production preparation of new models, once Citroën's general management had approved the prototypes built by the Bureau d'Etudes.

The six-in-line, push-rod OHV engine was again designed by Maurice Sainturat; family resemblance to the four-cylinder 11CV is obvious. It had the same bore and stroke (78mmx100mm), though two extra cylinders which gave a cubic capacity of 2657 litres and a maximum power output of 77bhp at 3800rpm.

A LEFT-TURNING CRANKSHAFT

This power plant became known as the 15 Six G* (G for à gauche/to the left/anti-clockwise) because its crankshaft rotated in the opposite direction to that in the 'normal' four-cylinder. This had to do with the fact that the three-speed gearbox had been completely redesigned to withstand the higher torque of the six-cylinder. To limit its length so that the new gearbox would not stick out too far at the front, it was equipped with three gearwheel shafts instead of two. After the war the gearbox was redesigned again and, from 1947, Citroën fitted the 15 Six D (D for à droite/to the right) engine in the Quinze.

To cope with higher speeds and cornering forces, the lower wishbones of the front suspension and the drivetrain were also modified. To improve driving comfort and prolong transmission joint life, both transmission shafts to the front wheels were equipped with a sliding rubber-in-torsion midsection. The function of these metal-rubber-metal components was to 'cushion' the transmission forces. Their technology was based on that of 'silent blocks' and their construction was similar to Michelin's 'Bibax' units, which were fitted on heavy trucks with tandem rear axles. Their use in the drivetrain of the six-cylinder Citroën was a direct result of the excellent relations between the Bureau d'Etudes of Citroën and the research department of Michelin. As André Lefebvre had regular contact

* The type designation 15 created some confusion with Citroën buyers in Britain, as the four-cylinder model assembled in Slough was called the 'light fifteen' in accordance with the British HP rating.

with the engineers in Clermont-Ferrand, there can be little doubt that he was instrumental in this decision.

The Quinze made its public début at the 1938 Salon de l'Automobile in Paris, and was the sensation of the show! Even if top speed hardly exceeded 135km/h, its fabulous roadholding permitted faster average speeds that other French luxury cars – such as those made by Delahaye, Hotchkiss and Talbot – found hard to beat. And it cost a lot less. So it is not surprising that, shortly after its introduction, this Citroën model became known as 'La Reine de la Route' (Queen of the Road). It also earned a rather dubious reputation as a fast getaway car for bank robbers ...

A PROTOTYPE THAT VANISHED WITHOUT TRACE

During the time that the Service des Méthodes prepared for production of the six-cylinder, Lefebvre was masterminding another project. Together with Forceau, Sallot and Léonzi, he began working on a successor to his Traction Avant. Some interesting information concerning this episode is available, thanks to a handwritten and finely illustrated booklet entitled *Les réalisations de votre père*, produced in 1967 by Lefebvre's devoted draftsman Jacques Léonzi (by then 75) for André's younger sons.

According to Léonzi, this design had the internal code 7-P-O. It seems that Lefebvre intended to preserve a large part of the body structure of the existing Traction Avant, but to improve the shape of the mudguards and rear end in order to reduce aerodynamic drag. In this he may have been influenced by the fastback fashion introduced in France with Peugeot's new – but still rear-wheel driven – 402, which in turn followed in the footsteps of American car makers such as Chrysler and Pierce-Arrow. At the 1936 Paris motor show, Peugeot even presented a 402 with a wind tunnel-tested four-door body with a large tail fin, designed by French aerodynamics specialist Jean Andreau. Although it was a concept car and just six were built, Lefebvre must have concluded that a new Traction should look more streamlined as well.

Lefebvre also wanted the new Traction to offer improved comfort and to have a better ride; to achieve this he had the front and rear suspension interconnected with torsion bars. (A similar construction was later used on the first prototypes of the forthcoming Deux Chevaux.)

Still preoccupied with intrusion of the engine block into the front of the passenger compartment, he had Odard design a radial engine, like those used in small aircraft. This power plant was so compact that it hardly took up three-quarters of the engine bay. Of interest is that in 1935 Lefebvre's mentor and friend Gabriel Voisin developed a six-cylinder radial engine intended for his mid-engined 'Voiture de l'Avenir,' which, unfortunately, never saw the light of day.

Léonzi recalls that a running prototype of the 7-P-O was built within about a month and presented to the general management, which obviously did not like it, or was reluctant to invest in tooling for a revolutionary replacement of the Traction that was actually selling quite well and contributing to Citroën's profits. Whatever the case, no more was heard about it and the prototype seemed to vanish without trace. "Only a few people have been aware of its existence," said Léonzi.

In the fascinating book *30 ans de Style Citroën*, co-authors Fabien Sabatès and Flaminio Bertoni's son, Leonard, have published a number of drawings and photos of scale models and 1/1 mock-ups, which Leonardo's father made around 1935-1936. One of these bodies could have served as a successor to the 11CV or the 7CV Traction Avant. The pictures show that the so-called A and B pillars (the frames of the front windows and the windscreen), are very thin. "Just the way Lefebvre liked them," says the accompanying text. It is hard to believe, though, that Flaminio Bertoni did these studies on his own initiative.

Reconciliation with Louis Renault

From 1935, life became easier as André Lefebvre's financial circumstances gradually improved. The Traction Avant now fulfilled the promise of its potential and sold quite well. It made money for the Citroën company and Lefebvre's bosses showed their appreciation, providing him with a company car – hardly customary in those days. However, as most of the time he was using test cars of the Bureau d'Etudes, he practically never drove it, so was allowed to buy a car for his wife, Claire, on favourable terms. André's son, Michel Lefebvre, remembers his mother's first car very well – a shining black or dark blue 11 Légère that bore the registration number 3277 RK4 – and also recalls that, from time-to-time, his father took him along to automobile races and air shows. André did not like the sensation of flying, but remained interested in planes, especially the evolution of the aviation industry, and so he regularly visited competitions and exhibitions to keep up with the latest trends in plane design.

When, despite a difficult start, it became clear that the Traction Avant was a huge commercial success, Citroën offered Lefebvre a company car for his personal use. In front of their home André took this photo of his wife, Claire, in the passenger seat of the 7CV. (Courtesy Collection family Lefebvre)

Claire, in turn, photographed her proud husband and their son, Michel. (Courtesy Collection family Lefebvre)

During one of these outings the pair ran into Louis Renault, who had a financial stake in the French airplane manufacturer Caudron. In the early thirties an angry Renault fired Lefebvre after an argument about the possibilities of front-wheel drive. However, with his Traction Avant Lefebvre had proved himself an excellent automobile engineer with brilliant ideas, and so now the master of Billancourt behaved much more courteously towards his former employee. Renault admitted that the front-wheel drive Citroën was a serious commercial competitor, but still doubted its return

Happy prewar years. From left to right: Michel, Jean, and their father, André, in front of the house at Plessis-Robinson. (Courtesy Collection family Lefebvre)

André Lefebvre was often invited as a visitor to the various aircraft exhibitions, air shows and aircraft competitions that were regularly held in prewar France. Because of his studying at the Ecole Supérieure de l'Aéronautique, he was well acquainted with many of those who mattered in the aviation industry, and they would let him roam around their planes because they respected him as the brilliant Chief Engineer of Citroën, responsible for the design of the oustanding Traction Avant.

Here we see Lefebvre – at extreme right – admiring the Caudron Aiglon of Madame Dupeyron and Mademoiselle Lallus at the start of the 'Twelve hours of Angers' flight in July 1936. (Courtesy Collection family Lefebvre)

on investment. In his own somewhat brutish manner he showed he regretted what had happened, and Lefebvre bore him no grudge, as he was happy working for Citroën.

THE GENESIS OF THE 2CV

There is absolutely no doubt that the TPV (Toute Petite Voiture/very small car) – which eventually became Citroën's Deux Chevaux – was the brainchild of Pierre Boulanger, who had the idea even before he became head of Automobiles Citroën.

Every time he drove on the narrow departmental roads in rural France, Boulanger was struck by the primitive means of transport the farmers used to take their wares to local markets: wheelbarrows, carts drawn by horses and sometimes even oxen, or worn-out and very old automobiles, mostly ramshackle passenger cars, from which the rear part of the body had been removed to transform them into pickup trucks. What these people needed, Boulanger reasoned, was an economical and reliable motorcar, and one they could afford.

A survey of the French automobile market in 1937 by Citroën's own researcher, Jacques Duclos, confirmed Boulanger's gut feeling that there was a market for a cheap and basic motorcar. Duclos found that many people could not afford a new car as prices had increased, whilst the purchasing power of the average French family had remained stable, or even decreased. It appeared that sixty per cent of Citroën's potential customers intended to buy a second-hand car costing less than 10,000 francs!

To manufacture a car that the masses could afford was, of course, in itself not a revolutionary idea, and had been the cornerstone on which Henry Ford founded his empire. During the twenties André Citroën and Herbert Austin in Britain made a fortune with their economical Cloverleafs and Sevens, and in the mid-thirties German and Italian manufacturers such as DKW, NSU and Fiat also tried their hand at producing a real 'people's car.'

The originality of Boulanger's approach was that such an automobile should not only be economical to buy, maintain and run, but be spacious and comfortable as well. Also, as it was primarily intended for farmers and professionals in rural areas, and not so much for the blue- or white-collar workers in the suburbs of the big cities, it could be a minimalist sort of vehicle, with just the bare essentials and no superfluous luxury.

THE TPV'S DESIGN BRIEF

Pierre Boulanger had asked Chataigner, one of his collaborators at Michelin, to draw up the technical specification (Cahier des Charges) for such a car. Boulanger's instructions to

A barn find. Some twenty years after they were hidden away during the first days of the German occupation of France, these three prewar TPVs were discovered in a barn not far from La Ferté-Vidame. Lefebvre and his team had used a lot of aluminium and other light metal parts in constructing the chassis and body, so, except for the mudguards, they were virtually rust-free. They are now on display (unrestored) in the Conservatoire Citroën. (Courtesy Hans Arend de Wit/Switchimage)

The TPV, predecessor of the Citroën 2CV, developed before WWII, had a water-cooled, two-cylinder boxer engine. To keep the price low there was no starter motor, and the engine had to be turned over with a starting handle. As with a motorcycle, it had just one headlight. (Courtesy Conservatoire Citroën/Hans Arend de Wit/Switchimage.

the engineers at Citroën: "Build me an umbrella with four wheels" has become legendary, though in reality the design brief for the TPV was more detailed:

- it had to be able to carry four adults plus 50kg of goods, or two people and 200kg of merchandise
- its dry weight should not exceed 400kg

- the engine must have a capacity in the lowest fiscal category; hence only 2CV
- a top and cruising speed of 60km/h was considered sufficient, while fuel consumption was not to exceed 5 litres/100km
- its suspension should permit the car to be driven over dirt roads or even through a field transporting a basket of eggs, without breaking a single one of them
- it had to be so easy to drive that a farmer's wife could take it to the market
- it must not cost more than 5000 French francs to produce

Boulanger – a very shrewd man – realised that even if it was relatively easy to put these specifications onto paper, to build such an unorthodox vehicle would be a great engineering challenge.

Maurice Broglie was officially the director of the Bureau d'Etudes, but, in Boulanger's eyes, this was primarily an administrative function. He called Broglie to his office and told him that he was convinced that André Lefebvre, with his unbridled fantasy and creativity, together with his dedicated team of talented technicians, was the man for the job. As a result, in 1936, Boulanger commissioned the Bureau d'Etudes to design and build a number of prototypes, and André Lefebvre was put in charge of the project.

It is in no small part due to Lefebvre's original thinking that the TPV became the car it did. Whereas in those days most cheap cars were scaled-down versions of larger models, Lefebvre came up with a completely different concept: a light and simple motor vehicle that offered the interior space of a full-sized automobile. He liked to explore new horizons, and building the Voisin racing and record machines had taught him how to turn unconventional ideas into reality.

Cyclops

That the TPV should have front-wheel drive was never disputed, and all options were open for the rest of the specification. Lefebvre told his team what Boulanger had said to him: "Even if only ten per cent of our ideas prove to be of practical value, it will be worthwhile to explore them all." With these words Boulanger gave Lefebvre the freedom to do what he thought necessary, and so he urged his collaborators to try out everything they could think of. Never before in the history of Citroën was so much time and effort spent on research and experiments as during the gestation process of the TPV.

Maurice Sainturat's engine department developed and tested a great variety of engines. The success on its home market of the small German front-wheel drive DKW even inspired the team to examine the possibilities of a two-stroke. As this required neither camshaft, valves or valve springs, it had the advantage of being lighter and cheaper to produce than a four-stroke. But such an engine also has some serious disadvantages, such as irregular idling, relatively high fuel consumption, and a fuel/oil mixture to lubricate the bearings in the crankcase and the cylinder walls. Probably, Citroën engineers feared that French farmers would forget to add the correct amount of oil to the tanks when filling up and thus damage the engine. In the end, they abandoned the two-stroke alternative.

In 1936 Fiat unveiled its famous Topolino 500, designed by Dante Giacosa. This small, rear-wheel drive two-seater had a 0.569-litre, water-cooled, side-valve four-cylinder engine in the front, with the radiator just behind the engine on top of the gearbox. In France, the Topolino was marketed as the Simca Cinq.

The pre-production TPVs manufactured in 1939 had a water-cooled, two-cylinder OHV boxer engine of 0.375 litres. Its radiator was located in the same position as that of the Fiat/Simca.

Boulanger followed the development of 'his' TPV with all the eagerness of an expectant father. He had the reputation of a real autocrat: a distinguished fighter pilot during WWI, he liked to have his hand on the rudder – quite literally – and as the boss of Michelin, and later of Citroën, in a figurative sense, as well. Besides, he wished to keep a firm hold on the purse strings of these companies. He was an exacting leader and not always easy to work with, but André Lefebvre's well-founded arguments were usually so persuasive that Boulanger often reluctantly gave in.

For example, Lefebvre managed to convince Boulanger that, in view of the requirements of the Cahier des Charges, it was essential to use aluminium for the chassis and body of the TPV, which would not only save weight, but also money as this light metal did not rust and so did not require painting. Aluminium was one of Lefbvre's favourite materials, and, through his training as an aeronautical engineer and his work with Gabriel Voisin, he was very familiar with its use. In those days the technology for welding aluminium or duralumin was not as well-developed as that for welding steel. Riveting was an option that was widely used in the aircraft industry, but being a more time-consuming and thus more costly operation than electric spot-welding, made aluminium construction less viable to mass-produce.

Nevertheless, the Bureau d'Etudes constructed various light metal chassis, and experimented with a ladder frame made up from large aluminium tubes that could serve as cooling ducts for the engine as well. There was also a composite chassis consisting of profiled aluminium between steel panels, and even one with plywood sandwiched between thin sheets of aluminium.

A consequence of constructing a vehicle with such an extremely low dry weight was that it required a suspension system able to cope with great load variation. Assuming that the car with just its driver aboard weighed 465kg, three passengers and 50kg of luggage or goods would add 245kg, taking total weight to 710kg; an increase of about 52.5 per cent.

An additional problem was that the TPV had to be comfortable, necessitating a very supple suspension. As most small, inexpensive cars of that time had rather stiff springs, this requirement posed an extra challenge, and led to a number of experiments with several types of independent suspension. To reduce excessive 'pitch' – the rocking movement that occurs when soft sprung cars are driven over undulating roads – Lefebvre insisted that these suspension systems had to be interconnected front and rear. This meant that when the front wheel moved upward over a bump, the rear wheel spring was pre-loaded or compressed, and so became firmer. Incidentally, in 1962 the same logic led Alec Issigonis to adopt the hydrolastic suspension system developed by Alex Moulton for the BMC 1100 and, later, the Mini.

The final TPV prototypes were equipped with interconnected torsion springs. But – as we shall learn – when the project was reviewed after the war, Lefebvre and his engineers replaced the torsion springs with a coil spring system that was simpler and more efficient. Between 1936 and 1939, the Bureau d'Etudes constructed and tested an impressive number of prototypes; insiders have counted at least 49 different TPVs. Most of these were built from duralumin and a few even had magnesium parts. Some body panels had washboard profiles, others just plain flat surfaces. Doors were made from steel, plywood or even canvas. One prototype even had revolving doors, giving alternate access to the front and the rear.

All of them were primitive and rudimentary vehicles; precisely what Boulanger had in mind. When someone from his commercial staff openly doubted if this was the sort of car their customers would find attractive, Boulanger retorted: "We do not intend to build a car to seduce people, but a car that will serve them."

To save on the cost and weight of a battery he even forbade the TPV to be equipped with an electric starter, so the engines had to be started with a starting handle as on the first Ford T models. For the same reason the prewar TPVs had a single headlight only, powered by a small engine-driven dynamo, just like a motorbike, which earned it the nickname of 'Cyclops.'

Boulanger's penny-pinching approach seems to have been contagious; Pierre Franchiset told Roger Brioult the following story: "By chance I discovered that the dies previously employed to press the rear mudguards of the old C4 trucks were the right size and shape for the front mudguards of the TPV. There was only one difficulty: the C4 mudguards were made from 1mm thick sheet iron, which would make the TPV too heavy. But Monsieur Simonetti, my boss at that time, came up with a clever solution. He took two sheets of 0.5mm sheet iron, greased their surfaces, stuck them together and put this sandwich under a press. When the dies came apart, there appeared a perfectly-shaped mudguard, with a nearly identical one inside it. Somehow, Monsieur Boulanger heard about our experiment and requested to see it for himself. He came down to the press shop, his hat loosely on his head and a yellow 'maize paper' Gitane cigarette stuck between his lips. When Simonetti showed him the two mudguards, the patron simply said: 'I knew we would succeed with this car.'"

MERCILESS TESTING

All TPV prototypes were mercilessly tested. At one point Michelin had tried to buy the Montlhéry track, but when this failed, invested heavily in Citroën's own test centre, situated near the small village of La Ferté-Vidame, about 120km west of Paris, in the department Eure-et-Loir. On the former property of the Dukes of Saint-Simon, in the middle of 800 hectares of woodland, Citroën had constructed a 2.5 kilometre-long track, where engineers and members of the test team could subject the cars to every imaginable type of trial in absolute secrecy.

Boulanger and Lefebvre often went there, not so much to take part in the test sessions but mainly to hear the opinions of the test drivers. From time-to-time they would also drive the prototypes.

Boulanger instructed Citroën's technical inspectors to take the exact measurement of the gradients and heights of all 'difficult' level railway crossings in France; the ten steepest were then exactly reproduced at La Ferté-Vidame test centre. The test drivers had to 'rush' the prototypes over these obstacles at full speed. If the engine or chassis touched the road surface or the rails, the suspension or shock absorbers were modified. But André Louis, a close collaborator of Boulanger, admitted to Roger Brioult: "To our great surprise one of the first clients ripped open the sump of his Deux Chevaux engine on a railroad crossing at Vernon. An inquiry proved that somebody had forgotten to put this one on the list."

THE FIRST PRE-SERIES

When the latest prototypes finally performed satisfactorily, around 250 pre-series TPVs were produced at Citroën's Levallois plant during the summer of 1939.

In early September the car was homologated by the Service des Mines as the Citroën Type A. Pierre Boulanger intended to introduce the new Citroën 2CV at the Paris Salon de l'Automobile in early October. But that exhibition had to be cancelled ...

CHAPTER
EIGHT
WORLD WAR II

On the first of September 1939, Hitler invaded Poland. Bound by previous treaties to help the Poles in the event of an attack by Germany, the United Kingdom and France declared war on Germany on September 3. The governments of both countries immediately proclaimed a general mobilisation, and industries had to switch to wartime production.

After the Nazis had overrun Poland – in a 'Blitzkrieg' of 36 days – they took time out to re-equip their troops and only minor skirmishes occurred along the Maginot Line, the belt of French fortifications at the Franco-German border. French and British forces remained on the defensive except at sea, where their fleets were heavily engaged in trying to halt the increasing number of torpedo attacks on merchant vessels by German battleships and U boats plying the waters of the Atlantic Ocean and the British Channel. Until April 1940, very little happened on the West European front, which is why this period is often referred to by Anglo-Saxon historians as the 'phoney war,' or, in Winston Churchill's words, the 'twilight war.' The Germans called it 'Sitzkrieg' ('sitting war') in contrast to 'Blitzkrieg,' and the French spoke of the 'drôle de guerre' ('funny war').

For the French population, however, the situation was not funny at all. To the horror of many French families – who well remembered the terrible losses suffered during the 1914-1918 war – husbands and sons were called up to serve in the armed forces. Those exempted from active duty because they were too old, were faced with an increased workload as their younger colleagues had left for the front lines. Production facilities had to be hastily transformed to manufacture equipment for military use. Soon, there was a growing shortage of basic materials, and metal use was restricted to the production of airplanes, armoured vehicles, army trucks and ammunition.

MILITARY VEHICLES WITH A *TA* ENGINE

Immediately after the outbreak of war, all development work on the TPV was halted and production of the Traction Avant drastically reduced. Because of their monocoque bodies, the French forces had no use for these cars, as army regulations – dating from 1902 – stated that military motor vehicles must have a chassis! Production capacity not needed for Citroën trucks (which did have a chassis) was used for the production of ammunition.

Around this time the French war ministry asked Boulanger to use Citroën's industrial know-how to manufacture a number of six-wheeled gun (artillery) tractors, originally designed by Laffly. As these gun tractors were to be powered by Traction Avant engines, Lefebvre became responsible for the engineering side of the transformation. As not only the Bureau d'Etudes was concerned, but also the Laboratoire (testing) and the Service des Méthodes (production planning), a young engineer named Pierre Ingueneau was appointed as the co-ordinator for the project, which was code-named W 15 T. The prototype was extensively tested in an abandoned quarry near Senonches (Eure-et-Loir), and in the spring of 1940, the French army finally approved Citroën's proposal for the modified Laffly artillery tractor.

Parallel with the work on the Laffly, Lefebvre and his team prepared a design for light armoured tanks also propelled by a Traction Avant engine. Interestingly, around that time the brothers Van Doorne (founders of DAF) in Eindhoven (Netherlands) built an amphibious surveillance vehicle for the Dutch army, the prototype of which was also powered by a Citroën TA engine. Designed to be driven forward and backward at equal speed, it proved very useful in hilly terrain and soggy marshland. However, neither of these vehicles ever reached the production stage.

Bureau d'Etudes destroyed

On June 3, 1940, at approximately 1.45 in the afternoon, German aircraft attacked Paris and bombed the Citroën works at the Quai de Javel, with, fortunately, no casualties as the wail of the air raid sirens had given ample advance warning. Besides, it was lunchtime, so most workers and staff were still finishing their meals in one of the many bistros surrounding the factory, or enjoying a sunny stroll on the banks of the nearby river Seine.

But the material damage was enormous. The right wing of the factory was in ruins, and a number of administrative offices went up in flames; the archives of the Bureau d'Etudes and the Service des Méthodes – where all of the technical drawings were kept – were completely wiped out by fire. Plans for the production of the Citroën-powered Laffly gun tractor and the approved prototype were also destroyed.

Exodus

After the bombing, work in the factory practically came to a halt. As the Wehrmacht advanced on the French capital, tens of thousands of Parisians fled the city to seek refuge with friends and family in the countryside, and the Citroën management decided to move the headquarters to the small town of Niort, in the department Deux-Sèvres. Nearly all of the Bureau d'Etudes employees and their families joined in this exodus, and were rehoused in the empty classrooms of a technical school in Niort.

June was to become one of the most catastrophic months in the history of France. On June 10, Mussolini's Fascist government joined forces with Hitler and Italian troops crossed the Italian-French border. The morning of June 14, the 6th German Army entered Paris, and two days later Paul Reynaud resigned as prime minister. On June 22, the French signed an armistice with Germany at Compiègne. The collaborationist government of Maréchal Pétain (a French war hero of WWI) then retreated to Vichy, leaving the northern and western regions of the country, including Paris, under German occupation.

Michel Lefebvre remembers that his father tried to obtain permission to establish Citroën's experimental department in Clermont-Ferrand; as that city was situated in the unoccupied zone this would have enabled work to continue on the new designs. Besides, André Lefebvre knew a lot of people there, thanks to his regular visits to Michelin's research and engineering staff. But the French authorities ordered all refugees to return to their homes, so the Lefebvres went back to the Paris suburb of Le Plessis-Robinson. As the workshops at the Quai de Javel were one big crater, Bureau d'Etudes personnel returned to the old buildings in the Rue du Théâtre, which they had used in the past. Not that there was much to do ...

Confusing times

For most French people the early years of WWII were very confusing. Germany was winning 'on all fronts'; France had lost her independence and the country was divided between the part occupied by the Nazis and the so-called 'free' zone in which the (non-elected) French government of Vichy ruled. Most French citizens detested the 'Boches,' but many also felt betrayed by the British. Some even blamed the defeat of France on the withdrawal of all British troops at Dunkerque, leaving their French comrades to fight the powerful German army alone. But that was not all …

To prevent the French navy from falling into German hands, Winston Churchill stipulated that all French warships and merchantmen should either join the Royal British Navy or be neutralised. Another alternative was to sail to the French dominions in the West Indies and stay there. Many of the crews of French vessels, anchored in seaports around the world, chose to join the Free French Forces of Charles de Gaulle.

However, Admiral Gensoul, commander of the strong 'Flotte de l'Atlantique' concentrated in the then French ports of Algeria, refused to comply with the British ultimatum. He informed the British envoy that he was awaiting instructions from his superior in Vichy, Admiral Darlan.

For Churchill the only thing that really mattered at that time was the survival of Britain and continuation of the fight against Nazi Germany, so when the French did not immediately accept his proposals he ordered the British fleet to "sink the ships." Accordingly, in the first days of July, nine French warships at Mers-el-Kébir and nearby Oran were destroyed with the loss of 1297 French sailors and 354 wounded. The media in France, controlled by the German occupying forces, gave only very subjective information about this 'treacherous' attack, which, of course, fuelled the feelings of deception many French had about their 'allies.'

But not everyone was fooled by the Nazi propaganda. Although this was a punishable offence, Pierre Jules Boulanger – who, as a young man, had worked in the United States – regularly listened to BBC radio, and so knew that the British government had proposed accompanying the French ships to safe ports in the West Indies. By refusing this opportunity the French naval commanders had not only taken the risk of their fleet being requisitioned by the Germans, but were also to blame for the death of so many French sailors.

Alternative fuels

In view of the shortage of petrol and gas oil, André Lefebvre teamed up with the French chemical engineer Freund with a view to sourcing alternative fuels for internal combustion engines. Lefebvre had some practical experience running Voisin's record cars on a mix of petrol and benzol, but did not have any scientific knowledge of petrochemicals. The two experimented with mixes of benzol made from coal, and alcohol (ethanol) made from sugar beet and other crops (today's biofuels), acetone, acetylene, and so on.

Yet, while the collaboration between Lefebvre and Freund sometimes had all the ingredients of an explosive mixture, it did not lead to a sensational breakthrough in the development of new fuels. As part of the research programme, the Bureau d'Etudes also investigated the effects of alternative fuels on engine performance and cylinder wear.

During this process a great number of 'gasogènes' (gas generators) were examined and tested. In these 'gasogène' installations coal, wood (charcoal), and even peat were transformed by smouldering into a combustible gas. Another solution was to use city gas, carried in bottles on the back or in a large balloon on the roof of a passenger car. As the refuelling of such a system depended on the proximity of a city gas depot, it was only suitable for taxis and other local means of transport. Citroën engineers concluded that, provided the carburettors and manifolds were adapted, a 'gasogène' was an acceptable proposition for those who could not obtain sufficient petrol coupons but needed to use their automobiles. Accordingly, Citroën acquired the manufacturing rights for the Imbert 'gasogène' equipment, and also fitted many of its trucks with 'wood burning' installations from other makes, such as Brandt and Sabatier-Decauville.

The only thing the Germans wanted from Citroën was the Type 23 and Type 45 trucks – and as many as possible! Pierre Boulanger and his right-hand man, Pierre Bercot, were regularly told that they must increase production – or else. The shortage of men and raw material, plus the factory damage inflicted by bombs, offered them an excuse to explain the systematic delays and limited number of trucks manufactured. They got away with it, thanks to the fact that a high-ranking German officer fell in love with one of their secretaries. This officer, who worked for the 'Kriegsverwaltungsambt,' the German organisation supervising the factories in occupied territories, was directly responsible for the quantity and quality of Citroën trucks to be produced for the German army. Fortunately, he was not a Nazi, but what was then known as a 'good' German. The little secretary must have been very charming and persuasive, because this German officer not only provided escaped prisoners with official papers and prevented the deportation of others, but also, from time-to-time, managed to get the Bureau d'Etudes some petrol, ostensibly for the purpose of testing the trucks prior to delivery.

Agricultural machines

The Germans did not allow Citroën to do any research or development work on passenger cars. Nevertheless, it was essential to keep Bureau d'Etudes personnel occupied, otherwise they could be transported to Germany and employed as so-called STOs (Service du Travail Obligatoire) – forced (slave) labour. This was one of the reasons why Lefebvre and his team were authorised to investigate the possibilities of using the engines and transmissions of the TPV and Traction Avant in agricultural machinery. An engineer by the name of Renard acted as project co-ordinator.

Such research was officially encouraged, as the Vichy government firmly believed that Germany would win the war, in which case only an efficient and highly mechanised agriculture could help France to survive economically, because the Germans would certainly want to move all important industrial activities, such as automobile production, to their own country.

Lefebvre drew up plans for a small motorised ploughshare, powered by the 0.375-litre water-cooled twin of a TPV, coupled to the transmission of a light truck. In his booklet for Lefebvre's sons, Léonzi noted that the Bureau d'Etudes also developed two larger agricultural tractors. The first was a four-wheel drive machine which had the 1911cc engine of the Traction Avant, a hydraulic clutch (fluid flywheel), and a hydraulic system for raising implements. The three-speed transmission was conceived by Forceau and his draftsman, Santa Maria. Accommodating the engine with its fluid flywheel and the transmission, including the front and rear differential housings, required a carter nearly 1.5m long. This was a problem, as the Citroën foundries were unable to produce such a large casting, so the project remained a bit of a white elephant.

Lefebvre planned to equip this machine with a pressurised (closed) liquid cooling system. Today, this is a common feature of nearly all cars and trucks, but at the time it was completely new. According to Léonzi, Lefebvre got this idea from a magazine article about engine cooling in fighter planes, which may well have been the case, as he read anything he could lay his hands on concerning the technical evolution of aircraft design. Even during the occupation of France such literature was sometimes available.

For example, the German propaganda ministry published a French language edition of *Signal*, which regularly published photos and descriptions of war material. So Lefebvre might have been aware that the Daimler Benz engines in the Messerschmitt 109, and the Rolls-Royce Merlins in the British Vickers 'Supermarine' Spitfire had pressurised and evaporative cooling systems that functioned on the principle of condensation, and were filled with a mixture of water and ethylene glycol.

The second agricultural tractor was much smaller, and had the engine of the 7CV Traction. Boulanger was intrigued by its possibilities and gave Lefebvre permission to construct a prototype, which was then tested not far from La Ferté-Vidame on the farm of a monastery near Soligny-la-Trappe in the department Orne – secrecy ensured!

Narrow escape

Achille Picard, one of Citroën's test drivers, was not only a trained technician but, above all, a clever troubleshooter who always found a solution to any given problem. He got the job of liaising between the Bureau d'Etudes and the Trappist monks to make sure that the tractor functioned well, and did so with great dedication.

Michel Lefebvre remembers that Picard, who – because of his frequent excursions to the monastery acquired the nickname 'le moine' (the monk) – regularly provided the 'équipe' at the Rue du Théâtre with fresh eggs, vegetables, and other farm products. Picard once told Michel about an incident that occurred during one of his 'missions.' As one risked a heavy fine and even jail for transporting food without an official permit, Achille had hid the goods in an empty (non-functioning) 'gasogène' installation mounted on a small two-wheeled trailer, while the towing Traction ran on the petrol attributed to the Bureau d'Etudes for road testing German trucks. However, one day the trailer broke free and, in his rear view mirror, Achille saw his fully loaded 'gasogène' disappear from sight: fortunately, it did not go far, and stopped at the side of the road without overturning. Just at that moment two French gendarmes on bicycles appeared. They were very friendly and, after inspecting Achille's driving permit and other documents, offered to push his car back to the stranded 'gasogène.' "Thank you for your kindness, but that is not necessary," replied a quaking Achille, who absolutely did not want these policemen to have a closer look at his lost trailer. "I have got enough gas left to get there." The policemen politely saluted and went on their way; luckily, they did not know that unattached gas generators could not possibly leave any gas in the carburettor system ...

Nightmare years

For André Lefebvre the years from 1940 to 1942 were a real nightmare. He missed the freedom of driving his cars where and whenever he wanted, and was even obliged to present himself every morning at the Bureau d'Etudes in the Rue du Théâtre as though he was a schoolboy. To visit his engineering colleagues at Michelin in Clermont-Ferrand in the 'free zone,' he needed an 'Ausweiss' from the Germans, a document that required a lot of paperwork, explanation and patience to obtain.

The men at the Bureau d'Etudes occupied themselves by building a simple electric single-seater, and a cheap bicycle with small wheels and a frame that was constructed like a 'monocoque' body. The electric vehicle was powered by a 24-volt motor, fed by batteries that could be recharged from the mains. It had a two-speed gearbox and could attain 30km/h. But Boulanger did not like it, and neither did he enjoy his ride on the bicycle; he lost his balance and crashed in front of all present in the middle of the workshop. That was the end of this 'dangerous' machine.

In all fairness, Citroën had available neither the steel, rubber nor other materials to manufacture such products. And projects such as these – and the agricultural machines already mentioned – could hardly satisfy Lefebvre's creative ambitions. In his work he was bored and unhappy and, to make matters worse, his personal life was overshadowed by even more serious problems. His beloved wife, Claire, was suffering from a very painful kidney disease that would eventually take her life. In those days there was no way to save her, as the dialysis treatment for kidney patients had not yet been invented. During her illness Claire was looked after by a very capable nurse, but the upbringing and education of his adolescent boys rested entirely on André's shoulders, and this proved quite a heavy burden.

A WARTIME CONSPIRACY – THE CITROËN H

Fortunately, Pierre Boulanger, who was witnessing André Lefebvre's frustration, provided him with a new challenge by instructing him to think about a successor for the TUB, telling him: "When this war is over France will need a lot of new vans. But we will not have much money to buy the necessary new machinery. See what you can do with the tools and components that we have."

Both Boulanger and Lefebvre were fully aware of the main weaknesses of the original TUB: it was underpowered and too expensive. Boulanger thought it wiser not to try and improve the existing model, but to invest in a new commercial vehicle that would be economical to produce in large quantities. In 1942 and in secrecry, Lefebvre began work on what was to become the H series.

In comparison to the original TUB the design brief for the new H specified:

- more loading space
- easier accessibility to the loading space at the rear
- better rear brakes and improved rear suspension
- a unit (monocoque) body construction for lightness (cost) and strength
- where possible, the mechanical components of the 11CV and/or the 15CV passenger cars had to be used

A small task force was formed consisting of André Lefebvre as Chief Engineer, Jean Cadiou (Director of the Bureau d'Etudes), Pierre Ingueneau (Direction de Fabrication), and André. Lefebvre asked chassis specialist Boisse, an engineer who, like him, had worked at Renault, to assist him with his sketches and calculations. It was agreed that the new van should have the 1.911cc, four-cylinder from the Traction Avant, rating 50bhp at 3800rpm. As in the TUB it was to be mounted in front of the three-speed gearbox which came from the six-cylinder Quinze, just as did the front suspension (torsion bars) and hydraulic drum brakes on all four wheels. The rear suspension consisted of torsion bars, but the one for the left wheel was placed 3cm behind the one for the right, resulting in a slightly longer wheelbase at the left side, but permitting easy loading, as the completely flat floor was only 35cm above street level.

Development of the monocoque body was entrusted to Pierre Franchiset, who, as we know, had also been involved in the construction of the first unit bodies for the Traction Avant. Franchiset came up with a box-like design: the square shape allowed flat rear doors and a large sliding door on the right-hand side. To avoid the necessity of complex dies and deep pressings, only the corners at the front of the roof were rounded. All of the side panels and doors had a number of small extruding 'ribs' that made them appear as if manufactured from undulated steel. In an interview with the French magazine *Citropolis*, Franchiset said that he had chosen this method to improve rigidity because it enabled him to use very thin sheet metal, which saved on weight. He admitted that this idea had already been used before in the aircraft industry; indeed, it reminded some of the fuselage of the Junkers Ju 52, a German transport aircraft and bomber, designed in 1932 and built up until 1945. The hinges for the doors and the top hinge of the bonnet were of the so-called Yoder type, made by folding and rolling sheet steel. Franchiset had used this system for the first time for the bonnet hinge of the Traction Avant in 1934.

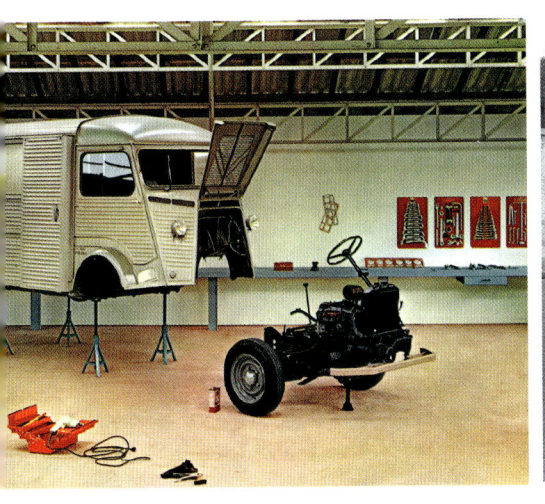

World War II

With its monocoque body and front-wheel drive, the concept of the H had a lot in common with that of Lefebvre's Traction Avant passenger car. Its engine was based on the two-litre unit of the 11CV, but the transmission was mounted behind the engine. Gearbox, clutch, final drive and front suspension originated from the six-cylinder 15.
(Courtesy Citroën Conservatoire)

Practical three panel tailgate and a large sliding door at the right side of the cargo area made the H a worthy successor to Citroën's prewar TUB.
(Courtesy Citroën Communication)

After the war the TUB was replaced by the front-wheel-driven Citroën H and HY utility vehicles, which offered a greater loading capacity and were also more economical to manufacture. The first mock-up, shown here, was based on drawings that were secretly made during the occupation.
(Courtesy Citroën Communication)

The box-like body of the Citroën H was inspired by ... an aeroplane. It seems incredible, but Pierre Franchiset, who was responsible for its construction, has confirmed that the idea to press small profiles in the body panels was inspired by the 'corrugated' fuselage of the German Junkers Ju 52 transport plane. (Courtesy Nico Braas, Aviodrome, Lelystad NL)

The H was ready for the 1946 Salon de l' Automobile, the first postwar motor show in Paris. But Boulanger refused to present it there because he knew that the factory could not produce it in sufficient number, and he did not want to disappoint potential clients. Thus, the H was launched a year later.

Apart from the characteristic corrugated body panels, it looked like a grown-up version of the pre-war TUB, and many French owners continued to call it 'ma tube.' In size it was 4.26m long instead of 4.04m; the wheelbase measured 2.53m (left) and 2.50m (right), compared to the 2.35m of its predecessor. It had a dry weight of 1400kg and a maximum payload of 1200kg. The factory claimed a top speed of 78km/h, and fuel consumption of 13 litres/100km.

The H, HY and later versions became immensely popular, not only in France, but also in Belgium, the Netherlands, and Portugal. A Citroën HY van can still be seen in the series *Louis la Brocante* (Louis of the second-hand shop) on French television.

CHAPTER

NINE

PARIS LIBERATED

On August 25, 1944, Paris – occupied for four years – was liberated after a week of turmoil and uncertainty.

Ever since the Normandy invasion Parisians had eagerly awaited this moment. With the Allied troops rapidly advancing, the Paris Métro, gendarmerie and police went on strike on August 15; the next day, the postal workers followed. Four days later communist-dominated résistance cells rose up against the German garrison, commanded by General Dietrich von Choltitz. Hitler told him to burn down the city; fortunately, Von Choltitz ignored Hitler's order.

Under General Eisenhower, the Allied high command had wanted to bypass Paris, but Charles de Gaulle convinced them that they must liberate the French capital. De Gaulle and his staff not only feared the vengeance of fanatical SS troops on innocent citizens, there was also a risk of an armed clash between different groups of the résistance, each of which wanted to seize power.

To prevent bloodshed the Free French Forces even threatened to make a dash for Paris on their own. Finally, on Tuesday 22, General Omar Bradley of the US first army gave Général Philippe Leclerc, commander of the French 2nd Armoured Division, official permission to proceed to Paris. It took bitter fights and bloody skirmishes, but with the help of the Americans and the French résistance, German opposition was quickly eliminated and Von Choltitz signed the capitulation of his garrison.

The next day Général de Gaulle made his victorious entry into the city. Snipers opened fire on him from the roof of a hotel, but missed. He addressed the enthusiastic crowd with the historic words: "Paris outraged! Paris broken! Paris martyred! But Paris liberated!" and the people of Paris danced in the streets ...

UNDER SUSPICION

André Lefebvre did not participate in the festivities as he was arrested on suspicion of having worked for the Germans, an accusation, it seems, that was based on the declaration of a jealous neighbour in Le Plessis-Robinson, where he had lived since 1938. Citroën's stylist, Bertoni, was also taken prisoner: he was considered an enemy because he had retained his Italian citizenship.

Pierre Boulanger, with powerful connections in the résistance and the new government, quickly got both of them out of jail. But pending enquiry by the 'purification committee,' Lefebvre was suspended and not allowed to resume his work at Citroën. He moved to the house of a niece, who lived close to the factory. There, his many loyal colleagues and assistants would drop by to discuss the projects they were working on, as shocked by what happened as he was. Lefebvre spent his forced exile drawing up plans and making calculations for future Citroën models. After some time he was cleared and reinstated as chief development engineer at the Bureau d'Etudes.

It seems an incredible coincidence, but Gabriel Voisin, Lefebvre's old mentor and lifelong friend, was also falsely accused of collaboration. Voisin himself believed that it was part of a communist-inspired conspiracy to nationalise the Voisin factory, which he did not even own any longer. He had to appear before some judges and, although not detained, he was never officially vindicated. However, some years later Président de Gaulle rewarded him with the 'Légion d'Honneur' because of his lifelong achievements for French aviation.

POSTWAR REVIVAL

Citroën was slowly recovering from its war wounds. Most of the smaller production facilities were still intact, but of the factory at Caen, in the invasion zone, only a few walls remained, and the various air raids on Paris had left their ugly mark on many parts of the premises at the Quai de Javel. The retreating Germans had also 'borrowed' a lot of vital production machines. The good news was that advancing Allied troops happened to discover most of them at a rail depot in Germany; undamaged, they were returned to their rightful owner.

After Maurice Norroy left Citroën in 1943 to take up a post at the COA (Comité d'Organisation de l'Automobile), Pierre Ingueneau was appointed Directeur de Fabrication. At Boulanger's request, Ingueneau and the Service des Méthodes looked into the possibility of manufacturing the chassis and body of the 2CV in steel, mainly because it was easier to mass-produce, but also because Boulanger feared that aluminium would be considerably more expensive after the war. As a steel structure was, of course, heavier than the light metal construction of the 1939 pre-series, it was decided to replace the water-cooled two-cylinder engine with an air-cooled one, thereby avoiding the weight of a radiator. Air cooling had another advantage as well; it made the engine completely winter-proof as it needed no antifreeze.

It has been suggested that the engine of the Citroën 2CV was based on BMW's famous flat-twin motorcycle, first constructed by Max Fitz and Martin Stolle in the nineteen twenties. However, considering all the facts, this seems unlikely. The original 0.375-litre two-cylinder boxer engine developed by Maurice Sainturat and his team for the prewar TPV was water-cooled, and BMW's motorcycle engines were air-cooled. Besides, Sainturat's design resembles his four- and six-cylinder TA engines; in particular, the operating mechanism of the overhead valves in the cylinder heads is comparable.

It is also well known that Boulanger was averse to paying royalties, so he would never have permitted his engineers to copy the design of another manufacturer, thereby risking a lawsuit over patent rights. Furthermore, BMW was neither the first nor the only manufacturer to produce motorcycles powered by horizontal two-cylinder engines: in 1907, the British motorcycle manufacturer Douglas introduced a 0.350-litre model with such an engine designed by W J Barter, and, in 1933, the German Zundapp factory brought out a K series that had a flat-twin developed by Xavier and Richard Küchen. During the mid-thirties, Gnome et Rhône in France also made motorcycles with air-cooled OHV, two-cylinder boxer engines, which, in 1937 and 1939, even broke several records at Montlhéry.

Various construction details and dimensions show that the postwar air-cooled Citroën flat-twin also differed considerably from the BMW machine. For instance, on the Citroën boxer, the pushrods commanding the overhead valves are located beneath the cylinder

World War II

The air-cooled boxer for the postwar 2CV was created by Walter Becchia. During his years with the French sportscar manufacturer Lago Talbot, he had invented a clever way to have the inlet and exhaust valves operating at an angle, allowing the construction of hemispherical combustion chambers, without resorting to the (costly) complication of an overhead camshaft. He used this system in his design of the Citroën engine. (Courtesy Citroën Conservatoire)

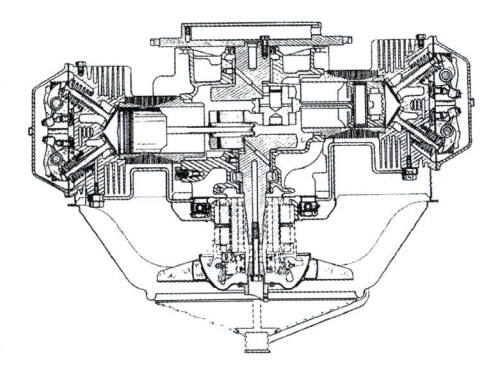

The cylinder head of a TPV engine with the valve cover removed. The pushrod and rocker arm mechanism controlling the OHV bears a striking family resemblance to that of the four- and six-cylinders designed by Maurice Sainturat. (Courtesy Hans Arend de Wit/Switchimage)

heads, with the camshaft turning below the crankshaft, while on the BMW, the pushrods are situated on top and the camshaft turns above the crankshaft.

The man responsible for the design of the air-cooled 2CV power units was Walter Becchia. This cheerful and clever Italian engineer had started his career in the competition department of Fiat in Turin. In 1924 he went to Britain to work on the legendary supercharged Sunbeam racing cars. As Sunbeam was associated with Talbot and Darracq, he regularly visited its factory in Suresnes near Paris. Being well aware of the growing influence of Mussolini's fascist movement, Becchia did not wish to return to Italy, and so when, in the mid-thirties, he was asked to take over from Talbot's chief designer, Vincenzo Bertarione, he decided to stay in France.

Anthony Lago, his new boss, asked him to design a hemispherical cylinder head to fit on the existing block of Talbot's pushrod-operated, OHV six-cylinder. The clever construction of the T150 cylinder head – which increased engine power without the costly complications of overhead camshafts – was later seen on the BMW 328 roadster, and also used by Peugeot, Chrysler, and other car manufacturers.

One of Becchia's responsibilities as chief engineer was the preparation of Talbot's racing and sports cars. Although these machines were quite successful, the company had insufficient financial means to develop a new 3-litre V16 engine that could compete with the Mercedes and Auto Union racers. Moreover, at the outbreak of WWII, all auto sport activities were halted, and in January 1941, Becchia joined Citroën as successor to Maurice Sainturat.

Dangerous experiment

The myth about the BMW probably originated from the fact that such a motorcycle did indeed influence Lefebvre's decision to use an air-cooled power plant for the Deux Chevaux. Flaminio Bertoni had owned a BMW motorcycle since before the war.

Becchia, who was all in favour of air cooling, asked his compatriot and friend to demonstrate to Lefebvre the strong torque and smooth, vibrationless running of his air-cooled twin. Lefebvre was not completely convinced of its efficiency, especially as, in a car, an air-cooled engine would have to propel a cooling fan that would absorb some of its power. But the fact that it did not need a radiator, and most non-wearing parts of the BMW were made of aluminium, tempted him to examine its possibilities more closely.

According to his son, Michel, this curiosity nearly cost his father, and a number of other Citroën employees, their lives. At Lefebvre's request, the Bureau d'Etudes acquired a BMW motorcycle that had been left behind by the Germans, and ended up in a war surplus dump. When it arrived, André Lefebvre, always impatient, immediately wanted to establish its power curve and ordered the engine to be put on a test bench. Fortunately, someone suggested that the BMW might be booby-trapped; it was known that retreating German SS troops sometimes put explosives in the cylinders of the machines they had to abandon, with the sparkplugs acting as an igniting mechanism. Explosive specialists from the French army were summoned. They carefully inspected the BMW and discovered that this was indeed the case. It's a miracle that nobody was hurt.

IMPROVING THE BASIC QUALITIES OF THE *TPV*

The decision to switch from a light metal chassis and body to an all-steel construction gave the Bureau d'Etudes the opportunity to carry out other modifications that would improve the basic qualities of the original TPV concept dating from 1939.

Lefebvre orchestrated the redesign of the flexible suspension, with its interaction between the movement of the front and rear wheels. Mercier – like Lefebvre an aeronautical engineer – and Paul Magès, Citroën's hydraulics specialist, built a prototype with a hydropneumatic suspension, which required compressed air with a pressure of up to 110 bar. For reasons of cost and because its pump also consumed too much power, this system was abandoned for the 2CV, but taken up again later for the DS.

Whilst Mercier and Magès were experimenting with hydraulics, Lefebvre directed Marcel Chinon and Renault, assisted by Barron, Boullay and Léonzi, to design a simple suspension system that would save weight, but also assure good wheel-road contact.

The same concept, but a world of difference: the prewar TPV and the 1948 Deux Chevaux have little in common. In fact, the small Citroën was completely redesigned for postwar production. (Courtesy Citroën Communication)

World War II

They came up with the solution that would be used on the new 2CV. The torsion bars of the 1939 pre-series were replaced by a construction consisting of horizontal coil springs, friction dampers (frotteurs) on the pivots of the suspension arms, and inertia dampers (batteurs) on the wheel hubs, the latter developed by Léon Renault, and consisting of a small, closed, vertical cylinder at each wheel hub, in which a weight – held by coil springs – could oscillate up and down. Their function was to reduce wheel hop (patter) by

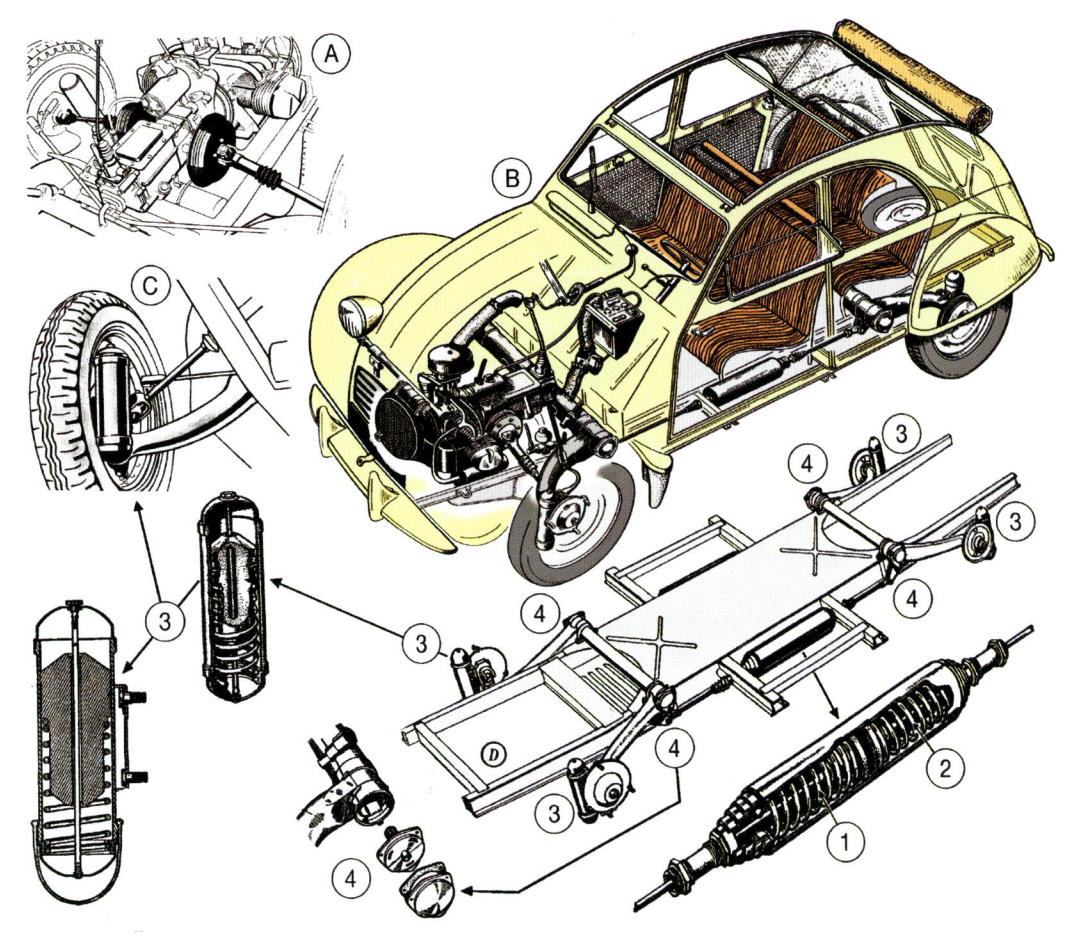

The 2CV that Citroën presented at the 1948 Paris Motor show was technically completely different from the one that should have been introduced in 1939. Its body (B) was made from steel, it had an air-cooled instead of a water-cooled two-cylinder engine, inboard front brakes (A), and two headlights. The independent torsion bar suspension was replaced by the ingenious system shown in this drawing. 1 and 2 The coil springs in their housing. These suspension units are mounted horizontally underneath the platform chassis (D). 3 The inertia shock absorbers, called 'batteurs' (also seen in drawing C). 4 The friction dampers, called 'frotteurs.' (Courtesy Citroën Communication)

coinciding the frequency of the oscillations with the hop frequency of the unsprung masses of the wheels bouncing on their tyres. To create room for these 'batteurs,' it was necessary to move the brake drums from within the front wheels to the differential housing. As every 2CV owner will confirm, this unorthodox suspension system worked quite well.

However, a strange phenomenon revealed itself during the first road tests. When driving the 2CV prototypes through the villages of rural France, all of the dogs would start to bark, but kept quiet when the accompanying Tractions drove by. It appeared that on certain road surfaces the oscillating weights produced a sound at a frequency that humans could not hear, but which drove dogs mad!

The horizontal coil springs were housed in a single cylinder at both sides underneath the chassis. The slightly curved front and rear suspension arms articulated on both ends of transverse tubes, which were located in the relatively strong midsection of the platform chassis, just fore and aft of the floor of the passenger compartment. While allowing plenty of vertical wheel movement, this arrangement limited deformation of the frame by torsional (suspension) stresses. It was a typical Lefebvre solution, one that he had already used on his first Traction Avant when he anchored the torsion suspension bars in the centre of the monocoque structure, thereby concentrating suspension stresses on this small surface.

Due to the fact that the weight of the flat-twin engine sat just over the front wheels, the 2CV had a low, forward-placed centre of gravity. Together with the extremely supple but road-hugging suspension system, this explains why the Deux Chevaux was so stable in crosswinds and handled so well, even if it did lean over in fast corners like a sharp-sailing dinghy!

Flaminio Bertoni did his utmost to improve the shape of the 2CV and make it more attractive, even designing a body with a more modern, slightly rounded nose and elongated front mudguards. This got him into trouble with Boulanger, who did not want such embellishments; he wished the 2CV to remain the sober, functional car that he had originally specified. Even a scale model painted in bright yellow made Boulanger see red!

The first of the postwar production Deux Chevaux already had two headlamps, but still had to be started by hand, although a device that could be operated from behind the steering wheel had replaced the starting handle; a pull-cord system, similar to that used on small lawn mowers and marine outboard engines. Rumour has it that Boulanger only agreed to have an electric starter motor fitted after his daughter was stranded with one of the early production models he had lent her. She found it impossible to restart the engine by pulling the cord and broke one of her fingernails trying! Disgusted and exhausted she took a taxi home.

The 2CV finally got two rear lights when, some seven years later, a new French law required all four-wheeled motor vehicles to have parking lights.

All traces of the TPV had to be destroyed

Before the first 'new' 2CV went into production Boulanger ordered all the TPV prototypes and the 1939 pre-series to be destroyed. However, some TPVs survived, and, around 1960, three very dusty prototypes were discovered in a barn not far from La Ferté-Vidame. The Citroën employees who had brought the cars there in 1940 made the farmer promise that, under no circumstances, would he ever reveal anything about these 'refugees,' and so he never did! His heirs found the cars by accident when they cleared out the farmyard.

Then there was the TPV that had been sent to Michelin in Clermont-Ferrand in 1939 for tyre testing. During all the war years it was used around the factory, and nobody realised that this little car, disguised as a small pickup truck, was in fact a unique Citroën prototype. Apparently, immediately after the war a Michelin employee sold it to a local scrapyard for its worth in metal. Fortunately, the scrap dealer discovered its historical value and saved it from destruction.

World War II

*To celebrate the 60th anniversary of the Deux Chevaux, Citroën organised a commemorative exhibition in the Cité des Sciences et de l'Industrie in Paris. Visitors could see its evolution from minimalist workhorse to cult car.
(Courtesy Hans Arend de Wit/Switchimage)*

An early 2CV pottering along a rural road in France, its natural habitat. It's almost possible to hear the sound of the engine! (Courtesy Johan van der Laan)

Rocking like a cradle

The general public got its first chance to see the new Deux Chevaux after Président Vincent Auriol had officially opened the Paris Salon de l'Automobile in October 1948. The press was shocked by its ugliness, as were most visitors. On the Citroën stand some tried out the seats, whilst others were rocking the cars like a cradle. It was treated almost like a fairground attraction and not as a serious proposition.

But opinion changed as soon as the first cars were delivered to the dealers. According to Boulanger's wishes, owners had been carefully selected by Citroën's commercial management, and, initially, only orders from farmers, self-employed craftsmen, priests, midwives, rural doctors and popular artists were accepted. Once the 2CV was in full production, the waiting list for it grew to over forty-eight months, despite its ugly body and standard drab metal-grey colour!

The huge demand for cars in postwar France was not the only explanation for this, as the economical and practical qualities of the Deux Chevaux attracted many who had never before bought a new automobile. In due course it became a cult car for unconventional individuals and today is a coveted collector's item. Between 1949 and 1990 an impressive 7,301,278 Deux Chevaux saloons and vans were manufactured in 15 countries. Tragically, Pierre Boulanger would not witness the incredible success of his brainchild.

A benchmark for the new Traction Avant?

That year, 1948, André Lefebvre went back several times to the Paris Motor Show, not so much to hear the comments of the visitors about the car he had brought to life, but because he was very intrigued by another exhibit. On stand number 80 in the Grand

Palais, the French inventor/designer Jean-Albert Grégoire showed his new Grégoire R as a bare chassis and as a four-door saloon. Like the prewar Amilcar 'Compound' and the AFG car that Grégoire had been developing during the period 1942-1943 in collaboration with the technical staff of Aluminium Français, his new design had a chassis made from Alpax (light alloy) castings. Shortly after the war Grégoire had invited Boulanger and Lefebvre to try the small AFG prototype with its air-cooled twin. At that time Grégoire was prospecting all the automobile companies that might eventually buy the manufacturing rights, but Boulanger was averse to paying royalties, and, furthermore, was convinced that the 2CV designed by his own Bureau d'Etudes was much more economical to produce. Eventually, Panhard acquired the project and used it to develop the Dyna.

It's not surprising that Lefebvre was interested in Grégoire's latest brainchild: it was the first postwar front-wheel drive car, and also incorporated many of the design features he already had in mind for the successor to Citroën's Traction Avant. The Grégoire R had a water-cooled, four-cylinder boxer engine with a 2 litre capacity, mounted ahead of the front axle. Body shape showed it had been developed with the help of a wind tunnel, but it lacked the elegance that a creative stylist could have provided. It had a top speed of 145km/h and used less than 9 litre/100km when driven on the French Routes Nationales at an average speed of around 80km/h. Lefebvre was convinced that the performance and fuel consumption of this new car would become the benchmarks against which his new Citroën would be measured, so needed to create a car that could better it.

According to his son, Michel, Lefebvre held Grégoire in great esteem as an engineer, notwithstanding the fact that he well remembered their unfortunate confrontation about the durability of Grégoire's Tracta joints, when Lefebvre had just joined Citroën's Bureau d'Etudes in 1933. Was this the reason for a certain uneasiness in their personal relationship? Or was it because both were, subconsciously, a little jealous of each other's achievements? Was Lefebvre, perhaps, envious of Grégoire's financial independence, thanks to the revenue of the many licences for his various inventions and constructions? Or did Grégoire's behaviour towards Lefebvre somehow convey that he had studied at the École Polytechnique, the 'grande école' of engineering in France, whereas Lefebvre 'only' attended the 'Supaéro' college, a less prestigious institute in the hierarchy of engineering faculties? Grégoire has written that he was always impressed by Lefebvre's tenacity, and the way his fertile brain found solutions to the most complex technical problems. And, secretly, he may have admitted to himself that Lefebvre's Traction Avant and 2CV were commercially much more successful than any of his own designs, and again the case with his latest creation ...

Grégoire had signed a contract with the old and established French car manufacturer Hotchkiss for the production and marketing of the R as the Hotchkiss-Grégoire. Previously, Peugeot had acquired a financial stake in Hotchkiss, and Maurice Jourdan, one of Peugeot's top executives, became a member of its supervisory board. Jourdan did not fancy front-wheel drive and was convinced that Grégoire's design – with its cast alloy chassis and all-aluminium body – would be very costly to produce. He did not like its styling either and advised Grégoire to seek help from Pininfarina in Turin, with whom Peugeot already had established an excellent relationship. But Grégoire thought he knew better, and everyone who had driven or tested the car – among them the well-known Belgian motoring journalist Paul Frère – was delighted with it.

When the Hotchkiss-Grégoire was finally presented at the Paris Motor Show in October 1951, its price tag was set at 1.8 million (old) French francs, a sum that could buy three 11CV Tractions or two six-cylinder Citroëns 15CV – and with cash to spare! It was even around 14 per cent more expensive than Hotchkiss' conventional top-of-the-range six-cylinder Anjou.

But body shape also proved a big stumbling block. The production cars had only four side windows instead of the six on the prototypes, which made the fastback rear end look rather cumbersome. As Grégoire remembered in his own memoirs, many wives and/or mistresses of well-heeled potential clients vetoed the purchase. At the end of 1954, after Hotchkiss had produced 247 units, it became clear that instead of making a profit, every Hotchkiss-Grégoire sold had cost the company a lot of money. Therefore, the board decided that Hotchkiss – which had, in the meantime, merged with Delahaye – would stop making passenger cars altogether and concentrate on the manufacture of light industrial vehicles (jeeps) for the military and fire brigades.

For Grégoire this was, of course, a terrible deception, even more so as, a year later, Citroën's DS – created by Lefebvre – made its sensational debut on the French market.

GEE, A MINI FRONT-WHEEL DRIVE CAB

Earlier in 1948 – some time before the first series of the 2CV rolled off the production line – the team at the Bureau d'Etudes was working on a completely different car: a mini front-cab van, powered by an air-cooled, two-cylinder boxer engine, similar to that of the 2CV but enlarged to 0.475 litres.

What Lefebvre had in mind was a versatile vehicle, for use not only as a handy and economic delivery van, but also a minibus, a taxi, or even a tiny camping car. Under his supervision and encouragement, a small task force consisting of the engineer Lagarde, chassis specialists Bernard and Boisse, and draftsman Lagary, developed a prototype.

For some mysterious reason the project received the codename Véhicule G, and, at first sight, the G looked like a scaled-down Type H van, crossbred with a 2CV. But it had a lot of original details. The front suspension was quite different from that of the 2CV; instead of single (forward pushing) wheel support arms, it had (right and left) two parallel-mounted suspension arms

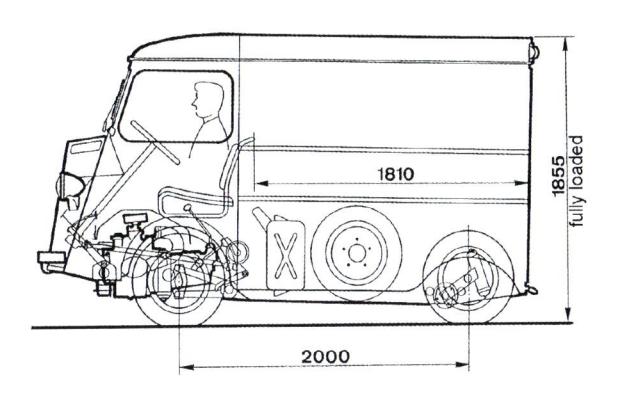

The G delivery van project was abandoned for economic reasons. The sole surviving prototype from 1948 resides in the Conservatoire Citroën at Aulnay-sous-Bois. Its compact size is clearly illustrated on this photo with the driver behind the steering wheel. Contrary to the prewar TUB and larger Type H van, the loading area of the small G has rear doors only and no sliding door at the right side. Courtesy Citroën Communication)

The engine of the G was based on the air-cooled, two-cylinder of the Deux Chevaux, but enlarged to 0.425 litres. and mounted under the floor of the front steer cab. This picture shows the starter motor and downdraft carburettor and air filter sticking out into the cabin. (Courtesy Hans Arend de Wit/Switchimage)

(a precursor of the front wheel support system later used on the DS), with a transverse torsion bar as the suspension unit. At the rear were trailing arms and transverse torsion bar suspension resembling the system used by the H. The sole surviving prototype – loaned by the Conservatoire Citroën to the French association of 'Les Amis du Type H' for exhibition on its stand at the 2008 Rétromobile Classic Car Show in Paris – did not have any shock absorbers. The driver sat practically on top ot the engine/transmission unit with a box covering the carburettor and air filter at his right-hand side. The wheelbase measured only 2.00m (some 50cm less than the H), total length came to 3.47m (compared to 4.26m for the H), and it was 1.68m wide and 2.03m high.

It was an ingenious small car but with one serious drawback: due to the location of the air-cooled twin directly under the cockpit floor, engine noise inside was much louder than in a 2CV. Ultimately, however, the G project was abandoned for economical reasons. At that time, Citroën's production capacity was already stretched to the limit and there was not sufficient capital to invest in another production line.

The management decided that it would be more sensible to manufacture the AZU van, which had the front of the 2CV and cargo space like a bicycle shed at the rear, and it could be produced on the assembly lines of the 2CV saloons, because both models shared the same platform chassis.

CHAPTER

TEN

ENJOYING LIFE AGAIN

With the black clouds of the war years in the past, André Lefebvre began to enjoy life again. Although recently turned fifty he did not feel middle-aged, and was still very dynamic and vigorous. His work was satisfying; his bosses mostly accepted his views concerning the future products of the company and allowed him a great deal of freedom. His staff and assistants, who hardly ever questioned his engineering knowledge or experience, admired him. Amongst his peers he was a celebrity, respected as the innovative and creative technical brain of Citroën. He had no dull administrative responsibilities, unlike Jean Cadiou, his Director at the Bureau d'Etudes, which department had grown from about 200 employees in the prewar period to nearly 700 in the 1950s.

In his personal life he was also quite happy. His third wife, Monique, had given him two sons, Alain and Philippe (Guy would follow later), and they lived in a nice house in L'Etang-La-Ville, an affluent suburb near St Germain-en-Laye in the Paris region.

His only regret was that he had never had any contact with Alice, the daughter by his first wife. In 1939 Alice, whom he had officially acknowledged, had

Monique loved children, and before her boys were born enjoyed taking care of Dominique, the daughter of Michel and Jeanine Lefebvre. André, by now approaching middle age, looks on. (Courtesy Collection family Lefebvre)

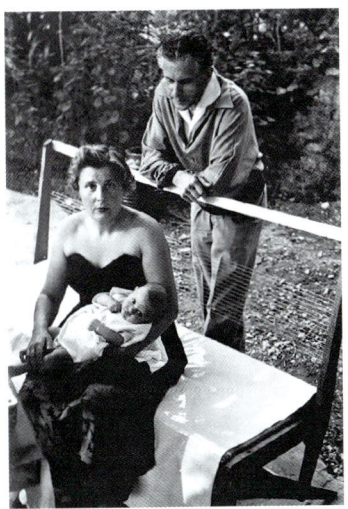

André with Monique and baby Dominique in their garden. Interesting detail; the seat was designed and constructed by André. Its frame was made from aluminium profiles, and it had a webbing of plastic wires for the seat and backrest, the same type of plastic webbing he intended to use for the seats of the Coccinelle. (Courtesy Collection family Lefebvre)

107

Family portrait from the early fifties. André and Monique with Alain and Philippe when they were still young boys. (Courtesy Collection family Lefebvre)

gone to England to study; then war had broken out and, in 1941, her mother – who had left him in 1918 – died. He did not even know where Alice lived. Fortunately, he and Monique often saw Jean and Michel the sons from his first and second marriages. They were both doing well.

Recently, Lefebvre had acquired an estate at Terrissole, amongst woodlands and vineyards, and close to the small town of Figanières near Draguignan in the south of France. His son Michel and his wife Jeanine had a house in that area. He contracted with some tenants – local farmers – to permit them to grow their produce on his fertile land and pay him rent in return.

The surroundings of Terrissole were ideally suited for testing cars, and no doubt this was at the back of his mind when he decided to buy the property.

Some years later, Monique and André enjoy a stroll on a sunny day. (Courtesy Collection family Lefebvre)

Situated between the city of Draguignan and a charming village called Figanières, Lefebvre's house at Terrissole was an ideal place for long weekends and family holidays. (Author collection)

In the early fifties, when Lefebvre and his team worked on the Citroën DS, he often managed to try out a prototype on the back roads in that area, and so the Terrissole property became a sort of unofficial test centre for the Bureau d'Etudes. (Courtesy Collection family Lefebvre)

When the DS was no longer a secret, André Lefebvre often travelled with his to the Var province just for the weekend. He liked the drive and enjoyed his conversations with Louis Proksch (on his left), who, for many years, was responsible for the agricultural exploitation of Terrissole. (Courtesy Collection family Lefebvre)

The VGD (Voiture de Grande Diffusion)

It is known that Lefebvre had been thinking of a successor for the Traction since 1935, and that year even built a running prototype, the 7-P-O, but, as will be remembered, this proposal was rejected by Citroën management. Between 1936 and 1939, Bertoni made a great number of sketches and drawings – even some scale models and full-size mock-ups – to show how the body of such a car could look. In those days, however, Boulanger was not really interested: the Traction was selling well and earning good money, and Citroën needed cash flow to invest in manufacturing equipment for the 2CV. After the outbreak of WWII, other projects had priority.

In 1946, Citroën resumed manufacture of its prewar passenger cars, the four-cylinder 11BL and B and the six-cylinder Quinze. By then concepts of the H-van and the new 2CV had been finalised, and the Service des Méthodes – together with the Direction de Fabrication – were preparing their production. However, Boulanger and his commercial staff recognised that, during the late forties, competition from major British car makers such as Austin, Ford, Standard-Triumph, Vauxhall, Nuffield (Morris-Wolseley-Riley-MG), and the Rootes Group (Hillman-Sunbeam-Humber) had become a serious threat in some of their European export markets, and in Britain itself. This did not yet worry them too much, as their home market in France and the French colonies could still absorb every car they manufactured. However, they agreed that, within a few years, Citroën would need to replace the Traction: although there was not much wrong with its performance or roadholding, it was beginning to look dated, as its shape had hardly changed since 1934.

GREEN LIGHT FOR A NEW CITROËN

The big question was: how to proceed? One possibility was to update the existing Traction concept with a more powerful engine and a modern body; the alternative was to start with a clean slate and create a totally new car.

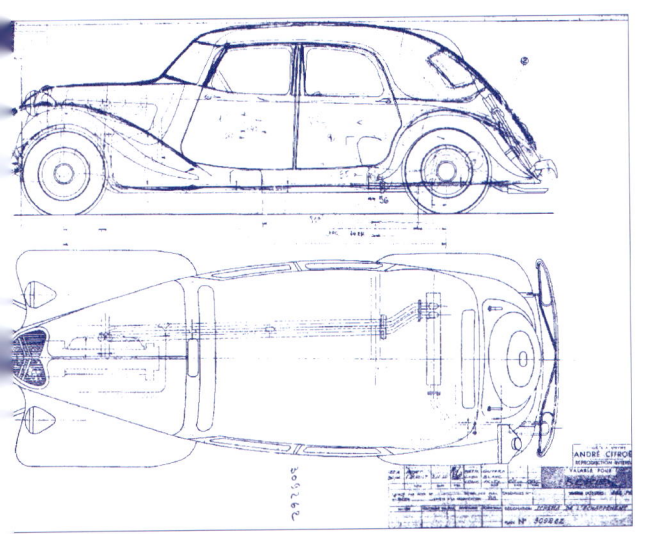

It took many years and thousands of sketches and drawings to develop a successor for the Traction Avant, which Lefebvre and Bertoni were already contemplating during the late 1930s. This draft shows a modernized body for the TA. The team made several feasibility studies and styling exercises, but Citroën's management had other priorities. (Illustration Citroën Communication, courtesy Leonardo Bertoni)

1948, Boulanger finally gave the Bureau d'Etudes the green light for the design of a new car that was then known as the VGD (Voiture á Grande Diffusion). This is a sketch by Bertoni.

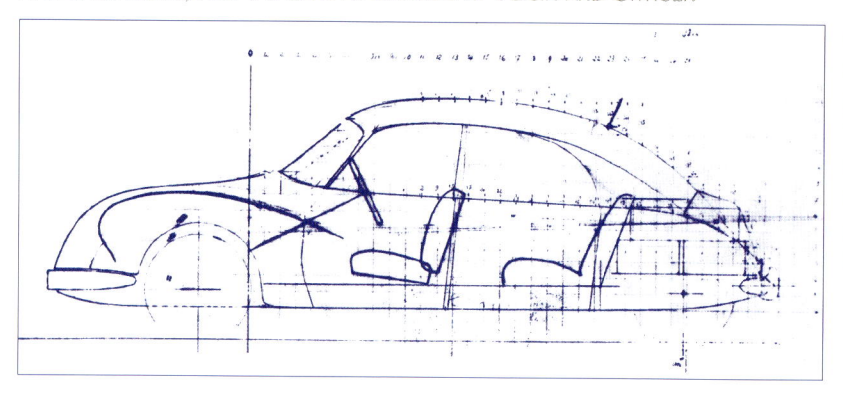

One of the first side view projections of the VGD. (Illustration Citroën Communication, courtesy Leonardo Bertoni)

It was a devilish dilemma that Boulanger and his staff discussed at length. The first solution required less investment in new tooling, but, as the Traction had proved, a new and advanced design could remain in production longer without the need for fundamental changes, with the added financial advantage of reduced tool and die depreciation.

André Lefebvre strongly favoured the second option as he felt that it was time for drastic rejuvenation. The successor to his Traction should have more comfortable suspension, lighter steering, higher cruising speeds and lower fuel consumption. At the same time, safety should be improved by means of better brakes and increased stability. All of this, in his opinion, required a completely new approach.

Lefebvre was never short of brilliant ideas and could also be very persuasive. In the end Boulanger gave in, but on certain conditions. He told Lefebvre: "It must be ahead of its time so we can produce it over a long period, but I don't want it to be as revolutionary as the Traction was when first introduced. It must have four large doors, a big luggage compartment and enough headroom at the rear so that back seat passengers can keep their hats on. Our clients are not seeking fancy streamlining and a high top speed. Cruising in comfort at a 100 to 130km/h and easy handling is what they like. A powerful engine with a three-speed box, as people don't like to change gears. And last but not least ... it must be less expensive to manufacture than the present models."

If Lefebvre was slightly disappointed by Boulanger's conservative 'Cahier des Charges,' he nevertheless started on the project with his usual energy and enthusiasm.

Boulanger's fatal accident

The man who had saved the Citroën Company from financial ruin and turned it into a profitable business died on November 11, 1950. While driving from Paris to Clermont-Ferrand, his car left the road near Saint Pourçain-sur-Sioule on the Route Nationale 9. He made this journey so often that he must have known every bend and curve of the road by heart. However, it was no secret that Boulanger was a fast driver and always tried to improve his own average speed on this stretch. It is equally possible that he fell asleep at the wheel because he was over-tired. Yet another theory is that his car was equipped with an experimental four-speed gearbox that had a different gate pattern than the three-speed one, and that Boulanger engaged a wrong gear by mistake. The real cause of his crash, however, will forever remain a mystery ...

For Citroën employees the death of their 'Patron' came as a great shock. They were used to Boulanger's management style; he had led the company through difficult times, and they trusted him to give direction to the postwar development and growth of the marque. What would happen now?

Rumour had it that Robert Puiseux, the top man of Michelin and thus Citroën's major stockholder, intended to sell the Citroën Company. General Motors again seemed interested and the names of Ford and Chausson came up as well. But, to everyone's relief, Puiseux himself took over the reins of the Société Anonyme André Citroën as Président Directeur Général, and appointed Pierre Bercot as Directeur Général. Antoine Brueder became Directeur Général Adjoint.

Quite naturally, André Lefebvre was distressed by the fact that, once again, a Citroën PDG, and a man he had known well, lost his life driving a Traction. Lefebvre had always appreciated Boulanger because he was straightforward, intelligent and absolutely dedicated to the Citroën company. He also admired the tenacious nature of Boulanger's character. But they had never enjoyed the same easy and cordial relationship that he had with his predecessor, Pierre Michelin. Boulanger and Lefebvre respected and accepted each other, but their relationship went no further.

With his new bosses, Robert Puiseux and Pierre Bercot, things would be quite different. Robert Puiseux (1892-1991), the son of Pierre Puiseux, a famous French astronomer, was an old acquaintance. While serving in the Armée de l'Air during WWI, Puiseux was apprenticed at the Voisin factory in Issy-les-Moulineaux, where he and André Lefebvre had met for the first time. Puiseux later married Anne, the daughter of Edouard Michelin, and since 1921 worked for the family business. One of his first accomplishments was to oversee development of the Michelin Pilote tyres, later to be followed by the revolutionary Michelin X radials. In 1937, after the tragic accident of his son, Pierre, Edouard Michelin appointed him co-gérant (co-director) of the Michelin company, the other director being Pierre Boulanger. When Edouard died on August 25, 1940, Puiseux was his obvious successor.

As it was impossible to obtain natural rubber for tyre manufacture, the war years were very difficult. By manufacturing prams, raincoats, toys and small trailers that could be towed by bikes, the company survived, however, and Puiseux led it through these black years and on to a postwar period of expansion and innovation. The family was closely involved with the résistance movement during World War II, and several Michelins were interned in concentration camps.

As General Manager of Michelin (and thus representing the major shareholder of Citroën), Puiseux often visited Boulanger in Paris, and nearly always dropped by at the Bureau d'Etudes to shake hands with Lefebvre and to talk about cars, at the Bureau d'Etudes. He was a fan of Lefebvre and his wife drove a Traction cabriolet. They also saw each other regularly in Clermont-Ferrand when Lefebvre went there to discuss technical matters with his colleagues at Michelin's Research Department.

CARTE BLANCHE

After Puiseux became Président-Directeur Général of Citroën, he handed control of the VGD project to Pierre Bercot. Bercot agreed to a redefinition of the project, convinced by Lefebvre that now was the opportunity to create a car that would be as far ahead of its contemporaries as the Traction had been in 1934. In fact, Bercot gave Lefebvre carte blanche to design the car as he saw fit, although did ask him to speed up its development.

To his colleagues and assistants Lefebvre outlined the objectives he had in mind: comfort, safety and operational economy, which implied, amongst other criteria:
- a suspension system that would set new standards for comfort
- light but direct steering
- predictable handling and excellent straight-line stability
- powerful and fade-resistant brakes
- a sturdy but lightweight (chassis) construction
- a spacious and light interior with comfortable seats

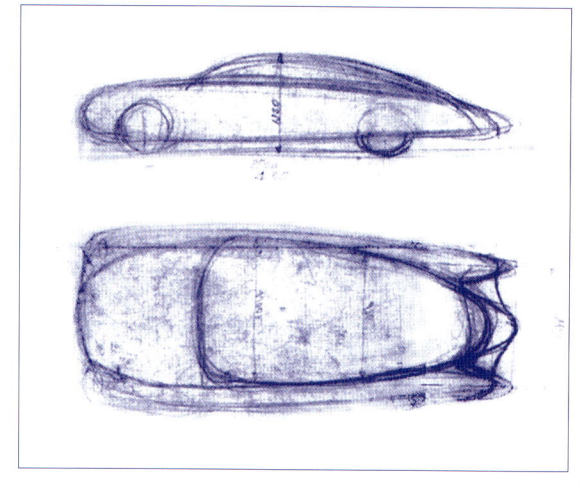

A rough sketch made in the late forties by André Lefebvre shows what he had in mind for the new Citroën. He intended to design a four-door saloon with comfort for five and the aerodynamic body of a fast sportscar. In those days this was a revolutionary approach. (Courtesy Collection family Lefebvre)

• functional aerodynamics for good performances and low fuel consumption
• the use of new materials to reduce maintenance and facilitate body repairs

Lefebvre even gave Flaminio Bertoni a rough pencil sketch of what the VGD should look like: as sleek as the latest jet aircraft!

Bertoni by now had his own 'Atelier Bertoni' styling studio at Citroën, and his award-winning sculptures had made him quite famous in the French art world. When recuperating from a nasty motorcycle accident, he had taken up the study of architecture and received his official diploma in 1949.

But Bertoni still greatly enjoyed designing automobile coachwork. Now a certificated architect, he had acquired the same professional status as the Citroën engineers, and had assistants to help with the heavy work. However, he remained an indefatigable artist and often worked from early morning till late at night, experimenting with innovative body shapes.

While Bertoni

This drawing by Flaminio Bertoni, master stylist at Citroën, illustrates how he gave Lefebvre's ideas shape and substance. He always liked to use a dark background for his renderings, because he believed that this way the light reflections on the body showed up better and thus gave a more realistic effect. (Courtesy Leonardo Bertoni)

Bertoni made innumerable studies for the bodywork of the DS. As a professional sculptor he had the gift to translate his ideas into three dimensional shapes. Here, we see him in his 'studio' with a beautifully finished scale model. (Courtesy Leonardo Bertoni)

made innumerable drawings, scale models and full-scale plaster mock-ups for the body, Magès was perfecting the precision engineering necessary for the revolutionary hydro-pneumatic system, incorporating the suspension, power-assisted steering, and power-assisted brakes. At the same time, Becchia was designing and testing new engines, among them an air-cooled and water-cooled six-cylinder.

WEIGHT IS THE ENEMY

Owners of these classic Citroëns may not like to acknowledge it, but the basic concept of the DS owes a lot to the Deux Chevaux. Like the 2CV the DS has a platform-type chassis, a body from which the panels – mudguards and doors – can be easily removed, and an independent suspension on all four wheels with interconnection between wheel movement at the front and rear. The DS is, of course, faster, more refined; its construction more elaborate and also more complicated. And it is certainly a more up-market automobile than Lefebvre's earlier design.

Apart from supervising the efforts of his colleagues, Lefebvre concentrated his brainpower on the chassis structure and drivetrain.

There were several reasons why Lefebvre decided that the VGD would have a platform chassis instead of the body-cum-chassis construction as used for the Traction. For one thing, the Citroën company refused to pay royalties to Budd for its patents concerning the building of monocoque bodies. It was also known that Budd had been engaged by Renault to help develop its new luxury model, the Frégate. A third consideration must have been that, because of the greater investment needed for a monocoque structure, the production run of the same body would have to be longer. Besides, the use of of a platform chassis wold make intermediate 'facelifts' or the production of other body variants (such as an estate) less complicated and therefore less expensive.

Of course, Lefebvre had no intention of abandoning his pursuit of lightness and strength and opted for a skeleton-frame with unstressed body panels. This creation resembled the concept pioneered by Charles Weymann and his partner, Maurice Tabuteau, in 1921, later modernised by the Milanese coachwork specialist Touring on its 'Superleggera' bodies. In the days when Lefebvre worked with Voisin, he had become familiar with the principles of the Weymann body. In Gabriel Voisin's opinion 'Charly' Weymann – a flamboyant and enterprising ex-WWI fighter pilot – was one of the few men in the coachbuilding business who understood that 'weight is the enemy.'

Lefebvre's approach was, of course, light-years ahead of Weymann, and even went a step further than Touring. His team constructed a sort of cage, made up of large and small steel pressings welded together. A top section, consisting of the roof support and A, B and C pillars, was welded to the chassis platform beneath, which was formed by a flat steel floor strengthened by high side- and cross-members, the engine bay at the front and support of the rear suspension at the back. This light structure helped provide a low centre of gravity, and proved highly resistant to horizontal deformation, though offered less torsional rigidity than a monocoque. It is likely that Lefebvre accepted this because his training as an aircraft engineer had taught him that a flexible metal construction would not fracture so easily – consider the flexing wing movement of an aircraft whilst it is taxiing. Whether the DS would pass today's ENCAP crash tests with high marks is another question, but in those days 'active' safety – the prevention of accidents – was considered more important than passenger protection or 'passive' safety.

As stated, the various body panels that formed the outer skin were not stress-bearing, thus, the front and rear mudguards, bonnet, roof, luggage cover and doors could be made of any sort of material. Lefebvre firmly believed that plastics were the material of

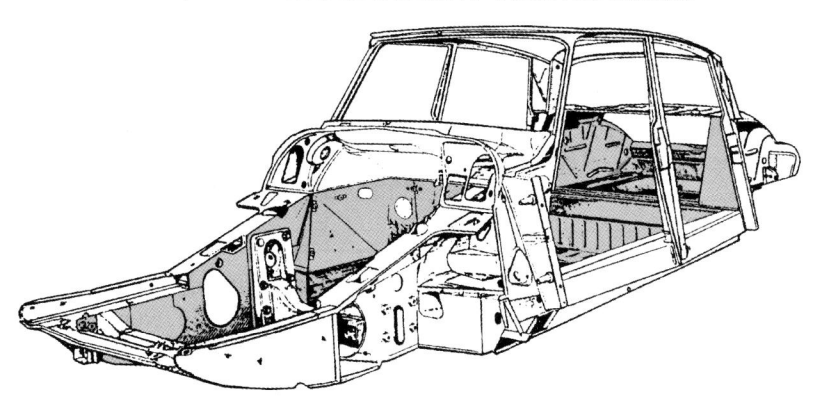

The skeleton of the DS is, in fact, a combination of a platform chassis and a space frame. The upper frame serves to support the roof panel. (Courtesy Citroën Communication)

Below: Lefebvre favoured the combination of a sturdy skeleton frame with non-stress-bearing and easy detachable body panels, primarily because it permitted the use of aluminium and plastics for these panels, but also because it made replacement of damaged body parts easier. To illustrate this feature, Citroën provided this photo in its publicity material. In some countries this proved counterproductive, however, as rival salesmen pointed out to potential clients that loose body panels did not provide adequate passenger protection. (Courtesy Citroën Communication)

Since his early days with Gabriel Voisin, Lefebvre was convinced that the right alignment of the front wheels was of vital importance for safe and pleasant steering characteristics. In order to provide 'centrepoint' steering, the axis of the kingpins at road level must coincide with the centre of the tyre. At that time this was achieved by a combination of wheel camber and kingpin inclination (A). (B) Fitting the front brakes inboard (near the transmission and not within the wheels), the upper and lower ball-joints of the front suspension, which act as a kingpin, could be situated within the wheel to permit the perfect 'centrepoint' alignment. This, together with assistance from the hydro-pneumatic system, gives the DS its light and precise steering. (C) Drawing of the double guiding arms of the right side front suspension (transverse links of equal length), the ball-joints and the wheel hub. (D) In order to reduce the turning circle, Lefebvre came up with the idea of tilting the transmission shafts slightly to the rear. During cornering this allows the transmission joint on the 'inside' wheel to function under a more favourable angle. (Courtesy RTA, Roger Brioult/Edifree & Citroën Communication)

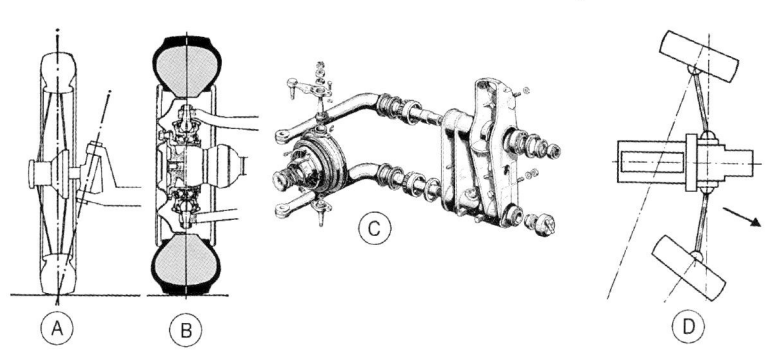

the future, and planned to have a number of these outer body parts made from fibreglass-reinforced plastic, which would be bolted, screwed or glued onto the steel inner frame. A big advantage of this concept was that the shape of some body parts, such as the front mudguards, could be changed without expensive alteration to the structure of the existing inner frame. Besides, these non-stressed body parts were easy to remove for repair.

Still, Lefebvre's major preoccupation was to prevent the car from becoming overweight. He asked one of the collaborators of the Bureau d'Etudes to painstakingly note the effect of all modifications and changes on total weight. These 'balance sheets' were kept up-to-date until the car's introduction, and it is thanks to these documents that we know that the early production DS19s, manufactured in September 1955, weighing 1159kg were just 68.90kg heavier than the 1954 prototypes.

DIRECT BUT EFFORTLESS STEERING

André Lefebvre realised that the steering of 'his' Traction Avant was very heavy at low speeds – his wife had often complained about it when parking her car – and that, even with the excellent new Michelin tyres, rough road surfaces could be felt in the steering wheel. He wanted the new car to have the precise and direct steering response of a sports car. At the same time, steering had to be as light as on a big American automobile. A logical step was to make use of power assistance, which was already common. An advantage of the high pressure system developed by Magès for the hydro-pneumatic suspension was that it could also be used for power-assisted steering (see *l'Autojournal* unveils 'La Bombe Citroën'). In fact, the Bureau d'Etudes had been experimenting with power steering on a Traction Avant as early as 1939.

Lefebvre was a perfectionist: the new Citroën's steering had not only to be direct and light but also completely free from road influences, so that, without any special effort from the driver, the car would stay on course on every type of surface, at any speed, and even if a front or rear tyre should have a blow-out. Accordingly, he and his colleagues spent a lot of time experimenting with the layout of the front wheels, the brakes, and alignment of the transmission shafts.

Their experience with the 2CV had taught them that mounting the front brakes at the transmission side of the driveshafts instead of – as was customary in those days – in the front wheels themselves, reduced unsprung mass. This was considered important as every bump in a road results in an upward movement of the wheels, and wheel and suspension arm mass determine the force of this vertical bounce.

Secondly, it also allowed perfect pivoting of the front wheels. Automotive technicians agree that, ideally, the axis of the horizontal movement (kingpin pivots) of a front wheel should come together at road level with the contact centre of the tyre and the road. In automotive jargon this is called 'centerpoint geometry,' or 'centerpoint steering.' It was one of the design principles that Gabriel Voisin and André Lefebvre had figured out together in the early 1920s and it is still valid today.

Moving the brakes from within the front wheels to the differential housing simultaneously achieved two objectives: perfect centerpoint geometry – as the kingpin axis could now completely overlap the vertical wheel axis – and, secondly, optimal reduction of the unsprung weight of both front wheels.

The engineers at the Bureau d'Etudes feared – and not without reason – that the streamlined, all-enveloping body which Lefebvre and Bertoni had planned would cause problems with cooling the inboard drum brakes, with severe consequences resulting from prolonged braking from high speeds, or descending steep mountain passes. Lefebvre always closely followed the latest technical developments in aircraft design and knew that, since the late nineteen forties, a number of airplane manufacturers had equipped their landing gear with disc brakes. So, in 1951, he asked Jacques Né, one of his colleagues, to study their potential for the VGD.

Né visited the French Patents office (Institut National de la Propriété Industrielle) in the Rue d'Amsterdam near the Gare Saint Lazare, to consult all of the patents covering this type of brake. A study of these documents revealed that the principle of such a brake had already been patented in 1902 by the British engineering consultant and inventor Dr Frederick Lanchester (1868-1946), and had effectively been used on Douglas sidecars as early as 1923. As Né saw in all the patents that the discs were gripped between two opposing pistons, he developed an experimental disc brake – called a frein à plateau = plate brake – which had two pistons at one side and a floating brake calliper. Né had studied naval construction, was a pilot in the French air force, and an enthusiastic motocross rider (he later became cross champion of Normandy). When Lefebvre discovered this talent he asked Né to try out several prototypes and report his findings, and, although Né's name hardly appears in books about the DS, his influence as a development engineer must not be underestimated.

After Lefevbre had to retire because of illness Jacques Né succeeded him at the Bureau d'Etudes, and was responsible for several sporting DS versions and rally cars, eventually fathering the Maserati-powered Citroën SM. But that's another story, so let's go back to Lefebve's idea to use disc brakes.

When in 1953 Tony Rolt and Duncan Hamilton won the '24 Heures du Mans,' the press wrote that this victory demonstrated the superiority of the disc brakes (developed by Dunlop) on its C type Jaguar. Nobody doubted that these new brakes had greatly contributed to success, as they had proved more resistant to heat – and therefore less prone to fading – than the large drum brakes on other competitors' cars. Once again Lefebvre's instinct had been right and the outcome of the Le Mans race convinced everybody at Citroën that the future DS should have disc brakes as well.

Another of the many 'unconventional' construction details of the Citroën DS is that both halfshafts, which transmit engine power to the front wheels, are slightly angled toward the rear. This has the advantage that, during full-lock cornering, the transmission joint of the wheel at the inside of the curve can swivel over a greater angle, resulting in effective reduction of the turning circle, which partly explains why the DS, with its 3.125m long wheelbase, has a turning circle of just 11m between curbs, which is 71cm less then the 'old' Traction Avant B 'Normale' with a wheelbase of only 3.09m. But there is a snag. When driving in a straight line the transmission joints must now also function under a narrow angle which, theoretically, will shorten their life. Lefebvre must have reasoned that this did not matter so much, as the up-and-down movement of the front wheels, following the suspension, means that those transmission joints are practically constantly working at small angles.

Some believe that the above-mentioned 'imperfection' in the layout of the halfshafts and transmission joints was an inevitable consequence of an effort to keep the wheelbase to a minimum. However, knowing that Lefebvre, just like his mentor, Gabriel Voisin, was a pragmatic technician who favoured unorthodox and sometimes controversial solutions, it's safe to assume that this was intentional, and both Sallot and Léonzi confirm this. As the severe bench tests at the Bureau d'Etudes had already indicated, the transmission joints of the DS were not prone to premature wear.

Lefebvre also decided that the rear track had to be some 20cm narrower than the front track (1m 50), and one of his reasons was that this permitted a more aerodynamic body shape – just as on the first car he had designed, the successful 1923 Voisin 'Laboratoire' racer. Besides, together with a smaller tyre size on the rear wheels (155 x 400) against (165 x 400) on the front wheels, it also improved handling.

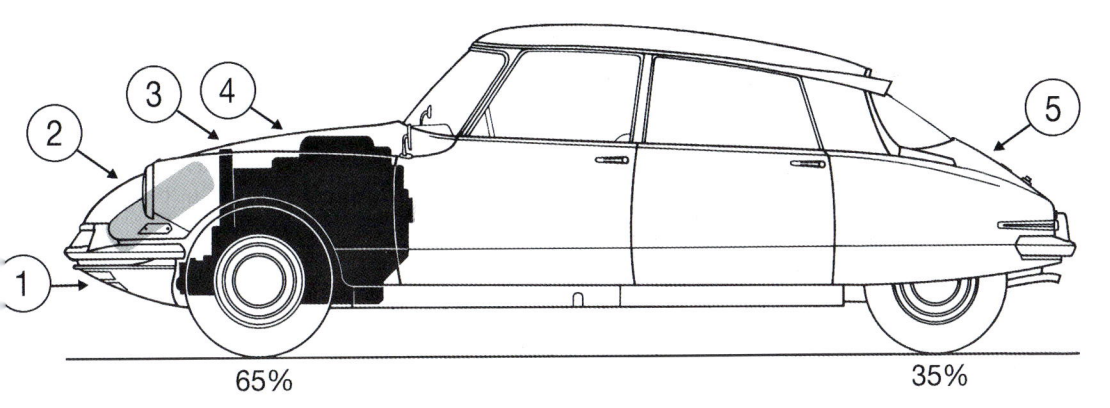

As with all the cars Lefebvre created for Citroën, the DS carried most of its weight on the front axles. Even with four people and their luggage on board, weight distribution was 60/40. This was the secret of its excellent stability, even at high speeds and in strong side winds. 1 Cooling. 2 Spare wheel. 3 Radiator. 4 Engine. 5 Luggage compartment.

Having most of the weight of a car on the front wheels is excellent for straight-line stability, though during fast cornering will cause strong understeer, which means that the front has a tendency to drift to the outside of a curve. The narrow rear track, in combination with the smaller tyres and low roll-centre of the trailing link rear suspension, somewhat counterbalances this understeer behaviour.

It must be said that, in Lefebvre's engineering vision, the main purpose of rear wheels – apart from keeping the car rolling on the road surface – was to ensure directional stability, somewhat like the vertical airfoil (rudder) at the tail of an airplane. In fact, the rear wheels of the DS were so lightly loaded that the car could be driven on one rear wheel only. The improved safety this provided was dramatically demonstrated on August 22, 1962 when an attempt was made to assassinate Général De Gaulle at Le Petit Clamart. Bullets punctured a rear tyre of his presidential DS, but the chauffeur managed to drive the car out of the ambush. Not surprisingly, Citroën used the phenomenon that a DS could be driven on only three wheels in publicity material.

There is still another example of Lefebvre's capacity to have his team find technical solutions offering more than one advantage. The windscreen wipers on the DS fall below the bonnet line when not in use, due, of course, to his preoccupation with reducing aerodynamic drag. But this was also a safety feature as, together with the low and plunging bonnet, these tucked-away windscreen wipers would limit injury should the car hit a cyclist or pedestrian.

HYDRO-PNEUMATIC SUSPENSION

The way that the suspension units of the DS were attached at both ends of the floor section of the passenger compartment bore the typical Lefebvre trademark. However, the suspension elements as such were certainly revolutionary, consisting of metal spheres in which Nitrogen gas was compressed by membranes activated by an hydraulic fluid under pressure; hence the term hydro-pneumatic. This system not only provided the possibility of interaction between the front and rear suspension, it also offered a number of other advantages.

The suspension units and the rest of the hydro-pneumatic master system installations were developed by Paul Magès, who, before being employed at the Bureau d'Etudes, had worked with Antoine Hermet at the Super Control department. There, one of his tasks was to find a solution for customer complaints concerning the brakes of the front-wheel drive TUBs.

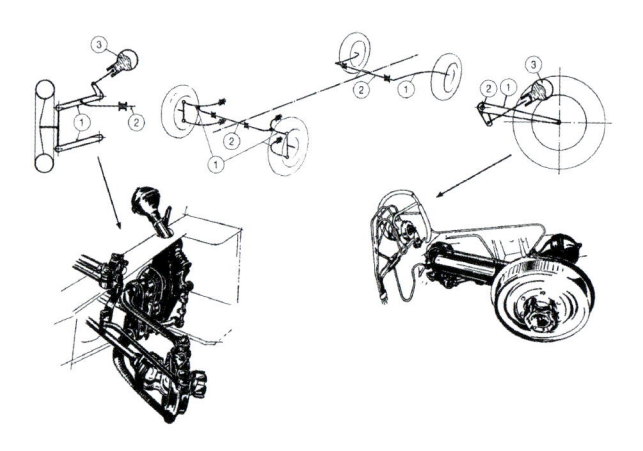

Schematic illustration of the independent front and rear suspension. 1 Suspension arms. 2 Torsion bar stabilisers. 3 Hydro-pneumatic spheres. The rear suspension units have single trailing arms. Those at the front consist of a pair of transverse links of equal length. All four units, including their hydro-pneumatic spheres, are bolted onto the body-cum-chassis structure. (Courtesy Revue Automobile (CH) & Citroën Communication)

With little or no cargo on board, insufficient weight on the rear wheels meant that the rear brakes tended to lock, which diminished stopping power and could also cause a nasty skid. As early as 1942 Magès found a remedy for this deficiency by designing a clever device that regulated hydraulic pressure to the rear brake cylinders, depending on the weight carried by the rear suspension. This brake force limiter was used for the first time on Citroën trucks with dual rear axles.

Pierre Boulanger was very impressed with this ingenious solution and transferred Magès to Citroën's Bureau d'Etudes, where he became known as 'Monsieur Hydraulique.' Although Paul Magès was 14 years younger, André Lefebvre warmed to his eager enthusiasm and appreciated the way he approached technical problems. Besides, Magès worked fast and used simple means to get things done. He was no dreamer, but a practical man, even if some of his colleagues thought his ideas too far-fetched. In this respect, Lefebvre discovered in Magès a kindred spirit and so they got on quite well.

Magès the magician

As he had to leave school when just 17 because his parents could not afford further study for him, Magès had no formal engineering training. By reading all of the literature he could find in technical libraries, however, he taught himself everything there was to know about hydraulics, braking and wheel suspension. He became obsessed by the idea of creating a suspension that would be supple when driving slowly, but would get firmer when speed increased. Once he discovered that air has approximately 500 times the flexibility of steel, he began experimenting with hydro-pneumatic suspensions.

In 1944, a prototype Deux Chevaux with a simple version of this system was ready to be tested. Sadly, it broke down within 20 minutes. However, Magès improved his design and in 1946 Boulanger, Lefebvre and Magès took another prototype to the 'torture stretch' at La-Ferté-Vidame. This time the hydro-pneumatic suspension functioned without fault and the car coped perfectly with all the irregularities of the test track. The system was too expensive to use in the 2CV and Boulanger asked Paul Magès if he could develop this type of suspension for a larger car.

Magès and Lefebvre then wondered: "Why only the suspension?" and Magès began working on a central hydro-pneumatic system that would also assist function of the steering, clutch, gear change and brakes.

Years later Citroën's PDG, Robert Puiseux, remembered that one day he went to La-Ferté-Vidame to join the test team. "At the proving grounds, one of the engineers offered to let me try a Traction which was fitted with a new, experimental suspension. When driving the car I discovered that it was much more comfortable than my own

Citroën. It absorbed road irregularities like a flying carpet and was very stable in curves. It was my first experience with the system that was soon after fitted on the rear wheels of the six-cylinder Traction H. [H for hydro-pneumatic.]

"Returning from my test drive I saw André Lefebvre and told him that, in my opinion, our new VGD should be equipped with a similar suspension. He looked at me thoughtfully, then grinned and said: 'Imagine, if we added a central high pressure system, we could also use it for power steering, power-assisted brakes and to provide a semi-automatic clutch which could help to make gear changing easier.' I asked him when I could try it and he replied: 'Give us four months.'"

Braking with a 'mushroom'

Paul Magès told Roger Brioult that one of his first long test drives with hydro-pneumatic-activated brakes nearly ended in disaster: "Lefebvre and I were both driving our 11CV Tractions on the winding roads of the Gorges du Verdon in the south of France. Lefebvre always drove very fast, especially on routes with a lot of bends, as long straight stretches were no challenge to him. But this time I was in front, as my car had the experimental power-assisted brakes and Lefebvre wanted to see if I could brake later than he did.

"Then, on a rather steep descent, I touched the brake pedal and it went all the way down to the floor. Of course, I started pumping, but at first nothing happened! I tried the handbrake as well, but was still going much too fast for the next bend. Suddenly the brakes gripped and the car came to a screeching halt. Heaven was really with me that time."

Afterwards, Magès tried to reconstruct what had happened. The high pressure pipe had sprung a leak, but that had little to do with the incident. He had been braking regularly over some distance so the brakes were already hot. Probably the brake linings were near fading temperature. The brakes only started to function again after he had repeatedly pushed the brake pedal to its very limit. Even without any further hydraulic pressure the leading brake shoes then stayed in contact with the brake drums because their friction produced so much heat that they locked together. Magès: "The drums were, in fact, so hot that I had to wait for nearly an hour before I could dismantle them. The brake shoe return springs came down in pieces and the brake cups had completely melted. I did indeed have a narrow escape, but I learned a lot from this mishap. The broken pressure pipe was just an unfortunate coincidence. But the 'free travel' of the brake pedal worried me a lot. That is why, for my own Traction, I designed a braking device that acted more directly."

This 'pédalo' – the small, mushroom-shaped brake 'pedal' – caused heated controversy within Citroën's technical department, and Magès admitted that he, too, had his doubts. Lefebvre also found it too revolutionary, as even the most experienced test drivers – including himself – did not easily get used to the feel of it. However, when Tudoux, one of the test drivers, reported that the immediate action of this brake 'mushroom' during an emergency stop had saved the lives of two children, most critics were won over. The advantage of this little 'knob' was that, contrary to a conventional brake pedal, it had practically no free travel, and thus effectively reduced the time and distance required to stop.

Terrissole

Testing of the various new features of the future DS required a great number of prototypes. Some of these looked like ordinary Tractions, whilst others used the bodies of other makes. An American Kaiser Henry J model, for instance, served as a rolling testbed for Becchia's new six-cylinder engines. Because La-Ferté-Vidame had only

At the family property, Terrissole, André Lefebvre's daughter-in-law, Jeanine Lefebvre, took this unique photo of a prototype that was secretly undergoing testing in the South of France.

limited possibilities for trying out cars at high speeds, and none for climbing, the prototypes were often driven on the Routes Nationales to the south of France and Lefebvre's property, which became a sort of unofficial test centre. It was a perfect hideaway; a rather secluded location far enough from the busy Mediterranean coast to prevent visits from curious tourists. Nearby, an abandoned freight depot that had once served the Draguignan-Grasse railway allowed the unloading of prototypes transported from Paris in lorries. A real advantage of this area was that, within a range of about 40 kilometres, there were plenty of hills and mountains. There was little traffic on local roads, so one could drive a car practically unobserved from sea level to heights of over 1000m. Besides – and this was very important – contrary to the well-known testing ground of La-Ferté-Vidame, the press was not (yet) aware of the fact that Citroën engineers sometimes tried out their secret prototypes around Terrissole. But that was about to change ...

Martians in the Var

It is a matter of local folklore now, but one day in the early fifties a photographer working for the regional newspaper *Nice Matin* received a tip that strange-looking vehicles were moving at great speed on the rural roads around Figanières in the nearby department Var. Could it be Martians on a reconnaissance tour? He went to the area indicated and, although he did not see any extraterrestrial beings, took some shots of an object that looked like a fast-moving tent on four wheels.

His editor published the photos and that particular issue of *Nice Matin* awakened the interest of the editorial staff of the Paris-based *l'Autojournal*. Founded in 1949 by Robert Hersant, this car magazine had an editorial formula based on critical road tests and investigative journalism, in direct contrast to the traditional French motoring press that was reputed to 'never bite the hand that fed it.' In other words, it hardly ever published anything that could displease its advertisers.

L'Autojournal – which had practically no branch-related advertising – was independent and aggressive. To inform its readers and increase circulation, it endeavoured to reveal the secret projects of the major car manufacturers. As soon as its managing editor, Gilles Guérithault (nicknamed Monsieur Scoop), saw the photos in *Nice Matin*, he dispatched some reporters and photographers to the south of France to find out more about this mysterious machine.

Lefebvre's son, Michel, who in those days worked for the Citroën test team and often stayed at Terrissole, clearly remembers what happened: "We drove in convoy, one ordinary Traction in front, one in the rear with the prototype between them. A canvas camouflage shroud hid the body that Bertoni had designed. Because of its unusual, rounded (aerodynamic) shape and grey paint, the men at the Bureau d'Etudes named it 'l'hippopotame' [hippo]. Suddenly, we all had to stop because another car came from a side road and blocked our way. The doors of this car flew open and men, armed with cameras, sprang from it. It was like a gangster film. They ran in our direction to take photos of our prototype. I was young and strong then, so I tried to prevent this. I grabbed one of them, his camera smashed on the pavement and I kicked it away. Its case flung open and I seized the film. He then tried to hit me, but the other test drivers came to my rescue, the men sprinted back to their car ... and fled. I think it, too, was a black Traction. "When my father, who was working in Paris, heard about the incident he was furious."

L'AUTOJOURNAL UNVEILS 'LA BOMBE CITROËN'

On 1 April 1952, *l'Autojournal* published a few pictures similar to those which had appeared in *Nice Matin*; two months later the magazine came out with a cover story about what it called 'La Bombe Citroën.' Its revealing 'scoop' had no photos, but did have a large and detailed cutaway drawing done by René Bellu, a brilliant illustrator who obviously knew quite a lot about automobile design. The article claimed that the car spotted in the Draguignan area had an air-cooled six-cylinder engine, but recently another prototype had been more closely examined near La Ferté-Vidame, and this was water-cooled. When Michel Lefebvre read this, he burst out laughing because the car *l'Autojournal* had tried to photograph near Terrissole also had a water-cooled engine, but as one of the exhaust gaskets had blown, it made a sound that could be mistaken for an air-cooled one.

However, for Citroën's management the publication was no laughing matter, as the drawing was uncannily close to reality and the description contained much factual information. Citroën decided to launch a judicial complaint against *l'Autojournal*, accusing it of industrial espionage. As a result, police invaded the headquarters of the magazine, confiscated dossiers – and even arrested a few editors for questioning! They were soon released, but other magazines and newspapers took up the story, and both *l'Autojournal* and Citroën got an enormous amount of free publicity.

No boxer

There was one thing the magazine did get wrong and this it could not help. *L'Autojournal* predicted that the new Citroën D would be a 10CV with a six-cylinder boxer engine, mounted ahead of the front axle. However, that was not to be.

As a matter of fact, Lefebvre did indeed originally plan such an arrangement, and had Becchia design an air-cooled and a water-cooled six-cylinder. With the former, Becchia and his assistant, Corner, ran into problems with cooling the second (middle) cylinder on each side. Another weak point of the air-cooled six was its noise: the mechanical clatter when cold and the whine of the fan were considered unacceptable for a car in the price category for which the new Citroën was intended, and is why development of the water-cooled six received priority.

Some say that this water-cooled six-cylinder was abandoned because it was too heavy. Apparently, bench tests showed that it also developed nearly 20bhp less than Beccia had promised. It seems that André Lefebvre was very disappointed by its performance and told Becchia so in no uncertain terms. Michel Lefebvre believes that solving the problem was just a question of time and money: mainly the latter. As one of the test drivers he tried out various six-cylinders and still does not think that there was much wrong with these 1.8-litre machines; all they needed was a little more development. He remembered that Becchia had experimented with two carburettors – one for each cylinder bank. Some of these more powerful engines were fitted in prototypes that were clocked at over 160km/h on a long straight road near Salon-de-Provence in the Rhône valley.

At any rate, in 1953 Citroën's management ordered the Bureau d'Etudes to stop all development work on the six-cylinder boxer for the time being and to revert to the faithful 'four' of the Traction. Probably, the Citroën management had finally realised that the production of a water-cooled six cylinder needed a far greater investment than first calculated, when it was still assumed that many parts for the air-cooled six could be manufactured with the same machine tools already in use for the air-cooled Deux Chevaux engine. Another problem was that implementation of the extra equipment needed for mass-production of a water-cooled six could take several more months, and cause further delay in the launching of the DS.

If Lefebvre could understand the point of view of his bosses, he was nevertheless quite upset, as the forward-mounted flat six was very much a part of his concept. But he had to accept the decision, even if it meant that he and his team were forced to redesign much of the car's front structure.

In the end the DS never got its flat six. The vertical four-in-line proved economical in production, offered acceptable if not brilliant performance, reasonable fuel consumption and great reliability. Besides, the DS was never a big money-maker as Citroën's management always refused to shell out the capital needed for the manufacture of a six-cylinder.

At the time of the decision to retain the four cylinder everyone at Citroën realised that the 'old' Traction engine was short on power. It is rumoured that Walter Beccia's assistant, Charles Poillot, made all the drawings for the new cylinder head in just eight days. This sounds incredible but not impossible, considering that the design of this new cylinder head was based on the same engineering principles Becchia had used whilst at Talbot. This new cylinder head was not made of cast iron, but of cast aluminium – a better heat conductor. Above all, it had (still push rod-operated) overhead valves 'inclined' under a V angle to give hemispherical (cross-flow) combustion chambers. Compression ratio was raised to 7.5:1. Together with other modifications, power output went up from 60bhp at 4000rpm to 75bhp at 4500rpm. The next step was to adapt the new, full synchromesh four-speed gearbox.

BACK TO THE DRAWING BOARD

Contrary to the flat six, the higher and heavier four-in-line machine could not be mounted in front of the gearbox/transmission unit. For one thing, it would not fit under the plunging bonnet that was so vital for aerodynamic reasons, and also there would be too much weight too high in the

For the DS engine Walter Becchia repeated the trick he had developed at Lago Talbot: he designed a new – state of the art – cylinder head, with pushrods operating the inlet and exhaust valves that were situated at an angle in the hemispherical combustion chambers. This new cylinder head was fitted on the lower end of the well-proven cilnder block that his predecessor had created in 1933 for the Traction. Becchia's construction improved the performance at minimal cost. (Courtesy Citroën Communication)

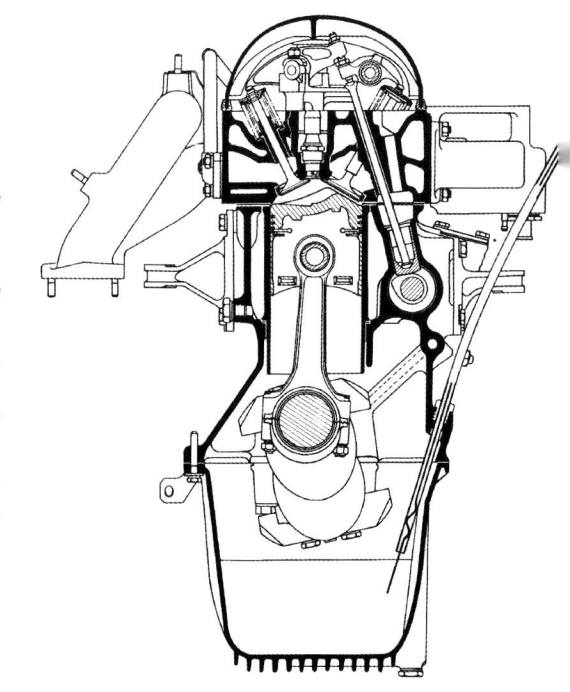

The decision to abandon the six-cylinder boxer and revert to the faithful four-cylinder block of the TA (again fitted behind the transmission) made it necessary to press a hole in the top of the firewall to allow removal of the number four sparkplug. (Courtesy Citroën Communication)

nose, thus spoiling Lefebvre's ideal centre of gravity.

All this frustrated Lefebvre more than the fact that the new car would have two cylinders less than originally planned. He was never very interested in engines, as long as they delivered the power required, but the change in engine position meant that the front part of the chassis structure had to be adapted to accommodate the vertical four-cylinder, which – as in the Traction – had to be located behind the differential, with the gearbox in front. The 'cradle' in which the four-cylinder was to be placed and the firewall between the engine and the passenger compartment had to be modified. Lefebvre could not prevent the rear of the engine once again intruding into the passenger front footwell; besides, it was necessary to press a hole in the monocoque structure, just in front of the windscreen in order to reach the sparkplug of the number four cylinder. Although these changes were quite drastic, they had advantages as well: now, the spare wheel could be moved from the rear of the car to the front of the radiator, which not only allowed a larger luggage compartment, but also gave the weight distribution Lefebvre had aimed for – two thirds of the mass resting on the front wheels.

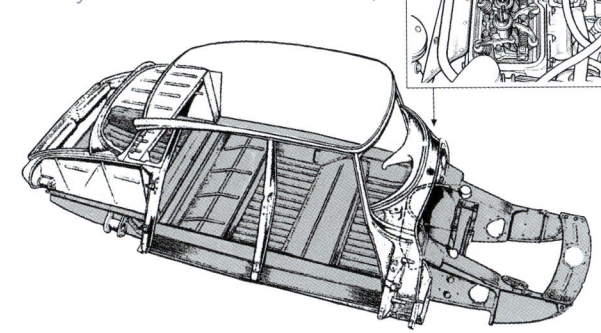

Of course, the body panels at the front – bonnet, bumpers, mudguards, and undershield – had also to be completely redesigned, a task that was entrusted to Bertoni and his team.

It was not the first time that Bertoni had to adapt his design, and neither would it be the last. In early 1955, and with the front end already accepted by the management, he modified the roofline, and, with a single masterstroke, gave the DS its unique styling. He raised the roof at the back over the large (Perspex) rear window, and prolonged the gutters to have them ending in what looked like small ice-cream cones. His assistant, Bosse, came up with the idea of fitting the rear direction indicators in them, giving the illusion that the DS was equipped with two very small rockets!

There were two reasons for this restyling: it improved headroom at the back and, at the same time, made the DS look completely different from the competition. This last consideration was probably the more important for Bertoni. At various motor shows during the previous autumn, he had noted that the fastback

About six months before the new Citroën was to be introduced, Bertoni decided to change the roofline at the rear. There were two reasons for this: he felt that the fastback style was going out of fashion, and he had also discovered that some rear passengers needed more headroom. His modification was a stroke of genius and gave the DS its characteristic appearance. (Courtesy Citroën Communication)

style (Peugeot 203, Ford Vedette) was going out of fashion; all the latest models had a notchback rear end with a pronounced luggage compartment. He must have been very satisfied to see that the famous Italian coachbuilder Pininfarina shared his views, as became clear when he introduced the remarkable Lancia Florida. This concept car would set the style for the future Lancia Flaminia, and later for the Peugeot 404 and the BMC range.

Bertoni finished his restyling operation barely six months before the planned introduction. But, as it did not involve too much retooling, his boss, Pierre Bercot, was so pleased with the result that he did not grumble.

A GODDESS ON THE STREETS OF PARIS

On Thursday October 6, 1955, at about eight o'clock in the morning, a brand new DS19 nosed its way out of one of the gates of the Citroën factory at the Quai de Javel.

It was probably the first time that a production DS19 mingled with the brisk Paris rush-hour traffic. At the steering wheel sat Paul Magès, with André Lefebvre next to him and, behind them, Jean Cadiou and Roger Prud'homme. Before they got into the DS Lefebvre had given Magès the keys saying: "You drive it. It's your baby as much as mine." That was Lefebvre's way of showing his great appreciation for Magès and for everything he had done to develop the most advanced suspension system ever.

On one of the Boulevards they were overtaken by an expensive chauffeur-driven limousine, with a good-looking lady in the back seat. While the limousine was passing them, she gave them a big smile and a thumbs up sign of approval.

Later that morning the French president, René Coty, being driven in his black Citroën 15 with a custom-made body by French coachbuilder Franay, arrived at the Grand Palais for the official opening of the Salon de l'Automobile. There, the new Citroën DS19 – which the media already called La Déesse (the Goddess) – made its public début.

STAR OF THE SHOW

The DS was the undisputed star of that year's Paris Motor Show. Media attention had been overwhelming as everyone wanted to see this revolutionary motorcar. The stand on which the new Citroëns were exhibited attracted so many visitors that it was almost impossible to approach the cars, though this did not discourage eager buyers, as the first day alone some 12,000 orders were taken; at the end of the show, Citroën had registered 80,000 potential customers.

The DS was indeed a totally new automobile concept. Apart from streamlined styling, panoramic windshield with its thin pillars, luxuriously soft seats, light interior and single-spoke steering wheel, its new hydro-pneumatic system was an absolute novelty as, up until then, the automobile industry had used hydraulics mainly for brakes, power steering, and in fully automatic transmissions.

On the same October morning that Lefebvre and Mages left the Quai de Javel to drive their DS on its maiden trip through the Paris traffic, photographers of Paris Match *were waiting outside the factory gates. The following weekend the popular weekly had an eight-page photo spread with the title: "Citroën has no secrets anymore." (Courtesy* Paris Match*)*

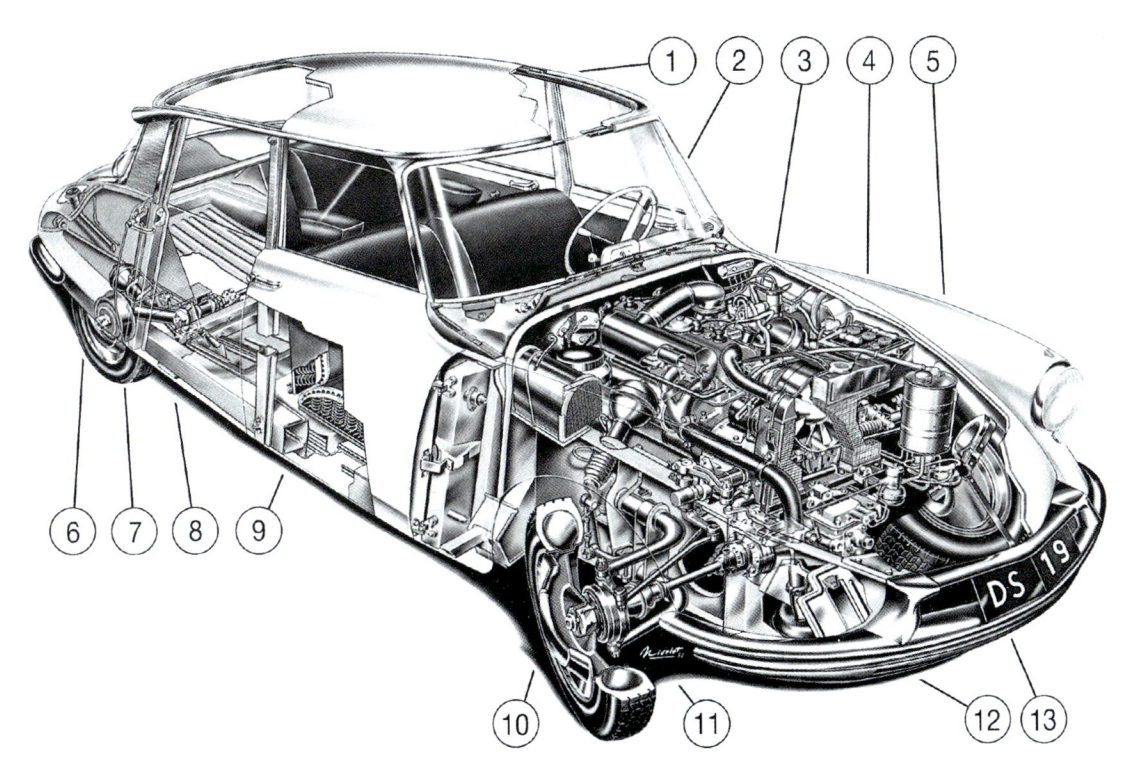

Under its futuristic exterior the 1955 DS was also full of surprises ... 1 Plastic roof panel. 2 Hydraulically-assisted steering. 3 Engine with hemispherical combustion chambers. 4 Battery under the bonnet. 5 Reservoir for the hydro-pneumatic system. 6 Smaller tyre size and reduced track at the rear. 7 Rear mudguards easily removable for wheel changes. 8 Self-levelling hydro-pneumatic rear suspension. 9 Strong steel side members for passenger safety (see also drawing of chassis structure). 10 Hydro-pneumatic front suspension. 11 Front wheel drive / double (Hooke) transmission joints. 12 Inboard front disk brakes. 13 Spare wheel in the nose. (Drawing by Charles Nivelet)

In the late fifties the Caravelle, an aeroplane that could carry 80 passengers, and the Citroën DS were considered icons of innovative French engineering and technology. Sud Aviation produced a total of 282 Caravelles and Citroën nearly one-and-a-half million DS and ID cars. (Courtesy Citroën Communication)

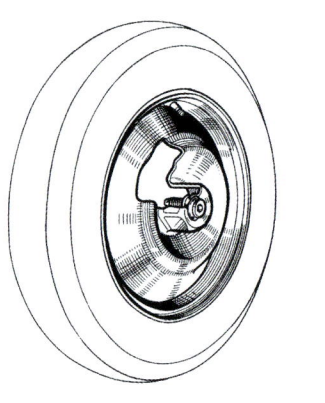

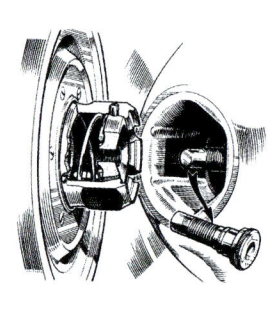

DS wheels have only one single fixing bolt which pulls outward a conically-shaped plug in the 'split' hexagonal hub, thus expanding the hub and thereby locking the wheel onto it. The system was designed and developed in close collaboration with engineers from Michelin. (Courtesy Revue Automobile (CH) & The Motor (UK))

The new Citroën had hydraulically-assisted steering, a hydraulically-controlled automatic clutch, a hydraulically-operated gearbox, hydraulically-assisted brakes, and a device that distributed braking power to the drum brakes at the rear, depending on the load on the rear wheels.

The hydro-pneumatic suspension allowed the driver to select three different chassis heights, which not only facilitated driving in snow but also changing a wheel in case of a flat tyre. A jack was not required as the hydraulic system would lift the car. The wheels were held by a single wheel nut; a system comparable to the so-called 'knock off' hubs on racing and sports cars.

Thanks to its unique body shape it looked like something from outer space. When a DS stopped in a street it drew gaping crowds, which were even more astonished when passengers got in at the back and the self-levelling suspension slowly lifted the car.

The press raved about the model, with some journalists calling it the 'Car of the Century.' The British magazine *The Motor* wrote: "This new Citroën caused enough effect to leave the rest of the Paris Show flat on its face."

No one at Citroën had expected such an overwhelming success, and demand exceeded their wildest dreams.

In the euphoria that followed, the management decided to speed up manufacturing

That the aerodynamic qualities of the DS equalled the aesthetic impact of its sculptured shape was, of course, the result of the close cooperation between engineer Lefebvre and Citroën's gifted stylist Flaminio Bertoni. Due to a drag coefficient of only 0.326, the DS – with its 1911cc engine developing some 75bhp – could attain a top speed of 150km/h. (These photos of a DS scale model during wind tunnel tests are published with kind permission of the Office National d'Etudes et de Recherches Aérospatiales at Châtillon in France, and by courtesy of Studio Kees-Jan Smit, 2064 XR Spaarndam NL)

The sloping bonnet and typical sturgeon's snout helped to reduce air resistance: the air needed for engine cooling was drawn onto the radiator via ducts in the protection shield on the underside of the bumper. At speed, this becomes a pressure zone.

and begin delivery right away. This decision was ill-advised, though, as the unprecedented and complicated hydro-pneumatic system of the DS was totally new. As the DS had for so long been a jealously-guarded secret, only a handful of people at the factory understood how it worked and knew what could go wrong. And things did go wrong in a big way in an emphatic demonstration of Murphy's Law: "If anything can go wrong, it will!"

OLIVE OIL

One of the main problems with the early cars was that they lost their 'lifeblood,' the hydraulic fluid, through leaks in the pipeline connections. When this happened a number of vital functions ceased: no more suspension, no more clutch, no more gear change, no brake assistance, and no power steering either. Apparently, the prototypes never suffered from those mishaps ...

According to Jacques Né, who, since 1951, was closely involved in testing and developing the DS, there were three problems: the quality of the hydraulic fluid, insufficient training of the workers on the assembly lines, and quality of the joints which, for the prototypes, had been provided by Lockheed, whilst first production models used another supplier.

A complicating factor was that the mechanics of most Citroën dealers did not know how to cope with these teething troubles. Viewing the engine compartment for the first time, they shied away, calling it 'a plumber's nightmare.' Besides, in the early days, the special synthetic oil (LHS, or liquide hydraulique synthétique) was extremely difficult to obtain.

Michel Lefebvre, in 1955 still part of Citroën's test team, had a rather comical adventure with one of the first production cars.

"I was asked to take a DS19 to the South of France. The Citroën dealer in Cannes had ordered the car for a very, very important VIP. There were no motorways yet, so I took the familiar RN 7 and was cruising happily along at about 90km/h when I felt the suspension giving way and the steering becoming heavy.

"As a precaution I had put a tin of LHS fluid in the boot and I knew what to do. I topped up the hydraulic reservoir and continued on my way. But after only some seventy kilometres the same problem occurred: and again fifty kilometres. By now my tin was nearly empty, so I drove very slowly to a service station. There they regretfully informed me that the special hydraulic fluid I needed was not commercially available yet, but I could use their phone to call the nearest Citroën dealer. That dealer could not help me either. Then I phoned Paris. When I had explained the situation to my boss, Roger Prud'homme, he advised me to go to the nearest grocery shop and buy a few large tins of the purest olive oil I could find. I had to stop the car several times to refill the reservoir. But thanks to the olive oil I reached my destination without further problems.

"Evidently, the dealer in Cannes was not too pleased when I delivered the car and told him what had happened. Not only did he have to find and repair the leak(s), he also had to flush out and purge the entire hydraulic system before filling it again with the LHS. I

Last engine check on an assembly line. The DS was at this point still a skeleton with engine, transmission, the hydro-pneumatic system and wheels. Roof and body panels were fitted later on. (Courtesy Citroën Communication)

Even today neither shape nor performance of the DS is outdated, a tremendous compliment to André Lefebvre, Flaminio Bertoni and all the others at Citoën's Bureau d'Etudes, who created this car over fifty years ago. (Courtesy Citroën Communication)

don't know if his client ever found out that his car had been driven on olive oil."

These early problems had repercussions on sales, as it took much longer than expected for the factory to deliver the planned number of cars. As a result, waiting lists grew steadily longer which, together with the problems associated with the first cars, caused many prospective customers to cancel their orders.

In due course all teething troubles were resolved and the DS took its place as a symbol of French ingenuity in the field of automobile engineering. When president Charles de Gaulle chose one for his personal transport, the DS became the official car for the ministries. The préfectures soon followed, and even outside France the qualities of this prestigious Citroën model were acknowledged. Paul Magès must have been proud when, in 1965, Rolls-Royce bought a licence from Citroën for the suspension of its new Silver Shadow.

During the twenty years of manufacture, 1,456,115 DS and IDs were produced.

CHAPTER

ELEVEN
NOT FOR SALE

The reputation of the revolutionary DS – and the team of technicians that had designed and developed it – spread outside of Europe. Philippe Lefebvre remembers a visit to their family residence in L'Etang-la-Ville by the editor-in-chief of one of Britain's leading motoring magazines, with an American colleague. It was not long after the DS was launched and he, Philippe, must have been six years old at the time. He was allowed to join the adults at lunch, which was served on the terrace outside the house. Both guests spoke French so he could easily follow the conversation. "The British journalist was full of praise for the qualities of the latest Citroën, and complimented my father on this achievement. Suddenly, the American said: 'Monsieur Lefebvre, I have been empowered by the Board of General Motors to offer you a position as Director of Engineering at their Technical Centre.' He pulled a cheque book from his jacket, put it in front of my father and continued: 'You can fill in the salary you want and the job is yours.' My father jumped up from the table and exclaimed indignantly: 'Tell your bosses that I am not for sale, I am not merchandise.'"

Lefebvre later told his son it was not the first time that someone had tried to lure him away from his employer and his team. Apparently, just before WWII, Professor Ferdinand Porsche had tried to persuade him to join his Engineering Consultancy Group, even inviting him to visit the new plant where his Porsche Typ 62, better known as the KDF (Volkswagen) 'Kübelwagen' was to be manufactured. At the time it must have been a tempting offer, but André Lefebvre remained loyal to his colleagues and friends at Citroën and Michelin.

Monique (left) and André seated next to his cousin, Annemarie, enjoying a quiet family lunch. According to his sons, their father made the table and the folding bench himself, using aluminium and plastics. (Courtesy Collection family Lefebvre)

CHAPTER TWELVE

THE COCCINELLE PROJECT

In 1953 – that is to say about two years before the introduction of the DS – André Lefebvre was already working on a new project.

It all began with the idea of a super Deux Chevaux which would cruise at over 100km/h. Boulanger's original (prewar) brief had been explicit: the 2CV was destined for use in rural areas and, at the time, in rural areas, a top speed of around 65km/h was considered sufficient. But times were changing, and Lefebvre and his bosses were convinced that, within a few years, there would be a substantial market for a family car that would be faster than the 2CV, though just as frugal on fuel, but lighter and less expensive than the luxurious DS. Valid arguments supported their vision, such as the booming postwar economy and plans for a network of fast toll roads in France.

In 1946, the French had inaugurated their first motorway. This Autoroute de l'Ouest (today, part of the A13 or Autoroute de Normandie) connected Paris (Porte de Saint-Cloud) to Rouen, and, within a few years had become a very popular and intensively used road. It considerably helped industrial development of the Seine valley and permitted Parisians to go for quick weekend trips to the Normandy coast, which explains why, in the 1950s, the French government was setting up regional organisations to finance, build and operate similar motorways (toll roads) to connect Paris with other parts of France.

The car Lefebvre had in mind was, in fact, the result of all the theories, experiences and convictions he had accumulated during his 35 years as an automobile engineer: an ultra-light, very aerodynamic, front-wheel drive four-seater, with plenty of room for luggage and/or children, powered by a small engine and with most of its weight in front. This concept was so advanced that it exceeded everything Lefebvre had created before.

SHAPED LIKE A DROP OF WATER

The Cs (several prototypes were made) – also known as 'La Coccinelle' (ladybird) and sometimes 'Goutte d'Eau' (water drop) – began life as a research exercise, to establish how far it was possible to go with certain design parameters. At the time, Lefebvre did not rule out that Citroën might eventually want to manufacture such a car in the new factory it was building near Rennes.

Lefebvre formed a small task force for this project, consisting of two engineers: Estaque, responsible for the structure, implantation of the engine and the drivetrain, and Roche, responsible for the suspension and roadholding. Two technical draftsmen, Léonzi and Laurain, assisted them.

Although Lefebvre had a lot of respect for Bertoni's artistic talents, this time he

Lefebvre's last concept... His C, 'Coccinelle' or 'Goutte d'eau' was a very unorthodox and innovative automobile concept. It was not intended to serve as a show car for exhibition purposes, as so many of today's concept cars are. Lefebvre started the project in 1953 as a serious study for a future mid-range Citroën, and incorporated all his designer's talent and experience into it. The two surviving prototypes in the Conservatoire Citroën are a testimonial to Lefebvre's daring and unconventional approach in automobile engineering ideas. In the end, Citroën's commercial management considered it too advanced for its time. (Courtesy Hans Arend de Wit/Switchimage)

For easy access Lefebvre equipped his Coccinelle prototypes with large 'gull wing'-type roof panels and two small doors opening horizontally. (Courtesy Citroën Communication)

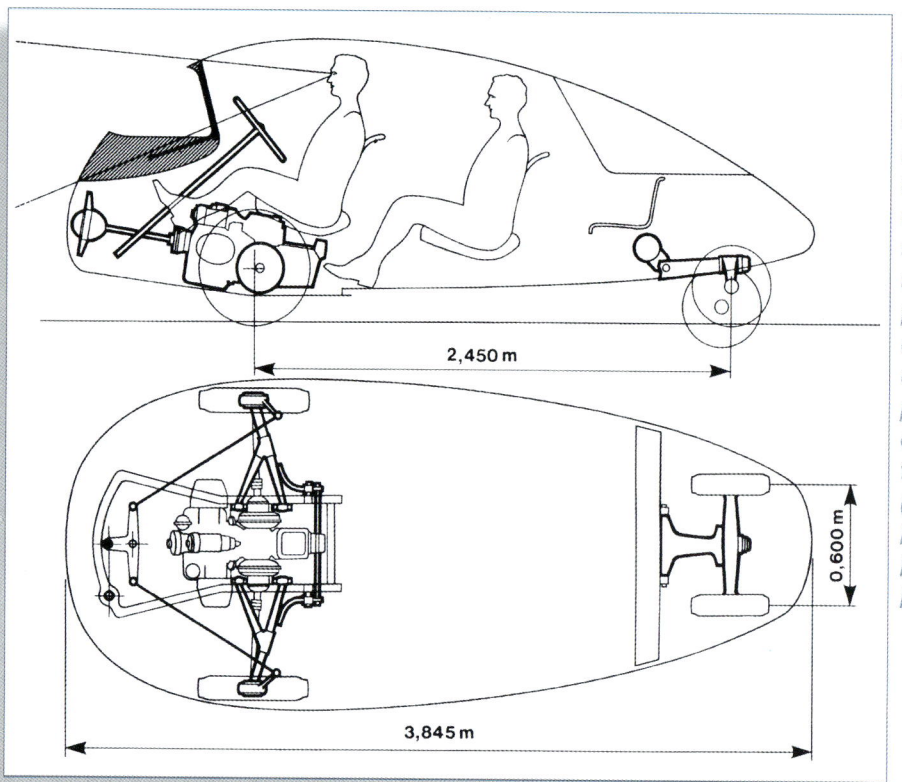

These drawings show the large front suspension, the narrow rear suspension, and the positions of the driver and passenger on top of the engine. (Courtesy Roger Brioult/Edifree)

The C was to be powered by an air-cooled twin, developed from the 2CV engine, so weight had to be reduced to a minimum. Note the backrest of the seats with a webbing of thin plastic wire, meant to be covered with a foam cushion. This prototype also has a single-spoke steering wheel, such as was used on the DS. (Courtesy Hans Arend de Wit/Switchimage)

From the side the C (it seems that there have been 10 prototypes) really looked like a raindrop, hence the nickname 'Goutte d'eau.' (Courtesy Citroën Communication)

wanted a more scientific approach to body design. Using logarithmic tables, Lefebvre, Léonzi and Laurain drew a shape that met their aerodynamic and aesthetic criteria. Lanoy, a colleague from another Citroën department and an enthusiastic mathematician, helped them with their complex calculations.

Apart from the engine, which, for economic reasons, had to be the 425cc flat twin of the Deux Chevaux AZ, the C was completely different from any other Citroën. The underside (chassis) of the car looked like a sort of shallow boat hull or large bathtub and was 3.60m long and 15cm deep. It was made up from duralumin (AU2G) sheet with cast alloy elements for reinforcement and for the suspension supports. In those days, welding light metal still posed practical problems as the thin oxide skin that always covers aluminium had to be cleaned and scoured just before such an operation. To circumvent this difficulty all these chassis components were glued together with Rédox, an epoxy product that had to be heated to 140 degrees. Although it was a revolutionary process for a car manufacturer, it could be used in mass-production. The streamlined body consisted of a light metal frame, covered by thin reinforced plastic panels. The first C, retrospectively named the C1, had huge 'gull wing' doors and a large canopy at the rear. This canopy and the side windows were made of Plexiglas or Perspex, a clear plastic much used in the aircraft industry since the war.

Perspex is light and practically unbreakable, but it scratches easily, which precluded the use of conventional windscreen wipers. However, Lefebvre and his team found a clever and original solution to this particular problem. The windscreen could be lowered and raised, the theory being that the driver could drop it slightly to look out through a small slit (just as in an armoured vehicle). The lower part of the windscreen then acted as a wind deflector carrying raindrops or snowflakes across the opening rather than through it, making a windscreen wiper superfluous. Estaque and Roche have assured Roger Brioult that it worked very well, and was a wonderful experience, especially when it snowed and the white flakes drifted up and away in front of one's eyes and disappeared over the top of the car. Brioult later discovered that Lefebvre's friend and mentor Gabriel Voisin had experimented with a similar idea on his 1949 Biscooter.

Even if on photos the C1 somewhat resembles a Messerschmitt 'cabinen roller' (bubble car), in reality it was a full-size passenger car with an original cab-forward body. Driver and front passenger sat just above the front wheels with the flat twin engine and transmission between them. Because of the aerodynamic roof line the rear seat was slightly lower than the seats in front. In the back there was room for luggage or two children. A hydro-pneumatic suspension system with three spheres – two for the front wheels and one at the rear – was developed by the engineer Bucan. The 12 inch front wheels were guided by wishbones and had inertia-type shock absorbers (batteurs). The wheelbase measured 2.45m, the front track 1.42m, and the rear track (trust Lefebvre!) just 60cm.

Too much understeer

During one of the trial runs at La-Ferté-Vidame, the first prototype overturned. Léonzi took all the blame, but Michel Lefebvre believes that it was his father who was driving. Both men left the wreck practically unscathed, although for some time André Lefebvre complained of stiffness in his neck. The cause of the accident was evident to everyone. With two aboard, the car had an exaggerated forward weight bias. Even under normal conditions it understeered, and during braking, this trait increased. Besides, the single suspension arm unit at the rear, called the 'Diabolo,' allowed the two small (8 inch) rear wheels not only to move up and down but also to swivel in order to follow road camber. This resulted in a self-steering effect, which did not help, either.

The C1 was so badly damaged that the Bureau d'Etudes had to build a second prototype with less weight on the front; then came a third ... and finally (in 1957) the C10, in which all of the design faults of the earlier experimental cars had been erased. The giant gull wing doors were replaced by roof panels that lifted upward, with, below them, two 'normal' doors that opened horizontally.

Those who have tested the C10 agree that it was pleasant to drive, with safe and predictable road behaviour. Its dry weight was just 382kg, top speed came to just over 110km/h, and cruising at 100km/h it used about the same amount of fuel as a 2CV did at 65km/h.

The soul was gone

It was a terrible shock for his collaborators at the Bureau d'Etudes when, in early July 1958, they learned that their 'patron,' André Levebvre, had been taken seriously ill and was partly paralysed. Estaque, Roche, Léonzi and Laurain bravely soldiered on and even finished the last prototype, but the project had clearly lost its soul. Although understandable, it is a pity that the C concept was then doomed to be shelved.

Without Lefebvre to defend the unconventional design and convince his superiors of the qualities and commercial possibilities of this futuristic car, Citroën's management decided not to take any risks. Instead, in 1961, Citroën introduced the Deux Chevaux-based Ami 6, with an air-cooled flat-twin engine, enlarged by Becchia to 602cc, and a body designed by Bertoni. Dry weight came to 620kg and it had a top speed of 105km/h. Within five years – and after the introduction of a five-door break version – it became the best-selling car in France.

On March 21, 2002, a commemorative plaque was unveiled at the rue du Théâtre, once the site of Citroën's Bureau d'Etudes, in honour of the men who created the automobiles that established the company's reputation as a trendsetting car manufacturer. A number of their descendants attended the ceremony. From left to right: Philippe Lefebvre, Guy Lefebvre, Michel Lefebvre, Jean-Michel Lefebvre (son of Michel), Alain Lefebvre, Leonardo Bertoni (eldest son of Flaminio), and, in the foreground, Bernard Citroën, André Citroën's eldest son. In the same 15th arrondissement, between the rue de la Convention and the rue Balard, can be found the rue André Lefebvre. Ironically, this is a pedestrian area. Automobiles – even Citroëns – are not allowed there. (Courtesy Jeanine Lefebvre)

POSTSCRIPT

André Lefebvre died on May 4, 1964, nearly six years after it was discovered that he suffered from hemiplegia, a condition which paralysed the right side of his body. Four days before his death he had enjoyed a picnic organised by his family to celebrate his turning sixty-nine and-a-half.

It illustrates Lefebvre's strong willpower that, when his doctors told him he would never again be able to use his right hand, he managed to teach himself to draw with his left. Fortunately, his brain was not damaged, although the paralysis seriously impaired his speech. Only his young son, Guy, and his grandson, Jean-Michel, sometimes managed to 'translate' some of the sounds he uttered. For someone who had always been very eloquent and who could explain the most complicated technical problems with a few well-chosen words, this was a terrible handicap. When his friends or former colleagues came to visit he communicated with them by writing short notes or showing them drawings.

By the end of July 1958, it had become clear that he would no longer be able to travel daily to Paris, so he quit his job with Citroën and stayed at home at 3 rue de la Garderie in L'Etang-la-Ville. As soon as he had mastered drawing with his left hand, he began working again, creating and inventing! Jacques Né, a close colleague and one of his successors at the Bureau d'Etudes, considered that some of the ideas Lefebvre developed during his illness were so outstanding that they should have been patented.

Notwithstanding the loving care of his wife, Monique, it was a depressing situation. All those who had previously worked with him found it difficult to look at him and see the sadness in his eyes. They remembered him as he had been before his illness: a strong and dynamic man, always on the move, bristling with new ideas, inspiring those around him; a brilliant and innovative engineer with a special way of approaching problems and challenges, who practised the process of 'lateral thinking' long before Edward de Bono invented the term.

André Lefebvre loved cars. He also loved designing them and driving them – fast. He did not like flying, though nonetheless remained true to his first love of aeronautical engineering, keeping in touch with the technical developments and production methods of the aviation industry. He was fascinated by the use of aluminium and duralumin, and by the application of real aerodynamics but he detested fashionable 'streamline' styling.

Lightness and effective streamlining were themes that dominated all his designs. After WWII, the many new man-made materials intrigued him, and his office and home were filled with objects made from acrylics, Perspex, fibreglass, nylon, and other synthetics. He was one of the first men in France to wear nylon shirts, and often visited Oyonnax in the department Ain, which was then the scientific centre of the French plastics industry.

His interest in and knowledge of these new materials explains why, for the DS, he not only used steel, cast iron, aluminium, stainless steel, zinc-aluminum-magnesium-copper alloys (Zamac) – and even two pieces of beech wood (to strengthen the towing hooks at the front) – but a roof made from glass-reinforced polyester, seats and carpeting of plastic foam covered with nylon jersey (cloth), a dashboard of solid (injected) nylon (Kralastic), and a – symmetrical – rear window of Plexiglas (Perspex). Many smaller parts were made from thermoplastics (nylon), polyvinyl chloride (PVC), polyamides (Rilsan), and polytetrafluoroethylene (Teflon). Most of these materials were chosen by Lefebvre and his colleagues in order to reduce weight or for their higher resistance to corrosion or mechanical wear.

André Lefebvre was born under the zodiac sign of Leo, and, from the many testimonials of all those who have known him, it is evident that he instinctively knew how to use his social skills. Women were attracted to him because of his sparkling eyes, but also, like most men, by his charming manners and quick wit. He was a born team leader, highly appreciated and well-liked by his peers and the majority of his colleagues, and many of them became his friends. He was a very warm and loyal person.

In their book about Flaminio Bertoni, the authors published an extract from a letter that the stylist wrote to Boulanger during his long stay in hospital, convalescing from his serious motor accident. In it Bertoni thanks Boulanger for the books that Lefebvre had brought him. His former colleagues agree that Lefebvre was considerate and always took good care of 'his' people, and not only when they were ill: if they had to work late he would arrange for a car to take them home.

However, it is no secret that he was also highly-strung and often nervous; he could, at times, be very bad-tempered, especially when he suspected that someone had neglected his job or had not told the truth. But he was never violent. His son Alain Lefebvre remembers that, once, when he was a young boy sitting alone in his father's Traction, he managed to release the handbrake. The car was parked on a slight hill and, with increasing speed, it rolled forward until a garden wall stopped it. His father, alarmed by the loud bang and the sound of crumpling metal, came running to the scene of the incident. He was raving mad, scolded Alain roundly, but did not spank him.

Alain also recalls that his father not only created trendsetting automobiles, but contemporary furniture, too. Once, he built a complete kitchen from aluminium and, for the living room, a very modern ceiling lamp using this same material. Then there were some ingenious toys that Lefebvre made, such as a kind of three-wheeled vehicle that his children used before they could walk properly. For their garden in the South of France he constructed a bench from aluminium profiles and, so it could stay out in winter, a webbing of plastic strings similar to the seats in the Coccinelle. "When Father was not toying with his slide rule or drawing, he was tinkering," says Alain. Lefebvre enjoyed working with his hands and was convinced that every engineer worthy of that name should be able to do the same.

Of course, Lefebvre – outspoken and from time-to-time sarcastic – had enemies as well. A few of his colleagues within the Citroën organisation were highly critical of him and of his achievements; they considered him too self-assured, even arrogant, and not the genius his successive bosses believed him to be. In their opinion Lefebvre's unbridled creativity was exaggerated; he always wanted to go too far. They also claimed that his obsession with unorthodox and unproved technology had cost the company fortunes, as both the Traction and the DS had at first been utterly unreliable. Such criticism is, of course, grossly unfair: Lefebvre was responsible only for the concept of these cars and not their production, nor for quality control. Perhaps they were simply jealous ...

It cannot be denied that Lefebvre's creations laid the foundations for Citroën's reputation as a technically advanced carmaker; besides, Citroën sold over 10 million units of the models Lefebvre and his team designed. There is no doubt that the standards of roadholding, comfort and fuel efficiency set by André Lefebvre's cars have influenced the automobile industry as a whole, and French manufacturers in particular.

Over the past fifty years the way cars are designed and built has changed considerably. Computer Aided Design and Computer Aided Manufacturing systems (CAD-CAM) have speeded the design process and enabled designers to visualise constructions without having to build a lot of prototypes. They can even simulate the operations on the production lines. The fierce competition in the motor industry has compelled the specialists in market research, product engineering, styling, manufacturing, marketing and sales to work closely together. Today's automakers not only have to respond to a constant evolution of the trends in the market, they have also to comply with numerous international and intergovernmental rules and regulations, such as limiting pollution during manufacturing and recycling processes, increasing passenger and pedestrian safety and, last but not least, reducing exhaust emissions by the development of cleaner engines. These have become the new challenges.

André Lefebvre worked in a previous era, a time when unorthodox and untried technical solutions led to innovations that paved the way for progress, a time when individual engineers with a clear vision could still put their personal stamp on the design and construction of automobiles.

In that respect Lefebvre was a real pioneer: a pioneer with a passion!

LEFEBVRE FAMILY TREE

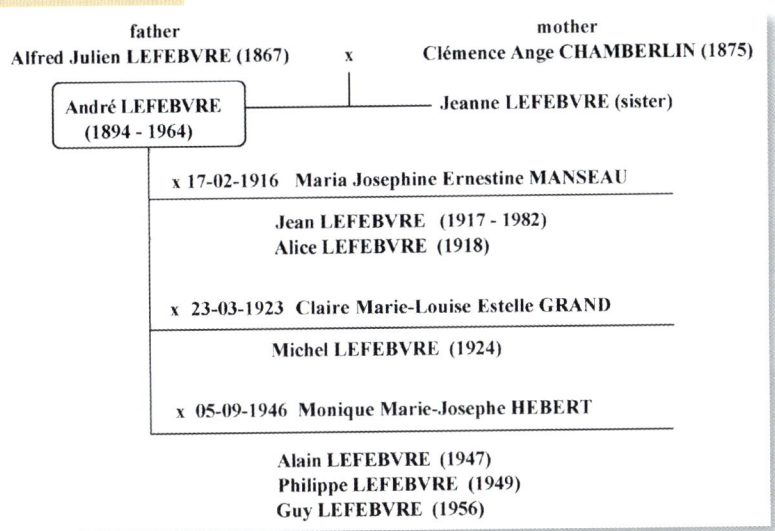

father: Alfred Julien LEFEBVRE (1867) x **mother**: Clémence Ange CHAMBERLIN (1875)

- André LEFEBVRE (1894 - 1964)
- Jeanne LEFEBVRE (sister)

x 17-02-1916 Maria Josephine Ernestine MANSEAU
- Jean LEFEBVRE (1917 - 1982)
- Alice LEFEBVRE (1918)

x 23-03-1923 Claire Marie-Louise Estelle GRAND
- Michel LEFEBVRE (1924)

x 05-09-1946 Monique Marie-Josephe HEBERT
- Alain LEFEBVRE (1947)
- Philippe LEFEBVRE (1949)
- Guy LEFEBVRE (1956)

HERITAGE

This passionate engineer has left a heritage of everlasting value. A great number of Tractions Avant, Deux Chevaux and DS/ID models have survived the ravages of time, and are cherished today by their owners as collector items or for daily use. By a recent estimate about 500 Citroën clubs worldwide have approximately 40,000 enthusiastic members. Citroën's current management considers these three icons of Lefebvre's creativity to be important milestones in the history of the company.

At the inauguration of the impressive new showroom on the Champs Elysées, these three 'old timers' had a place of honour among the company's latest flagships – and with good reason. A closer look at Citroën's most recent offerings, such as the C6, the C4 Picasso, the C-Crosser, and some futuristic show cars, reveals that they still carry traces of DNA from the Lefebvre/Bertoni era. Following a long tradition – and in direct contrast to some of their competitors – all have front-wheel drive, even the most prestigious models.

The latest Citroëns are technically advanced automobiles, with all the state-of-the-art electronic equipment and options available. Moreover, they also have an unmistakable and highly individualistic architecture that sets them apart from other cars in their category. The new C6, with its aerodynamic shape and uncluttered lines, has the subtle elegance of a French haute couture dress. Passers-by still stop to admire it, and, since its introduction in 2005, it has also become the benchmark for comfort and drivability. Just like the DS in its time, it is a worthy 'state carriage' for the Presidents of France.

If critics complain that because of all the safety and emission regulations – plus Citroën's own ambitions to equal teutonic quality – the C6 has put on so much weight that the performance of its smallest and most thrifty engine suffers, one can only remind them that the original DS19 was no sprinter either!

Citroën's design director, Jean-Pierre Ploué, and his team have shown they are true innovators, daring to make bold aesthetic statements. At the same time they manage to emphasise Citroën's traditional identity, without reverting to retro shapes. One explanation could be that Ploué's grandparents owned a Traction Avant, a DS and a Deux Chevaux; these cars must have made a strong impression on him when he was a boy. Be that as it may, the newly-designed C5 berline and break (station wagon) display a purity of line and sophisticated chic that will not only seduce faithful Citroën owners, but will also certainly attract other car buyers looking for style and comfort in the highly competitive premium class.

The will to discover and exploit new solutions is still very much alive at Citroën, as is illustrated by the C-Cactus concept car. Developed by Emmanuel Lafaury, who also designed the C-Métisse, the spectacular red metallic show car impressed thousands of visitors at numerous international motor shows with its sculptured shape. Diesel-powered hybrid technology and large gull wing front doors – plus swivelling rear doors – demonstrate that the C-Métisse was mainly intended as a futuristic vision of a four-seater Gran Turismo.

The C-Cactus has other ambitions: it is a research project meant to evaluate the possibilities of a truly ecological four-seater with a hybrid HDi drivetrain, eventually to be sold for the same price as an entry level family car.

To achieve this objective, the designers and engineers had to:
- simplify all mechanical parts
- combine several functions in a single component
- reduce the number of parts by leaving out everything that is not essential to the running of the car, or to the comfort and safety of its occupants

An example: the doors of Lafaury's C-Cactus consist of only two parts, whereas the doors of an average modern car have twelve. It all comes down to reinventing the automobile, starting with the basic needs of present day car owners. In many ways it is a process requiring wit, intelligence and the ability to select the right technical solutions, similar to those that, 50 years ago, resulted in the Deux Chevaux.

History repeating itself? That seems unlikely, though it is certain that the findings and experiences of the C-Cactus design team will one day be applied in some of Citroën's future production cars. The C-Cactus project clearly demonstrates that curiosity and creativity still go hand-in-hand at Citroën, just as they did in the days when André Lefebvre was the driving force of the Bureau d'Etudes …

APPENDICES

APPENDIX 1
SLEEVE-VALVE TECHNOLOGY

During his 16 years with Voisin, André Lefebvre had a lot to do with sleeve-valve engines. Today, this type of engine has practically disappeared, which is why it seems appropriate to give some background information on these machines and explain how they worked.

In 1908, Charles Yale Knight from Chicago was granted a British patent for his double sleeve-valve system, and in 1910 this construction was patented in the United States. Although the principle of the sliding or sleeve-valve was known and used in steam engines, Knight was the first to adapt it to four-stroke petrol engines.

He developed a system of two concentric cast-iron sleeves (thin-walled tubes), interposed between the engine's pistons and the cylinder block. Near the top of these sleeves there are two diametrically opposed ports, and the pistons slide in the inner ones, which act as the cylinders.

The sleeves are moved up and down by short connecting rods, operated by the equivalent of a camshaft, usually a small crankshaft, which rotates at half the speed of the main crankshaft. The sleeves move in such a way that during the inlet stroke the ports of both sleeves are opposite each other and free the inlet passage.

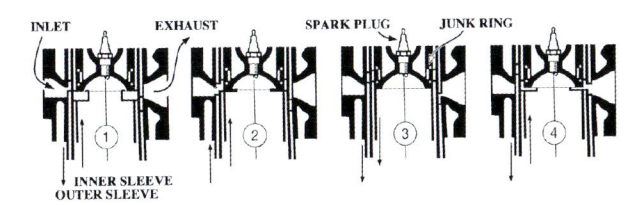

The movements of the sleeve valves during a four-stroke cycle.
1 The inlet port opens and the exhaust port closes at the beginning of the suction stroke. The inner sleeve rises and the outer sleeve descends. 2 The exhaust port is closed and the inlet port closes at the beginning of the compression stroke. 3 The ports in the inner sleeve are moving up into the cylinder head, where they are sealed by the junk ring during the period of maximum pressure and temperature at the beginning of the firing stroke. 4 The exhaust port is already well open at the beginning of the exhaust stroke. The sleeves are now moving into the position shown in 1. As with any four-stroke engine, the complete cycle of suction, compression, firing and exhaust takes two revolutions of the crankshaft.

During the exhaust stroke the two other ports in both sleeves establish a connection with the exhaust manifold.

In the Knight engine each cylinder has two sleeves, operated by a connecting rod that transmits movement from the crank of the small crankshaft to this sleeve. The pistons move up and down within the inner sleeve.

In the first quarter of the twentieth century the Knight system was adopted by a number of manufacturers of luxury automobiles. There were several reasons for this: their fully lubricated sliding motions made them extremely quiet compared to the tappet clatter of the poppet valve engines, and they were also free from detonation or pinking, even with high compression ratios. This was because the sparkplugs could be located in the exact centre of the combustion chamber and there were no objects (hot valve heads) that could cause self-combustion. Their high compression efficiency allowed excellent torque characteristics; in other words, great pulling power.

Sleeve-valve engines were also more reliable, meaning no more burnt exhaust valves, leaking valve stems, bouncing, floating or broken valve springs, damaged valve seats or expensive 'decoke and valve grinding jobs.'

The sleeve-valve engines had disadvantages as well, however. They were more expensive to manufacture and had high oil consumption; the greater reciprocating mass of the sleeves prevented high rpm, and thus restricted their specific output (bhp / litre), and friction between the two sleeves made these engines harder to

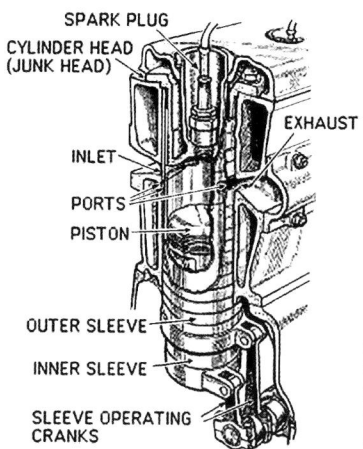

Cutaway drawing revealing the inside of a sleeve valve machine.

turn over when starting, especially if the oil was thick on cold winter days.

One of the first car manufacturers to obtain the Knight patent was the British Daimler Company, and the 1909 Daimler produced for HRH King Edward VII had a Knight engine.

In 1910 Panhard et Levassor in France followed suit and produced sleeve-valve engines in various sizes. During the 1930s, many were fitted in Paris buses and also in the AMD armoured car. Panhard et Levassor remained faithful to sleeve-valves for its 'Dynamic' models up to 1939.

By 1913 Knight licensees in Europe included Peugeot and Mors in France, Minerva in Belgium and Mercedes in Germany.

A Mercedes-Knight took 5th place in the 1913 Indianapolis 500 race. That same year John North Willys purchased the Edwards Motor Company. The purchase included a Knight sleeve-valve licence. Willys also bought the Overland Company, moved its manufacturing operation to Toledo, Ohio, and changed its name to Willys-Overland. By 1914, it was the second largest carmaker in the USA, after Ford. With annual sales as high as 50,000 units, the Willys-Knight became the world's best-selling sleeve-valve-engined automobile. Smaller American manufacturers using the Knight patent were Stearns, Stoddard-Dayton and Columbia. The Canadian company Russell in Toronto, also made Knight engines.

Gabriel Voisin was in fact a late adapter, joining the sleeve-valve club in 1918 when he acquired the Knight licence, together with the manufacturing rights of the M1 designed by Dufresne and Artaud.

It is interesting to note that Voisin was the first to build a V12 sleeve-valve engine. He presented a prototype at the Paris Motor Show of 1921, but it never went into production because it was very complicated and expensive to make, and Voisin, at that time, could barely satisfy demand for his four-cylinder cars.

In 1928 Gabriel Voisin took up the idea again and developed a V12 with a cubic capacity of nearly 12 litres, which was used in the 1929 record machine. A smaller one, with a capacity of 4.885 litres, was fitted in the Voisin C18 production cars.

Two years earlier, in 1926, the British Daimler Company introduced its first Double Six model with a 7.136-litre V12 sleeve-valve engine. The company's new Chief Engineer, Laurence Pomeroy – already famous as the man responsible for the 1911 Vauxhall 'Prince Henry' – designed it.

But getting back to indefatigable genius Gabriel Voisin: in 1935 he designed a radial slide valve seven cylinder intended as a mid-engine for a small car. It was tested in a C14 chassis but his lozenge-shaped 'Voiture de l'Avenir' remained a scale model. Then, at the 1937 Paris Motor Show, Gabriel Voisin presented as a world premiére the V12L, a 12-cylinder-in-line sleeve-valve machine that was mounted in his personal streamlined 'Aérosport.'

Advances in metallurgy and lubrication, and development of such innovations as sodium-cooled valve stems and hydraulic valve lifters, gradually made poppet valves quieter and more reliable. As sleeve-valve engines were more costly to produce, they lost their advantage and, between 1935 and 1939, gradually disappeared from under the bonnets of automobiles.

Until the end of his life André Lefebvre kept in touch with his mentor and old friend Gabriel Voisin. At the 1936 Paris Motor Show, Voisin exhibited this impressive motorcar with a 12-cylinder in line sleeve valve engine. For a long time Gabriel Voisin used this 'Ailée' coupé as his personal car, and its aerodynamic shape undoubtedly influenced Lefebvre's first sketches of the future Citroën DS. (Courtesy Meurisse, Paris)

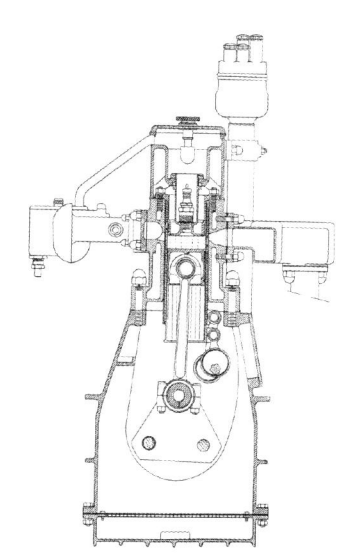

Cross section of a six-cylinder 14CV Voisin engine (first series), as installed in the C11 (1926-1929).

APPENDIX 2

Production figures & engineering achievements

André Levebvre's creativity contributed to the creation of ten million cars.

Make	Model or type	Production year(s)	No units made
Voisin	C6 Course/Laboratoire (Tours)	1923	4
Voisin	C8L (Grand Prix de l'ACF)	1924	1
Voisin	C9 Grand Laboratoire (GP de l'ACF)	1924	3
Voisin	C10 Petit Laboratoire (GP de l'ACF)	1924	1
Voisin	Record car (4-litre 18 CV SS)	1925	1
Voisin	Record car (4.9-litre 6 cyl)	1926	1
Voisin	Record car (7.9-litre eight-in-line)	1927	1
Voisin	Record car (12-litre V12)	1929	1
Voisin	Record car (4.9-litre V12)	1930	1
Citroën	7 and 11CV Traction Avant	1934-1957	759,123
Citroën	7-P-O (prototype)	1936	1
Citroën	15CV Traction Avant	1938-1955	48.448
Citroën	TUB (utility van and ambulances)	1939-1944	1748
Citroën	TPV / 2CV (prototypes and pre-production)	1936-1939	circa 250
Citroën	Type H (utility van)	1948-1981	483,289
Citroën	Deux Chevaux (including AU vans)	1948-1990	7,301,278
Citroën	Type G (prototype 2CV utility van)	1948	1
Citroën	DS & ID	1955-1975	1,456,115
Citroën	Coccinelle (prototypes C1>C10)	1953-1958	10

TOTAL **10,050,247**

Engineering achievements

1916-1917 Design and construction of an undercarriage with brakes, rubber suspension and shock absorbers for the Voisin night-bomber.
1919-1920 Improving the reliability and performance of the four-cylinder sleeve valve engine of the Voisin C1.
1922-1923 Design, construction and testing of the Voisin C6 Course or 'Laboratoire' racing cars for the GP de Tours.
1923-1924 Design and construction of the Voisin C9 or 'Grand Laboratoire,' the Voisin C8 L and the Voisin C10 or 'Petit Laboratoire' for the GP de Lyon.
1924-1925 Design and construction of the four-cylinder Voisin record car that set the 6 hours world record at 1,032,28km, with an average speed of 172km/h.
1925-1926 Design and construction of the six-cylinder Voisin record car that established a record over 100km, with an average speed of 185.49km/h.
1926-1927 Design and construction of the eight-cylinder Voisin record car that set the 24 hours world record at 4,383,84km, with an average speed of 182.66km/h.
1928-1929 Design and construction of the V12 Voisin record car that in 10 days set the record for 30,000km at 133.531km. On September 25 it had to abandon its attempt to achieve 40,000km because of the collapse of one of the front wheels.
1929-1930 Preparation of the V12 Voisin that achieved the 50,000km record.
1929-1931 Feasibility studies with Gabriel Voisin concerning the construction of a front-wheel drive Voisin with a V8 engine. Due to financial problems, this project did not materialise.
1931-1933 Developing the Renault 40CV at the Bureau d'Etudes in Billancourt. Evenings and weekends spent at home drawing up plans for a medium-sized front-wheel drive passenger car. This project was presented to Louis Renault, who refused to discuss it.
1933-1934 Design and development of the Citroën 7CV Traction Avant, codenamed PV (Petite Voiture) in just over 13 months.
1934 Development of the wide body Citroën 11 B and the Citroën 22CV with a V8 engine, both using the technology of the Traction Avant.
1935 Feasibility study of the 7-P-O together with the Citroën engineer Oudart. This was intended to be the successor to the Traction Avant, but with a more comfortable suspension and a radial engine under the bonnet. Citroën management rejected this project.
1936-1938 Assisting in the development of the six-cylinder Citroën 15 (Quinze) Traction Avant, which used the body structure of the 11B.
1937-1939 Design and development of the Citroën TUB (Traction Utilitaire Basse), the first small cab forward van, with front-wheel drive, powered by the engine of the Traction Avant 7CV.
1936-1939 First studies for the TPV (Toute Petite Voiture), which was to become the Citroën Deux Chevaux.
1938 Experiments with an automatic transmission with extensible pulleys, driven by a metal belt, Comparable to today's CVTs.

1939 Development of a six-wheeled gun (artillery) tractor for Laffly, to be powered by the engine of the Citroën Traction Avant.
1939 Design of an armoured car to be powered by the engine of the Citroën TA.
1940 The French army accepted the proposal for the Laffly, but on June 3, 1940 German bombs destroyed Citroën's Bureau d'Etudes and all the prototypes and drawings.
1940-1941 Experiments with alternative fuels for cars and trucks, together with the French chemical engineer Freund.
1941-1942 Construction of a small electrical single-seater car.
1942 Design of a cheap bicycle with small wheels.
1941-1942 Construction of a prototype for a small tractor, driven by the engine of the 2CV.
1941-1942 Design and construction of a prototype for a four-wheel tractor, driven by the engine of the Citroën 11CV and equipped with an hydraulic clutch.
1942-1946 Design and development of the front-drive H-vans, a cab-forward concept similar to the TUB, but with a monocoque body and powered by the engine of the 11CV.
1947-1955 Design and development of the VGD (Voiture á Grande Diffusion), which was to become the DS.
1953-1958 Design and construction of a number of prototypes for the 'Coccinelle' or 'Goutte d'Eau,' this was an ultra-light, streamlined four-seater passenger car. It had the hydro-pneumatic suspension system of the DS and used the two-cylinder engine of the Deux Chevaux.

APPENDIX 3

BIBLIOGRAPHY & SOURCES

BOOKS

La tragédie d'André Citroën / Sylvain Reiner 1954.
50 Ans d'automobile, l'histoire de Tracta et autres tractions avant / J A Grégoire 1954.
Mes 10.000 cerfs-volants / Gabriel Voisin 1960.
Men, Women and 10.000 Kites / Gabriel Voisin 1963.
Mes mille et une voitures / Gabriel Voisin 1962.
Nos étonnantes chasses / Gabriel Voisin 1963.
French vintage cars / John Bolster 1964.
Les Réalisations de votre Père / Cahier privé pour les fils de A Lefebvre par Jaques Léonzi 1967
Great designers and their work / Edited by R Barker & A Harding.
Lost Causes of Motoring / Lord Montagu of Beaulieu & Michael Sedgwick.
La traction, en 300 histoires et 150 photos / Jacques Borgé & Nicolas Viasnoff 1975.
The designers / L J K Setright, 1976.
André Citroën, l'Aventure est au bout du quai / Sylvain Reiner (reprinted 1977).
André Citroën, les chevrons de la gloire / Sylvie Schweitzer & Fabien Sabatès 1980.
Citroën 1915-1935, Des engrenages à la chaîne / Sylvie Schweitzer-Lyon 1982.
Citroën: L'histoire et les secrets de son Bureau d'études / Roger Brioult-Edifree 1987.
Guide de l'automobile française / Jacques Rousseau & Jean-Paul Carron 1988 & 1993.
André Citroën / Jacques Wolgensinger 1991.
Toutes les Voisins / René Bellu-Studio Gemot.
Citroën Traction Avant / Jon Pressnell.
Citroën DS, The Complete Story / Jon Pressnell.
Citroën 2CV, The Complete Story / M White.
Automobiles Voisin, 1919-1958 / Pascal Courteault 1991.
André Citroën, 1878-1935. Le risque et le défi / Sylvie Schweitzer-Fayard 1992.
Le type H; le cube utile / Wouter Jansen & Fabien Sabatès-Massin.
Flaminio Bertoni; 30 ans de style Citroën / Fabien Sabates & Léonardo Bertoni 1998.
André Citroën, The Man and the Motor Cars / John Reynolds 1999.
Chassis Design: Principles and Analysis / William F & Douglas L Milliken 2002.
Daring to be different (Citroën) / John Reynolds 2004.
The Classic Citroëns 1935-1975 / John Reynolds 2006.
Les Hommes de la 2CV? André Lalanne et les anciens de Citroën.

MAGAZINE ARTICLES

The experiences of an 'apprentice' at Voisin Leroy-Motorkampioen 1928
Sleeve-valve 12-cylinder Voisin / *The Autocar* October 4th 1929.
Gabriel Voisin et les records / Serge Pozzoli - *Album du Fanatique de l'Automobile* 1970.
Prophet without honour: The 1923 Voisin 'Laboratoire' Cyril Posthumus - *The Motor* 1966.

THANKS & ACKNOWLEDGEMENTS

This book could never have been written without the help and encouragement of many people. It is extremely difficult to write a biography about someone whose work and technical genius you admire but have never met; therefore, I am particularly indebted to André Lefebvre's sons. Michel, the elder, and his charming wife, Jeanine, told me many fascinating stories from Lefebvre's youth and anecdotes from the time Michel himself worked as a test driver for Citroën during gestation of the DS. Jeanine, who remembered her father-in-law as a very attractive man, gave me a number of pictures; among them one she had taken when a top-secret prototype of the DS was hidden at the family retreat at Terrissole. Alain, Philippe and Guy, André's younger sons, were equally helpful. Alain and Guy spontaneously opened up their family archives to supply me with some unique photos of their father during his Voisin years.

Then, I have to thank Roger Brioult who kindly gave me permission to quote from interviews in his well-documented books – Citroën; L'histoire et les secrets de son Bureau d'Etudes. Philippe Ladure, knowledgeable president of the French association 'Les Amis de Gabriel Voisin,' gave me valuable background information about this brilliant and highly individualistic aircraft and automobile manufacturer. He also introduced me to Philipp Moch, who reconstructed the famous C6 Course which gave André Lefebvre his first chance to prove his talents as a designer and racing driver. Concerning Voisin's aviation past, I received useful advice from the Service de Documentation of the Musée de l'Air et de l'Espace at le Bourget near Paris.

Johan van der Laan has a busy and responsible job at the Institute for Automobile Management IVA at Driebergen in the Netherlands. He is a connoisseur of classic Citroëns, especially the 2CV and DS, and in a Deux Chevaux completed the Peking to Paris memorial run, about which he wrote the book *Peking Duck*. I very much appreciated his offer to read the draft of my manuscript during his summer holidays. He also drew my attention to some interesting technical details of these Citroën models. I am equally most grateful for the help of Gro Hoeg, International PR Manager Citroën, Anne-Marie Michel of the Médiathèque of the Direction de la Communication at Citroën, and Jean-Claude Lannes, Yannick Billy, Catherine Jeannin, and Anne-Lise Colombel of the Conservatoire Citroën at Aulnay-sous-Bois, which houses a most impressive collection of early Citroëns and prototypes.

I should not forget Pascal Richard of l'Autojournal who sent me reprints of the magazine articles revealing the secrets of the DS, long before it was officially introduced.

When in the Terrissole area I met Jacky Michel, still active in apiculture, who vividly remembers the time when the Lefebvre family visited for holidays.

Then, of course, I must mention the man who is in fact directly responsible for this book. At the occasion of the anniversary of the Citroën DS in 2005, I asked Erik Verhaest, enthusiastic director of Public Relations of Citroën in Amsterdam, if he could recommend a biography or in-depth magazine article about its creator, André Lefebvre. He replied: "I have never seen such a publication and if it existed I would certainly have heard about it. So, if we agree that the man deserves a book, you will have to write it yourself!"

Erik also introduced me to Hans Arend de Wit of Switchimage, who has become a friend and took many splendid photographs for this book.

Last, but not least I want to thank my wife, Barbara, who patiently assisted me with the research for this book, and is responsible for many improvements in the text.

Gijsbert-Paul Berk
Airion, France

INDEX

Adler 51, 59, 63, 79
Andreau, Jean 82
Artault, Ernest 14, 15, 140
Aubade, Paul d' 66
Auburn Cord 51, 52, 55
Autonacional SA 53

Barron, Mr 100
Beccia, Walter 99-100, 113, 121, 122, 134
Bendix 63
Bercot, Pierre 4, 92, 111, 124
Bernard, Marius 19, 21, 27, 35, 39, 43, 54
Bernard Mr 105
Bertoni, Flaminio 65, 72, 75, 82, 83, 97, 100, 102, 109, 112, 115, 118 120-124, 128, 133-135
Bertoni, Leonardo 82, 112
BMW 38, 79, 98-100
Boisse, Pierre 94, 105, 123
Borgé, Jacques 71
Boulanger, Pierre-Jules 4, 73-76, 78, 79, 84, 86-89, 92-94, 96-98, 102 104, 109, 110, 118, 130, 135
Boullay, Mr 100
Bourdon, Pierre 73
Brioult, Roger 5, 64, 88, 119, 133
Broglie, Maurice 60, 61, 62, 86
Brueder, Antoine 111
Brull, Charles 62, 63
Bucan, Mr 133
Budd 51, 58, 60, 64, 65, 113

Camusat Mr 62
Cardiou, Jean 94, 107,124
Chataigner Mr 84
Chinon, Marcel 100
Christy, John Walter 51
Citroën, André 4, 5, 15, 58-62, 66, 67, 70-74, 84
Corner, Mr 121
Cuinet, Raoul 65, 66, 72

Dauvergne, Mr 32
Decarne, Albert 33
Dinthilhac, Mr 46
Doorninck, Co van 48
Du Castel, Mr 73
Duclos, Jacques 76, 84
Dufresne, Louis 14, 15, 18, 33, 140
Duray, Mr 26, 28

Estaque, André 130, 133, 134

Forceau, Alphonse 61, 62, 82, 92
Fortin, Raphael 25, 26, 39, 61
Franchiset, Pierre 65-66, 75, 88, 94, 95
Franzen, Paul 73

Gauderman, Mr 30, 32
Gaz de Paris 43, 48

Giacosa, Dante 86
Giffard, Pierre 6
Gnome et Rhône 53, 98
Grégoire, Jean Albert 51, 59, 63, 104, 105
Guyot, Mr 27

Hermet, Antoine 73, 74, 117
Houdin, Mr 63

Imperia 51, 54
Ingueneau, Pierre 89, 94, 98
Issigonis, Alex 87
Issi-les-Moulineaux 12, 32, 35, 44, 111

Jeantaud, Charles 50
Jouffroy, Maurice 73
Jourdan, Maurice 104
Julien, Maurice 61, 66
Julienne, Mr 36, 39

Kiriloff, Serge 41, 44, 46
Knight (sleeve-valve system) 14, 15, 139

Lafaury, Emmanuel 138
Laffly 89, 90
Lagarde, Mr 105
Lagary, Mr 105
Lamberjack, Dominique 16, 17
Lamy, Eugène 53
Lanoy, Mr 133
Latil, Georges 50, 51
Laurain, Mr 133, 134
Ledwinka, Hans 50
Ledwinka, Joseph 51, 59
Lehideux, François 54-55
Lemaire, Pierre 66
Léonzi, Jacques 61, 82, 92, 100, 116, 130, 133, 134
Lockheed 127
Louis, André 88

Magès, Paul 100, 113, 115,117-119, 124, 128
Marchand, César 17, 27, 36, 37, 39 42, 44, 45, 48, 72
Marchand, Eduard 48
Mercier, Pierre Etienne 100
Michelin (company) 65, 81, 80, 87,102, 126
Michelin, Edouard 73, 74, 78, 79 111
Michelin, Pierre 4, 73-75, 78, 79, 111
Miller, Harry 51, 55
Moch, Philipp 5, 20, 22
Montell Mr 61
Montlhéry 33, 35, 44, 47, 61
Morel, André 26, 30, 32, 34, 41, 44

Né, Jacques 116, 127, 135
Nordlinger, Théo 61
Norroy, Maurice 73, 98

Oudart, Mr 61, 82

Picard, Achille 93
Piccioni 30, 32
Pillipon, Anthony (Tony) 41, 42
Pininfarina 104, 124
Ploué, Jean-Pierre 137, 138
Poillot, Mr 122,
Pomeroy, Laurence 140
Pommier, André 67, 72
Porsche, Prof Dr Ferdinand 19, 50, 79, 129
Pozzoli, Serge 34
Présalé, Leroy 44, 45, 48
Prévost, Pierre 59, 66, 73
Prud'homme, Roger 66, 71, 124, 127
Puisseux, Robert 4, 110, 111, 118

Renard, Mr 92
Renault (company) 33, 36, 56 60, 94, 113
Renault, Louis 4, 33, 54, 55, 83
Renault, Léon 72, 100, 101
Rivolier, Charles 63
Robin, Louis 61
Roche, Alain 130, 133, 134
Rogé, Mr 39
Rohr, Hans Gustaf 51, 59,
Rosengart, Lucien 51, 59
Rougier, Henri 19, 20, 26-28, 30, 32
Roux, Mr 39
Ruxton (company) 51, 55, 59

Sainturat, Maurice 65, 72, 80, 81, 86, 98, 99
Sallot, Georges 75, 82, 116
Santa Maria 92
SARL Lefebvre 14
Sauzay, Maurice 25
Seagrave, Henry 26
Sensaud de Lavaud, Dimitry 60-62
Serre, Charles 55, 60
Silvani 27, 28
Simonetti 88
Strasbourg 19, 20

Talbot 82, 99, 122
Toublan, Georges 78
Tours 20, 21, 25, 31
Tudoux, Mr 119

Vialet, Fernand 39, 42
Voisin, Charles 15
Voisin, Gabriel 4, 5, 11-13, 14-16, 19-48, 52-54, 58, 61, 64, 71-72, 82, 87, 98, 113, 115, 116, 118, 133 140

Wall Street Crash 46, 50, 57
Weymann, Charles 113

Yacco 42, 43, 46-49, 72

Zenith 22, 42